# CLAMBAKE

With best wishes,

Kathy Neustadt

**Publications of the American Folklore Society**
New Series

*General Editor,* Patrick B. Mullen

# CLAMBAKE

*A History and Celebration of
an American Tradition*

KATHY NEUSTADT

The University of Massachusetts Press
*Amherst*

Copyright © 1992 by Kathy Neustadt
All rights reserved
Printed in the United States of America
LC 91-45599
ISBN 0-87023-782-9(cloth); 799-3(pbk)
Designed by Jack Harrison
Set in Adobe Caslon by Keystone Typesetting, Inc.
Printed and bound by Thomson-Shore, Inc.

Library of Congress Cataloging-in-Publication Data
Neustadt, Kathy, 1951–
    Clambake : a history and celebration of an American tradition /
  Kathy Neustadt.
       p.  cm. — (Publications of the American Folklore Society, new series)
Includes bibliographical references and index.
ISBN 0-87023-782-9 (alk. paper) — ISBN 0-87023-799-3 (pbk. : alk. paper)
1. Clambakes—United States—History.   2. Clambakes—Massachusetts—Allen's Neck—History.
3. Festivals—United States.   4. Festivals—Massachusetts—Allen's Neck.
5. Allen's Neck (Mass.)—Social life and customs.
6. United States—Social life and customs.
I. Title.   II. Series: Publications of the American Folklore Society.   New series (Unnumbered)
GT2956.U6N48   1992
394'.3—dc20                           91-45599
                                         CIP

British Library Cataloguing in Publication data are available.

*This book is published with the support and cooperation of
the University of Massachusetts, Boston.*

*For Casey and Nicky,*
*who may someday even want to read this*

# Contents

# Acknowledgments

I have been blessed with help at every stage and in every aspect of this project. Roger Abrahams, Margaret Mills, and Don Yoder from the Department of Folklore and Folklife at the University of Pennsylvania guided me through the vicissitudes of the doctoral process and have remained supportive and helpful resources ever since. To Roger goes particular thanks for his help in propelling this book toward publication and putting me in touch with Paul Wright at the University of Massachusetts Press, who, among other supportive acts, has never once asked me to justify a study of clambaking. Kathryn Grover, who contributed clarity and polish through her editing, gave this work its closest and most constructive reading.

Jim Baker, Bill Weaver, Betty Little, and Nancy Jenkins, all experts in their fields, have been generous with their time and knowledge, and the obscure references to shellfish practices that they have passed along to me have added enormously to the historical narrative. I owe a specific debt to Sandy Oliver, who first directed my attention to the "squantum" connection, and to Bob St. George, who introduced me to the Forefathers' Day "feast of shells" and to many other choice references besides: every researcher should be blessed with such friends. Nanepashemet, curator of the Wampanoag Indian Program at Plimoth Plantation, has earned my profound intellectual respect and gratitude for his contributions to my understanding of some very subtle aspects of cultural politics that, among other things, have played a role in the history of the clambake. I have also benefited from his historical knowledge, his critical thinking, and, perhaps most of all, from his willingness to be a character, a foil for the native American perspective, in the clambake story.

Joe Ofria, of The Image Inn in Arlington, and Joe Thomas, the man who *is* Spinner Publications in New Bedford, have provided me, first and foremost, with the photographic images that I needed to tell my story. More important, they have turned their good eyes toward my project and inspired me through their own creative work to explore my interest in texture and community further.

It is an absolute fact that without the help of my family—immediate, extended, and spiritual—there would be no book, on clambakes or anything else. Love, encourage-ment, and child care have been the sine qua non of my ability to produce this text, and there are more people to thank for these gifts than I can possibly name here: I am grateful to, and for, all of them. Casey and Nicky, for their part, have had to do the most accommodating of Mommy's other "progeny," and I can only hope that having educated palates in the realm of clambake will somehow serve them well in the future.

As the clambake project has grown in scope, so has the number of people who helped me out. Approaching a group of strange men working around a clambake fire has never been easy for me, but, without exception, I have been made to feel at home. Watching the crew at the Fire Station Bake in Russells Mills has become a perennial pleasure; Carl Flipp of Leighton's Clambakes and Sandy Favazzo and Phil Demetri of D. M. Roberts Clambake Caterers generously allowed me to watch them work; Eliot Knowles, Jr., made me part of the guest list at his bake on the beach; and Donald Carr and Steve Howland at the Smith Neck Clambake took me in like a long-lost relative. Charlie Peters, Earl Cash, Jr., and the other gentlemen at the Mashpee Pow-wow might well have wondered why this woman was poking around while they were trying to get a clambake together, but they were tolerant and gracious above and beyond the call.

To Raymond Davoll, who runs most of the clambakes-for-hire in the Allen's Neck area, and Peter Gonet, the bakemaster of the Allen's Neck Clambake, I owe particular thanks for letting me, literally, get in their way as I followed them around asking questions and taking pictures. Raymond and Peter were the key players in the decision to take the Allen's Neck Clambake to the Smithsonian Festival of American Folklife on the Mall in Washington in 1988, for which I am—and, I believe, their community is also—still very grateful.

Finally, then, to the people of Allen's Neck goes the lion's share of the credit for whatever is good or interesting about this book. It is their Bake and their lives that have inspired me and kept me plodding on, trying to capture some of its beauty and power in words. "Grace" is the word that often comes into my head after a day of fieldwork, a day of clambaking, or a day spent there among the people I now think of as my friends. I am grateful for this grace in my life and hope that some of it has found its way into this work.

# CLAMBAKE

# Introduction

*It is very rare in country life, where high days and holidays are few, that any occasion of general interest proves to be less than great. Such is the hidden fire of enthusiasm in the New England nature that, once given an outlet, it shines forth with almost volcanic light and heat.*
—Sarah Orne Jewett, *The Country of the Pointed Firs* (1896)

O N  T H E  T H I R D Thursday in August 1984, I attended my first clambake at Allen's Neck. I had been invited to join the crew of my vacationing relatives at this popular local event by my aunt Louise, who, as a relatively recent resident of the area, had been attending the clambake for about six years. It was good fun and great eating, she assured me, and added that a budding student of folklore would probably find it of particular interest. And so it was that with baby Nicky and three-year-old Casey in tow, I found myself approaching an unassuming grove of trees in which a large number of people were bustling about, engaged in activities whose meaning escaped me.

Between a dullness of mind caused by two years of graduate studies and the general fogginess that results from sleep deprivation, my first impressions of the clambake were vague, at best. I remember thinking that it was going to be like church suppers and community fund-raising dinners I had attended elsewhere, only that the food would be more traditional and regional than at those pancake suppers and chicken barbecues. It was only after the rake-out performance was drawing to its conclusion, as I watched the parade of tarps go by and felt the tears welling in my eyes, that I realized something much more powerful was afoot here—something that I wanted, even needed, to know more about.

In the seven years that have followed, I *have* come to know more about the Allen's Neck Clambake, and although I now have relatively normal sleep patterns and no longer suffer the stresses of an acolyte to academe, I still find myself deeply moved by the forces that come together in this event. A couple of hundred hours of audiotape, reams and reams of transcriptions and field notes, an extensive bibliography, and several thousand photographic images later, I offer up, by way of this book, some of what I have learned about the American tradition of clambaking in general and its manifestation in the Allen's Neck community in particular.

I could never have guessed in 1984 how a simple fieldwork project would become so much a part of my life—not when I began interviewing the individuals who participated most directly in Clambake, their returning rela-tives, and the "summer people" who came to eat; not as I expanded my focus to include other local clambaking crews and clambake caterers; and not even as I started spending more and more hours looking for the origins of this venerable New England tradition in archaeological reports, old diaries, local histories, and tattered travel guides.

My involvement in the project deepened in the face of—and, no doubt, to some extent in response to—the nearly unanimous bemused and often slightly patronizing reaction on the part of people around me. "Studying a clambake," people would say with a smirk, "must be really *tough* work." "A clambake?" others would ask quizzically. "What's there to study? What's there to know about a clambake?" "You're working on a theory chapter? What theory? The deeper meaning of a clam?" I am used to these responses by now—as folklor-ists in general have to become used to the "triviality barrier"[1] which dogs many of their research areas—and this book will either satisfy these skeptics or confirm their suspicions.

The book is divided into three sections, representing the three major ap-proaches that I have taken to the study of the clambake. The first section is historical and traces some of the social, economic, political, regional, and cultural forces that have shaped the tradition of clambaking over time and created a storehouse of symbolic potential, as well as a context for its con-tinued physical practice. Each of the first three chapters investigates specific themes relating to the "native" origins of the clambake—in relation to archae-ological studies, nationalistic politics, the development of industrialization and leisure, and a variety of related cultural themes. In the process of constructing a reasonable chronology, the nature of "tradition" itself has become an additional topic for discussion.

Section Two focuses specifically on the clambake at Allen's Neck, not merely as an example of a clambake in situ, but as a cultural phenomenon in its own right. In chapter 4, I present some of the unique factors—historical, ecological, and religious, in particular—that have affected the Allen's Neck community and provided the context for its century-old feast. With this ethnographic portrait as its backdrop, chapter 5 sketches a rough history of the Allen's Neck Clambake over the past hundred years, noting some of its major traditional elements and the aesthetic sensibility that it has engendered. The final chapter in this section is a detailed description of the technical and culinary components of the clambake presented by the people of Allen's Neck, which reflects and further defines the group's notion of a "proper bake."

The final section views the clambake from a more abstract vantage point. Chapter 7 undertakes a critical examination of some of the more popular theories that deal with central elements of the clambaking tradition—food, ritual, and festival. In addition to the insights these theories provide, the increasingly evident lack of fit between the hypotheses and the clambake serves, in turn, as the basis for a more intensive look at the theoretical models themselves. In the final chapter, after considering some of the central narratives and themes associated with the event, I suggest my own quasi-theoretical perspective and interpretation of the "meaning" of the Allen's Neck Clambake.

This organization is not only structurally practical, but it makes it possible for readers to pursue their particular interests more easily. Although I have struggled mightily to make all of the sections readable—by, among other things, relegating some of the finer points of scholarship to footnotes—I have also tried to make each section stand on its own. It is my hope that this presentation will prove equally interesting to amateur, professional, local, and culinary historians; to folklorists, anthropologists, and Americanists; to clambake enthusiasts and Allen's Neck community members; and to my mother.

To all of these potential readers, however, I would like to make it clear that this study makes no claim to being all-inclusive, on any of its levels. The historical component, though certainly exponentially more rigorous and extensive than any hitherto produced on clambakes, is neither exhaustive nor absolute. In terms of the Allen's Neck Bake itself, there is fieldwork material that I have not used, and, no doubt, information that I have yet to gather. And in the theoretical discussion, I have made a conscious effort to limit, rather than expand, the number of hypotheses to be discussed. Less committed to the idea that truth can be attained through discovering the "right" data, I have been more intent on examining how right-ness gets defined, expanded upon, and made traditional.

As an example of my selective process, I am aware of traditions of clambaking that exist in other areas along the eastern seaboard—most notably in Rhode Island, Maine, and in parts of Long Island—but I have chosen to focus here almost completely on southeastern Massachusetts, where, I would argue, the tradition was most fully and elaborately developed. I have attempted a reasonably complete explication of some major facets of clambaking, and I anticipate—indeed, I hope—that this study will stimulate others to bring forth new materials, new citations, and new hypotheses to add to the story.

As an additional cautionary note, I would like to share the perception I have often had of my study of clambaking—that it is a hall of mirrors, in which the reflections of reflections make it nearly impossible to grab ahold of anything "true" or "real." For example, there is the Yankee tradition of clambaking, and there is the Indian tradition of clambaking, and there is the Yankee tradition of doing an Indian tradition, and so on;[2] the difference between the idea of the clambake (either as "popular imagination" or as scholarly abstraction) and the hands-on experience of it is another source of serious confusion. One of the difficulties I have encountered in drawing together this broad range of perceptions of the clambake—many of them in direct conflict with one another—is that, in striving for a "chorus of voices," I have as often as not felt assaulted by a cacophony.

A definition of the Allen's Neck community itself—so central to the discussion of its clambake—has also proved to be elusive, since the boundaries that divide insiders from outsiders are so mutable, even mercurial. Making a distinction between Clambake workers and Clambake ticket-holders, for instance, is too simplistic and involves more exceptions to the rule than it does effective examples. A schema that places the Clambake Committee at the inner circle, surrounded by the members of the Allen's Neck Meeting as the larger core group, with summer people, then tourists, representing the outer circles is more defensible and certainly tidy, but it also does not reflect the dynamic nature of the group's identity. Community membership, for better or worse, seems to be more like a state of mind than an organizational chart, and at Allen's Neck, at least, there are no participants who are so far out of the community as to be incapable of perceiving themselves to be the opposite.

Clambaking is ancient and new; it's "traditional" and it's "invented"—and, depending on where you stand theoretically, it can be an "invented tradition" and/or traditionally invented. There are right ways of doing a clambake—"proper" ways—and a multitude of other ways that are never actually wrong. A clambake can be nothing more than "a convenient way to have a big feed for a lot of people," and it can also be a "sacramental meal." The reality of clambake, its "true story," clearly depends on where you are standing and what lenses you choose to look through.

This message was made intensely clear to me when, not so long ago, I met with a group of executives from the Walt Disney World Company who were touring the Northeast to gather ideas for the food and beverage component of a new Disney resort in Florida being built around a turn-of-the-century New England theme. As a leading "clamologist" (I have the calling cards to prove it), I was invited to join them for breakfast—a breakfast, I might add, of the most remarkable proportions, with four or five plates full of "regional" specialties spread out in front of each person. They quizzed me extensively about every aspect of the clambake and brainstormed how they might put on an "authentic" clambake in their new banquet hall. After indicating that an indoor bake was not exactly authentic, I found myself responding to their crestfallen looks by assuring them that in manipulating the clambake to fit their technical and marketing needs, they were well within a time-honored "tradition" of clambaking.[3] I still believe that this is true.

Situated in the midst of historical narrative and theoretical debate, the story of the Allen's Neck Clambake has been the topic most dear to my heart. It has also entailed the greatest personal challenge of this work. In all ethnographic studies, there is an inherent tension between the interpretations of the analysts and the interpretations of those whom they study; in the context of "invented traditions," the tension is between the critics of "authenticity" and those who experience their lives as real. While it would be naive to argue, in the case of the Allen's Neck Bake, that the meaning of the event rests *entirely* with the statements and themes expressed by its community, it is equally unsatisfactory to give the final and privileged word to the scholarly community, no matter how self-reflexive and relativistic its pronouncements attempt to be. I have tried in my conclusions to account for both perspectives.

What follows is the product of several years' worth of research, interviews, and analysis—my attempts to "know" something about this place through its clambaking event. Ironically, what has proved most valuable to me in this search has come when I put down the books, turned off the tape recorder, and stopped *thinking* altogether. It is then—it seems clear to me now—that I started finally to *feel* something about Allen's Neck, to let my experiences in that place teach me what it was that I needed to know. It's not that I suddenly thought like an insider—I never will be that, I know—but it was something like feeling "at home."

Transcribing the taped interviews, I finally started hearing the wind in the background as it whistled through the trees at the edge of the cornfield, where the smell of manure was signaling the beginning of growing season. I could lower my camera and expectations of capturing "the perfect clambake photograph" and give myself over to the smell of cooking rockweed and the memory of tearing its slippery fingers from rocky anchors and the feel of the wind on my face as I rode in the back of Al's truck astride a mound of wet weed. And just as I was beginning to be able to see in the open fields and rubble of stones the phantoms of ancient buildings no longer standing, I thought I could make out in the words of these people the shapes of their lives, so foreign and enriching to my own.

But my conclusions are neither neutral nor authoritative, no matter how effectively my authorial "voice" may convey these impressions.[4] It is my voice, after all, imperfect like all the rest, constrained and limited in its own ways. It has been important for me to recognize that, poised awkwardly between participation and observation, my presence is also not neutral or negligent, but has had an effect on the tradition and the community that I have been attempting to document.[5] Of course, I would like to think that my presence at Allen's Neck, if not completely positive, has at least been essentially benign, but even this position is something I can never take for granted.

The positive responses I had received from the people of Allen's Neck to my first attempt at writing about Clambake were, to a large extent, the impetus to take the study further. As a producer of texts, even on this minor level, I already felt implicated in the larger issues of cultural politics and poetics; as a major participant in packaging the Allen's Neck Clambake for presentation at the Smithsonian Institution's 1988 Festival of American Folklife, my fate as a cultural commodifier was sealed. Having deftly sold the idea of performing a traditional New England clambake on the Mall in Washington, I then had to figure out how to bridge the gap that arose between the needs of the festival programmers and those of the Allen's Neck folks, who were flattered to be invited but not at all sure that they actually wanted to participate.

From a research point of view, I learned more about the nature of the Yankee character through observing the negotiations and interactions at the cultural interface of the festival than I had to date in the more "natural" context. It turned out, happily, after the balking and stalling were over, that the festival experience was deemed a major success by everyone involved, but particularly by the people of Allen's Neck, the nine who were paid "performers" and the other forty–plus who chartered a bus and made the trip to Washington for the long weekend. Participation in the festival in Washington remains a source of positive memory and pride for most of the people in the Allen's Neck community, and a number of them even refer to it as a high point in their lives. I am grateful that this could be true.

I had a dream about Clambake during the festival stage of my research: in the midst of the grove, an array of microphones had been set out for each of the participants, and behind them a series of floodlights. The thing that upset me most in the dream was that the people of Allen's Neck were the ones doing the "producing"—Ila Gonet, efficient as always, was testing the mikes; Willy Morrison was making sure that there was proper exposure on the stage where he was going to serve as emcee—and my hypnagogic sense upon waking was that I had ruined the clambake. Anxiety dreams like this one have a role to play in keeping a person who mucks about in other people's traditions honest, and I have struggled to stay aware of the responsibility that fieldwork at least *should* entail. Although at this point it is too early for me to tell what the effects of being publicly "traditional" will have on the tradition itself—how clambaking on the Mall will affect the clambake at Allen's Neck—I need to be prepared for the likely event that there will be some.

The clambake is a unique American folk tradition that has what I have found to be interesting connections and rich resonances with other aspects of American culture and history. By examining this tradition in detail and in one particular community, I have tried to demonstrate the creativity, artistry, and even "transfiguring powers" that it entails. If the reader comes away with any sense of this power, or with a suspicion that art and sacred rituals might be embedded all around us, at every turn, then I have, indeed, said enough.

# Prologue:
# The Bake

AT 7:30 A.M., as the mist burns off the surrounding cornfields, a small group of people begins to gather in the stand of trees where Allen's Neck and Horseneck Roads meet. Peter arrives first. He parks his pickup next to the stone wall and hops out to survey the still and silent scene. Everything is in order: the summer's growth of long grass has been cut back, the dead trees felled; tables and benches have been laid out on the cross-beamed stumps; the firewood is stacked and dry next to the weathered concrete slab; the rock pile is ample, and the rockweed, dumped yesterday, is still moist and fragrant under the old tent canvas. Best of all, the sky is completely clear.

Within a few minutes, Peter is joined by his cousin, Burney; his girlfriend, Cathi; Burney's wife, Julie; and Julie and Burney's infant daughter, Corey. Neighboring kids come strolling over to be conscripted, willingly, to help build the fire. Willy drives up to drop off the kerosene and heads back to pick up his grandson and the remaining supplies from the store, despite his bad back. As newcomers arrive, yawning and stretching, they quickly form a line and begin passing the melon-sized rocks from the pile by the side of the road to the wooden cribs being constructed on the concrete slab.

Gordon unpacks the sausage, butter, and tripe from his van, while his brother-in-law, Karl, helps to cover the long tables from the enormous roll of brown paper. Their grandchildren, recently arrived from various parts of the country for the occasion, begin preparing the food. The sound of their banter as they get reacquainted drowns out the birds, and they cut and season and twist first sausage, then fish, and finally tripe into small, "penny candy," brown paper bags. They load the bags into the weathered wooden trays and stack them next to some trees, out of the way.

Pies and loaves of brown bread begin to arrive, some of them still warm from the oven, and are cut by some women and teenaged girls sitting along the tables back by the cookshack. Paula attends to the brown bread. She cuts it with care and spreads the pieces evenly around the paper serving plates. The old pie rack is carried out of the shack and, listing badly, soon begins to fill up. Some of the younger boys start to congregate nearby, talking and laughing, their eyes riveted on the rack and its toothsome cargo. Two other boys drag out the old sign and carry it to the road, where they lean it against the stone wall.

Vehicles come and go with great purpose. Raymond drops off the fish and heads down to the beach with the clams—the missing ten bushels are on their way from Maine, he reports, due in around 9:30; he'll be back. Ila backs up the Peugot, and she and her daughter unload its contents onto the handicrafts table—homemade aprons, quilts and pot holders, dried ornamental flowers, and wooden toys. Jewel-colored jams and jellies, just-picked vegetables, and Muriel's famous Jim Dandies are spread out across the adjoining food table. Cathi takes off in her pickup for Tiverton to buy the corn, which is just now being picked.

Karl's three-week-old great-grandson is passed from relative to relative, until he falls asleep in his basket under the trees. Corey, after helping with the kindling and twisting a bag or two of sausage, sits with the grapes her mother has brought for her and eats and plays. Both of her grandmothers, Elsie and Norma, stop from time to time to snuggle with her as they go about the work of setting up their table. Lewis Cole, the minister, is regularly drawn aside by senior menfolk to be regaled with stories of how this all used to be done, how it was "way back when." And just as the fire is being lit in one part of the grove, Zachary Smith, at the advanced age of nine years, flirts with a rite of manhood as he considers the challenge to take his first taste of raw tripe.

Away from the tables, back in the trees, the corn is being stripped of most of its leaves, the sweet potatoes hacked into pieces. Onions sit waiting in aluminum pots, surrounded by mounds of corn husks. The stacks of wooden trays grow higher and more numerous, as this stage of the preparations is nearly completed. Now that Burney has tended to it, the fire is burning evenly and hot, and red flames flare high into the air. "I call this the altar of burnt sacrifices," jokes Lewis, standing nearby. "It reminds me of primitive religious rites."

Down on the beach, a group of men and a few women kneel in the sand around two rowboats filled with water and clams. They lift out the bivalves one by one and inspect them, tossing the cracked, smashed, and open ones into one bucket and "the good ones" into another. Against the backdrop of the ocean's rhythmic surging, voices flow and laughter bubbles to the surface. Wooden racks fill up with clams and are stacked in the back of Raymond's truck, to be driven back to the waiting fire. But before they go, Gus will perform his almost zen-like ritual, shaking and running his hands over their shells one more time as he listens for a kind of silence, a hollow rattling—the sound of one dead clam.

Back off the beach, cars are beginning to line the narrow country roads that edge the grove, as people holding tickets and silverware begin to arrive. The stillness of morning has given way to the din of midday. The scene is suddenly filled with bright colors, floral prints, and the sheen of pearls. The new arrivals move adroitly toward the sale tables to acquire pot holders, jars of pickles, and loaves of freshly baked bread. Women hold up aprons; children push wooden toys through the rough-cut grass. First kitchen, soon to be dining hall, the grove is now a marketplace.

Meanwhile, a group of men in work clothes—dark greens, grays, and blues—starts to gather around the fire—Peter and Burney; Burney's father, Allen; Raymond, back from the beach; Ralph Macomber (Fat Mac, as he's called), the burly sawyer from Acushnet; a few young newcomers, who will literally sweat their first encounter with the fire; and a few old men, who have done their service and earned the right to watch. Julie, her hair tucked up into a baseball cap and dressed in a flannel shirt, jeans, and heavy boots, quietly joins them.

A little before noon, a hush descends over the grove. Workers and guests alike begin to form a circle around the fire. Slowly at first, but with increasing speed, Julie and the men step into the fire and, with long-handled pitchforks, pick up the ashen logs and smoldering sticks that are the last remains of the three-hour fire and carry them away from the slab. Next, moving forward and backward in a dance choreographed by intense heat, they lift and toss the

rocks to the sides. Shielded by his worn fireman's coat and rubber boots,
Raymond runs down the middle of the slab, where the heat is most intense,
pushing the coals and cinders aside with a metal scraper until the slab is clear.
Quickly they toss the rocks back into place, and Fat Mac, red-faced from the
heat and wielding a homemade wooden tool, remolds the igneous bed to its
proper size and shape.

Almost before the silent crowd can take a breath, the sweating crew begins
pitching rockweed from the nearby pile onto the rock bed, which is still white
with heat. The sound is like spitting oil, the smell is heavy and pungent; a
thick smoke billows upward. Appearing and disappearing through the steam,
the workers carry the trays filled with food to the slab and stack them carefully,
but blindly, on top of the rocks and the rockweed. Here a tray of striated gray
clams, there a flash of bright orange sweet potatoes; neat rows of brown bags
in brown racks; white corn peeking through the brilliant green of tender
husks. On the very top are placed the shiny silver-foiled pans of dressing.
"Let's go," says Burney, and the parade of men carrying canvases aloft begins.
They lower and drape tarp after tarp over the food and, finally, they seal the
edges with additional rockweed.

For the next hour, as the food cooks, people mingle and chat.

"Burney, hi. Mrs. Dodge. I'm just stopping by for my annual hello. Is your
mother here today?"

"Yeah, she's on the first table. You haven't met my wife before, have you?"

"Last year, for one brief moment. Hello."

"So, how are you? Is David still around Boston?"

Conversations overlap each other; sentences started in years past are pro-
jected into the future. "See you next year," they all conclude.

Before long, a new circle has formed around the steaming food, this time to
hear Lewis deliver the prayer. His quiet voice drifts in and out of hearing, ". . .
the larger family back together again . . . ," drowned out sporadically by the
wind and other talk. "Heavenly Father," he intones, "we thank you for drawing us together in this gathering of family and friends. We thank you for your
providence of nature, from farm and from water, and we thank you for the
friendship and fellowship that has developed over the years. We ask that
everyone may be blessed by this gathering, and that we may be together again
next year. We pray through Jesus Christ, our Lord."

While the crowd stands, still in silence, Fat Mac steps forward and pulls up
an edge of the canvas cover. He reaches into one of the bottom trays, and
stands back, holding a single, steaming clam in his hand. All eyes are now on

him. He removes the gray morsel from its shell, pops it in his mouth, looks once around the circle of expectant faces, and pronounces in his booming, resonant voice, "It's good."

As if a spring had been released, everyone is suddenly in motion. They quickly open the steam oven, pulling back the tarps, and haul out the bottom trays of clams first. Guests scurry back to their seats while men carry trays of food from the fire to the serving tables. Women and children move the food from the trays to bowls and baskets and rush off to their assigned tables to "wait on" while the food is still hot. Around the eating tables the waiters and waitresses go, then back to the serving tables, then out again with more food.

Before the hour is over, some 600 people will have consumed 26 bushels of clams, 200 pounds of sausage, 165 pounds of fish and 175 of tripe; 75 dozen ears of corn, 3 bushels of sweet potatoes, 100 pounds of onions, 30 trays of dressing, 15 loaves of brown bread, 50 pounds of butter, a dozen large watermelon, and more than 50 homemade pies. Before another hour is past, the remains of the meal will have been swept up and taken to the dump, the serving dishes washed and put away, tables and benches taken up and carried back to the cookshack. Soon everyone will go home, sated and tired, and, in the empty lot, the birds will be heard again. The only signs that anyone has been there are a few charred pieces of wood and some warm, melon-sized rocks.[1]

The Allen's Neck Clambake in southeastern Massachusetts has been going on like this for more than a hundred years. It was started in August 1888, when the Allen's Neck Friends Meeting organized an outing on the beach for its Sunday school. Within a few years, the now-annual clambake had become so popular that the Quakers opened it to their friends and neighbors and began charging a fee. Today, the Allen's Neck Clambake—with its local reputation for being the best of the "traditional New England clambakes"—is still a major event in the area's festal calendar. Attended by more than five hundred paying customers and involving nearly one hundred volunteer helpers, it is the primary fund-raiser for the Friends Meeting and easily the community's largest social affair. A large-scale reunion and homecoming, a seasonal fes-tivity and celebration of community, the Allen's Neck Clambake is also, according to one participant, "our most holy day." How all this could have come to pass is the subject of this book.

## Section One

# THE NEW ENGLAND CLAMBAKE: A HISTORY

*'Cause the Indians did it like that, and the people here now want it done the same way.*
—Raymond Davoll, bakemaster, Nonquitt Clambake, July 20, 1985

Indians,[1] it is said, discovered clambaking first. Back before history, they had learned how to cook clams and other seafood in pits dug on the beach, using hot rocks for heat and wet seaweed for steam. When the Pilgrims arrived, the Indians taught them how to do these clambakes, along with a lot of other useful things, and this tradition was passed along, unbroken, in Yankee culture from generation to generation, down to the present day.

Or at least that's how the story usually goes, asserted and "proven" time and again in the reports of archaeologists and antiquarians, in various culinary histories, in journalistic, literary, and poetic renderings, and in the testimonies of enthusiastic modern-day clambakers and clam eaters. A statement such as "The Pilgrims learned the ingenious technique [of clambaking] from the Indians"[2] is a succinct presentation of an idea that is not only commonly accepted but that has also substituted for other, more rigorous attempts to chronicle the presence of this unique foodway on American soil. The fact that there is no direct proof for this particular history of clambaking marks the beginning of the story I will try to tell.

A closer study of the evidence suggests that instead of being a seamlessly

15

organic development, the transmission of a clambake tradition has been uneven, at best, and, at worst, shows signs of having been extremely "unnatural." However we may ultimately judge its role within native American cultural practices, the clambake within a Yankee context has been consistently manipulated for a variety of purposes. Particularly during the late nineteenth century, when clambaking reached the zenith of its popularity, the clambake appears as a by-product of a combined romantic and capitalistic fervor.

"Invented tradition" is the term historians Eric Hobsbawm and Terence Ranger have given to phenomena like this—revered folk customs and ritual complexes that appear to be based on older social orders but that are, in fact, constructed and reconstructed by different groups and generations in such a way as to legitimate existent institutions and values—particularly relating to national and political identity. Hobsbawm defines invented tradition as "a set of practices, normally governed by overtly or tacitly accepted values and of a ritual or symbolic nature, which seek to inculcate certain values and norms of behaviour by repetition, which automatically implies continuity with the past. In fact, where possible, they normally attempt to establish continuity with *a suitable past*. . . . The peculiarity of 'invented' traditions," Hobsbawm continues, "is that the continuity with [the historic past] is largely factitious" [italics mine].[3]

The purpose of this historical section is to explore the fallacies, as well as the "facts," and to examine the "invented" nature of the American tradition of clambaking. Rather than seeking to debunk the Indian-to-Pilgrim chronology of the clambake—to prove it spurious and thereby to dismiss it—I intend instead to follow the path of invention of this tradition to the larger historical and cultural trends that undergird it. In addition, by unearthing the historical artifacts of clambaking—both "real" and "invented"—that make up its interpretive repertoire, I also hope to be able to display the diversity of symbolic values associated with clambaking over time that explains, to a large extent, why the practice has survived and often flourished.

# 1

# Early Evidence

*Nobody knows much about the history of the clambake. There have been a lot of assumptions made, but we've never had to prove them.*
—Jim Baker, historian, Plimoth Plantation, March 22, 1988

T O THE EXTENT that popular belief in the prehistoric origins of clambaking ever even requires substantiation, people have widely assumed that these origins are documented somehow by archaeological studies. Food historians in particular, eager to flesh out the story of the earliest American gastronomic experiences, have tended to extrapolate broadly from the more cautious findings of archaeologists (when they have consulted them at all). The confident, authoritative histories of native American culinary habits that have resulted attest ancient clambaking practices pleasingly similar to those of today and reaffirm the myth of their transference from native to newcomer.[1] Archaeological research, however, provides no such proof for the native American origins and ancestry of the clambake.[2]

What archaeologists have uncovered about precontact indigenous American seafood practices is much more circumstantial. William Ritchie's excavations on Martha's Vineyard, for example, indicated that "shellfish exploitation" in southeastern Massachusetts goes back at least four thousand years.[3] Ritchie's study of the island's shell middens—the ancient rubbish heaps—allowed him to obtain the stratigraphic and chronologic data necessary for his

Indians offering the bounty of the New World welcome Roger Williams to Rhode Island. Engraving by Johnson & Fry Co., New York, 1866. Courtesy of the Rhode Island Historical Society.

book, subtitled *A Framework for the Prehistory of Southern New England*. Within this framework, Ritchie was able to conclude, among other things, that shellfish gathering was one of the oldest of "a series of different cultural manifestations" that characterized cultural adaptations to the marine environment during Archaic times, beginning as early as 2270 B.C.[4]

In *The Archaeology of New England*, Dean Snow offered additional information about factors that shaped the use of shellfish in the region. Snow noted that during the Early Horticultural Period (1000 B.C.–70 A.D.), a drop in water temperature occurred that caused a decrease in the population of a number of varieties of shellfish. There was, however, Snow added, "a relative

and perhaps absolute increase in the abundance of soft clams (*Mya arenaria*)
over the same period. These changes in natural abundance are reflected in
changing frequencies of their relative abundance in coastal archaeological
sites."[5] The reduction of other available food sources simultaneous with the
increase of the soft clam apparently served as the point of origin for a regional
dietary habit among native peoples—a habit that laid the foundation, at least,
for the later practice of white inhabitants feasting on these same clams.

In addition to the midden pits, the "shell heaps" found throughout the New
England region have been another source for scholarly projections about
shellfish consumption by native populations. Shell heaps were numerous and
large, and, according to Howard Russell in *Indian New England Before the
Mayflower*, were "to be met at oyster harbors and clam banks on the Connecticut shore, the largest (24 acres) at Milford, and all about Narragansett Bay.
Banks of waste still remain at Apponaug (translated "Shellfish") in Warwick,
Rhode Island. There were dozens of spots on Cape Cod. In Maine, clam
banks, scores of them, have been identified at Damariscotta, Sheepscot Bay,
Medomack, York, Deer Isle, and other beaches. Many are or were three feet
deep and some ten to twenty acres in extent."[6]

Unmistakably a raw form of evidence of the importance of shellfish to the
area's original populations, the mounds have also been interpreted as proof of
an early practice of drying and smoking large quantities of shellfish for winter
use—an activity that European immigrants witnessed later, during their initial
period of contact. The association of the shell mounds with seasonal activities
links them additionally to the widespread conjectures about annual migration
patterns. William Simmons, in his ethno-historical portrayal of New England's indigenous peoples, has stated, "Residence patterns varied with the
season through a cycle of dense inland winter villages, to spring fishing camps,
to dispersed summer homesteads by cornfields near the sea, to isolated inland
hunting camps in autumn and early winter."[7]

While the deposits of shells confirm for archaeologists and anthropologists
the prominence of shellfish preservation and consumption in the life of these
native communities before the arrival of Europeans, they represent something
quite different among local people of the present day who have encountered
them: they are taken as simple proof of the ancient heritage of Indian
clambaking. In the popular imagination—where larger associations of native
American culture with abundant gaming, feasting, and celebration already
exist—the association of shell heaps with clambakes makes perfect sense.[8]

Around Allen's Neck in particular, people use words like "we are told," "they say," and "tradition states" to express the long-term and widespread belief that clambakes were held regularly throughout the region by its original inhabitants, the Wampanoag Indians, and that the practice came down to their ancestors from this source.[9] A tribal confederacy of thirty villages spread across southeastern Massachusetts from Cape Cod to Narragansett Bay (including the islands of Nantucket and Martha's Vineyard), the Wampanoag, or Pokanoket, were the same people who welcomed the Pilgrims upon their arrival.

According to the published and unpublished works of local amateur historians, the Wampanoag held annual clambakes in a number of nearby locations. "We are told that the Indians of Old Dartmouth used to have annual clambakes at two places, at least, in the town," Gladys B. Gifford wrote in her *History of Old Dartmouth from 1602 to 1676*. "One of these was held near the shores of Apponegansett (now Padanaram) and the other at Paquachuck (now Westport Point). The exact spot where the Paquachuck clambakes were held is fixed for us by tradition at a place west of the present village and known as Cape Bial, so named for Abiel Macomber."[10] Other sites include "a little point of land facing the Acushnet River" in New Bedford, called "Smoking Rock," and another near the mill pond off Gifford Road in Head of Westport.[11]

Ginny Morrison, a lifelong resident of the area and a member of the Allen's Neck Friends Meeting, remembers this last location from her childhood: "Up at the Head of Westport, you head north on Gifford Road, and there's a river that comes meandering down through a meadow. And when I was a kid going to school in that area, there was a great big huge mound, right beside the river. And the people always said that the Indians from inland came down in the spring and summer for their summer camp in the area, and that's where they had clambakes, and those were mounds of shells. Whether it's true or not, I don't know, but that's what they used to say."[12]

These days, with more land being developed and divided up, the local kids rarely come across shell heaps or mounds. But when today's older generation was young, evidence of the earlier Indian presence was still tangible and vivid. They studied it in their school lessons about King Philip's War, in which their own village of Russells Mills had been destroyed; they handled the arrowheads that their fathers' plows tossed up in the fields; and they played among the Indian burial ground and ancient Indian shell heaps along the shorelines. Being "born among the shells," as one member of the Allen's Neck Clambake crew describes it,[13] resulted in a vernacular archaeological sensibility, which, like its professional counterpart, shifts back and forth between artifacts and conjecture to produce a form of local knowledge about the land and its former inhabitants. Within this framework, the evidence of Wampanoag clambaking, although still officially circumstantial, has nonetheless satisfied the local inhabitants.

The lack of official archaeological proof for the Indian invention of clambaking involves more than just a matter of questioning the belief modern-day Yankee clambakers hold that they are continuing a tradition of native American ancestry. More significant in the larger context of cultural politics, acknowledging the lack of evidence involves questioning the beliefs held by modern-day native Americans themselves that clambaking is part of *their* heritage. In the history of white-Indian relations in this country, where a great deal more than the attribution of clambaking origins has been at stake, the dismissal of native traditions—another kind of local knowledge—has often had dire consequences.

In these interactions, White has almost always made Right. And not only White, but Write—the presence of literary, written artifacts—so that, lacking what the ruling white culture has determined to be proper documentation, native history and culture have been consistently relegated to the realm of belief and folklore, not knowledge or fact.[14] Even today, archaeology and anthropology, the sciences of the unwritten, have had uneven success in providing proof of native claims to such inheritances as land, treaty agreements, and tribal status.[15] From a native American perspective, then, a "scientific" challenge to the Indian ancestry of clambaking is nothing particularly new.

Even the opposite response—in this case, the widespread, popular attribution of the clambake as an Indian invention, which is, after all, never based on native sources or testimony—testifies more to the low value whites have placed on the clambake as an actual cultural property than it does to their benevolent recognition of native traditions as independently valid and worthy of respect. For whites to say that the clambake has an Indian origin has given nothing away; in fact, as the history of Yankee clambaking unfolds, it will become clear that even through this attribution, whites, and not Indians, have been the ones to gain.

However tangential or even overblown these matters of cultural politics may appear on the surface, they have persistently dogged this investigation of the clambake, and I would like to make them explicit at the outset. The notion of invented traditions, clearly a valuable historiographic tool for teasing out the constructedness of some of our most sacred cattle, requires an additional sensitivity to "multi-vocality"—an awareness of the existence of "many voices"—if it is to accommodate the number of perspectives that this, or any other time-honored tradition, actually involves. For example, as I will eventually argue, it is possible for the clambake to be a part of native American cultural inheritance *and* an invented tradition within white culture.[16]

Dateline: mid-June 1987, Plymouth, Massachusetts. Dressed only in a hand-stitched leather loincloth, a young Indian boy carries a smoking pine cone in a stone bowl from the fire at the center of the campsite to the nearby pile of twigs and wood. He hands the bowl to a young man standing next to the pile, who takes the pine cone and, pushing back his braids, blows on it, igniting the brush and leaves with its sparks. As the two Indians work, a cluster of white schoolchildren under the careful eye of their teachers point, poke, and jostle each other, while some of them dutifully take out their Kodaks to record the Indian clambake.

Despite the fact that archaeological proof for precolonial clambaking does not actually exist, clambakes at the Wampanoag Summer Campsite once constituted an integral part of the summer programming at Plimoth Plantation, the living history museum in Massachusetts that attempts to re-create life at the Plymouth Colony in 1627.[17] Nanepashemet, curator of the Plantation's Wampanoag Indian Program, explains that "what makes sense"—as well as what is available and practical—is often a necessary element in the public interpretation of a native American cultural past. Standing at the edge of the fire, tossing in commercially hewn cordwood, Nanepashemet notes that the popular Wampanoag clambake demonstration is a case in point.

Invisible, certainly, to the gaggle of schoolchildren on a field trip, some very complex issues undergird the performance they witness in innocence as historical "fact." From the perspective of many anthropological critics of culture, even if this "Indian clambake" had rigorous documentation to back it up, it would still be, at best, an objectification and recontextualization of native American experience, and, at worst, a dangerous misappropriation.[18] According to anthropologists Richard Handler and Jocelyn Linnekin, "Western common sense, which presumes that an unchanging core of ideas and customs is always handed down to us from the past" is insidious, and is part of an historical consciousness that strips other peoples of their own history in order to create a globally accepted, "hegemonic" or homogenizing model of cultural identity.[19]

Summer clambake at Plimoth Plantation, 1987 (Nanepashemet, standing at mid-range, at right). Photo by Kathy Neustadt, 1987, courtesy Office of Folklife Programs, Smithsonian Institution.

Himself a Wampanoag, Nanepashemet would, according to this perspective, be doubly implicated in this drama of cultural struggle—aiding the "oppressors" in recasting his culture in their own terms and for their own oppressing purposes. But that is not the only way to look at it. In fact, Nanepashemet's participation in and attitude toward the clambake is precisely the "voice" that has consistently been missing from the chorus of food historians, archaeologists, local Yankees, and even critics of culture. His position deserves closer examination.

Nanepashemet "knows his history": he knows the documents of the early white settlers, and he knows the traditions passed down from his Indian ancestry. His professional as well as personal responsibility at Plimoth Plantation is to act as proprietor of his own culture; his task, to find ways to present and interpret the "Indian ways"—his own cultural heritage—to non-Indians, for the most part, but also to other native Americans. And Nanepashemet— knowing what the historical and archaeological research says and doesn't say— believes the clambake to be a native tradition. "I tend to think that it wasn't a big formal deal because basically our staple foods were from the garden—corn, beans, and squash—and the important ceremonial times would be for the harvesting and the thanking for the corn . . ." he says. "[A clambake was] a way of feasting, cooking food in the summertime, near the shore. A lot of times native people would be foraging along the coast for shellfish and things like that—it was a convenient way to have a big feed for a lot of people."[20]

His is a portrayal of native clambaking without romanticized drama, without eulogies to the "linear and irreversible" nature of time.[21] It is an account of a practice not tinged with awesome venerability, as most non-natives' renderings are. Because Nanepashemet perceives clambaking to be part of his own culture—ongoing and still vital for him—there is none of the feeling of vestigial survival and no image of the Indian as filling "a pathetic imaginative space for the dominant culture . . . always survivors, noble or wretched."[22] His is clearly a different voice.

In nearby Mashpee, an "Indian town" for more than three hundred years,[23] the clambake put on at the annual Fourth of July "People of the First Light Annual Pow-wow" is of the style Nanepashemet describes—practical, convenient, and adaptive, as well as festive. Displaying none of the self-consciousness that surrounds a clambake like the one at Allen's Neck, the Mashpee bake is relaxed, flexible, even a bit helter-skelter. Some years, when it's not convenient, it isn't held at all. No air of the inviolable surrounds it: wood is tossed onto the fire without any particular design, workers show up and disappear without apologies, the timing is adjusted to suit the buying public's needs, and no one holds forth on how it should be done or how it has always been done. It is as unmarked an activity as a backyard cookout would be for many American families.

This kind of "Indian clambake," the kind performed by Indians themselves, highlights another issue that reappears throughout the history of this tradition: who actually owns the clambake? Is it Nanepashemet and the people of Mashpee who, according to their traditions, are the descendants of the first clambakers? Is it Plimoth Plantation, who has Nanepashemet in its employ and whose historians, in general, have been entrusted with interpreting our "sacred texts," the documents of our nation's origin? Is it the people of Allen's Neck, with a century of clambaking under their belts, or the pavilion owners who have made a business of the feast?

Or is it the children—"our future," we call them—and the ticket-holders, who as tourists and seekers of knowledge have exchanged legal tender for ownership of history, photographic truth, and hands-on, mouth-on, firsthand gastronomic experience? Conjecture, caricature, traditions, and assumptions abound in the quest for the origins of the clambake. Archaeological evidence in one network is traditional inheritance in another; making one man's prehistoric source another man's culture. However destabilizing this thought, close scrutiny of tradition has a way of making it clear that even science, history, and common sense are relational issues.

If the origins of clambaking are lost in the misty realms of the prehistoric past, then the transfer of the clambake from native American to white culture is equally shrouded in the glorified myths of American national origins. On the one hand, what is known about native American culture in the 1600s has been derived wholly from the accounts of the early English settlers, sources that, as one historian points out, reveal more about the observers than they do about the observed.[24] Information about the English experience during the early years of settlement, on the other hand, has been so thoroughly filtered through a constructed national saga as to have been rendered into nearly whole-cloth inventions which fulfill varying presentistic, self-affirming needs rather than more serious historical ones.

"The aboundance of Sea-Fish are almost beyond beleeving and sure I would scarce have beleeved it except I had scene it with mine owne Eyes," wrote Francis Higginson in his 1630 report, *New-Englands Plantation*.[25] But about clambakes Higginson had nothing to say. Feasting of any kind was far from common, and during the winter of that same year, according to Cotton Mather, "The only food the poor had was acorns, ground-nuts, mussels, and clams," and a man "inviting his friends to a dish of clams, at the table gave Thanks to Heaven who 'had given them to suck the abundance of the seas, and the treasures hid in the sands.'"[26]

Mather's reference to prayers of thanksgiving notwithstanding, other testimonies suggest that this appreciation of the sea's abundance was not universal during the early years of settlement. The English, who depended largely on the knowledge and technologies of the Indians for their survival, had to eat what was available during these early years—eat or starve—but they apparently did not unanimously feel that they had to like it.[27] Whereas oysters were embraced gustatorily almost from the beginning,[28] other shellfish was not. As culinary historians Root and de Rochemont have noted, "It is on record that in the 1620s the Pilgrims fed clams and mussels to their hogs with the explanation that they were 'the meanest of God's blessings'"[29]—and mussels, at least in the Allen's Neck region, are still considered "trash food" today.[30]

"Come Over and Help Us,"
seal of the Massachusetts
Bay Colony from 1629 until
1692, when the motto was
changed and the Indian figure was shown brandishing
a sword. From Joseph B.
Felt, *Annals of Salem* (1845).

Root and de Rochement have explained this phenomenon as an English resistance to foreign foodways: "The initial hardships of the colonists were to a considerable extent the result of their own shortcomings. A minor one was characteristic unwillingness to accept any change in their eating habits; one suspects that the Pilgrims, dire as was their need, did not give as much attention as they should have to collecting food which they did not like (fish, shellfish and lobster, among them)."[31] So low was the status of the clam for human consumption that recipes for its use rarely appeared in English cookbooks, and Hannah Glasse's 1747 *Art of Cookery,* which includes a recipe for Muscle (clam) Pie, seems to have been the first cookbook in the American colonies to include the clam within the edible and enjoyable category.[32]

If the English settlers were ill disposed to welcome clams with open arms, they were even less inclined to adopt new methods of food preparation. Culinary historian Betty Fussell has proposed a general psychological resistance among newcomers to the technical novelties of the host culture: "Indian methods of roasting shells in their campfires or steaming them in earth pits would have seemed to the new settlers a reversion to the barbarisms of their own Celtic tribes." Less speculatively, she asserts, "As soon as they could, they substituted pots and pans," and on this point there is considerable substantiating literature from the period.[33] As early as the 1650s, at least one visitor to the colonies had testified to this same trend, noting that as food was becoming more abundant in the New World, English foodways were reappearing: "They have not forgotten the English fashion."[34]

An additional obstacle to the possibility that a tradition of native clam-baking would have passed smoothly into the English culinary repertoire, of course, is the actual history of the relationship between indigenous peoples and English newcomers. The peaceful interaction between the New England Indians and the Puritans, so critical during the early years of settlement and so

King Philip (Metacomet or Pemeta-com), son of Massasoit, drawing by Palo Alto Pierce in Ebenezer W. Pierce, *Indian History and Genealogy* (1878).

much the focus of the historiographic romanticism, came to an abrupt and violent end during King Philip's War, 1675–1676, in which the settlers suffered severe losses and the Wampanoag were brought to near extinction.[35]

The tolls of the war have been variously reported, but the impact is generally agreed upon: in little more than fifty years, the English colonists had effectively routed out the Indian populations of Connecticut, Rhode Island, and Massachusetts.[36] Good feelings toward the original host culture and the inclination to celebrate Indian heritage did not appear among the non-native population for at least another hundred years, and then only after native culture had been all but eradicated throughout the region.

Despite the widespread belief that clambaking was an uninterrupted American tradition that changed hands during the early years of colonization, a more careful study suggests that such a chain of events is unlikely. In place of the simplistic Indian-to-Pilgrim transference of knowledge, what appears instead is a general resistance by the English to foreign foodstuffs and technologies and a subsequent re-embracing of their own customary foodways, all within a climate that became increasingly inhospitable to cultural exchange of any kind with native Americans.[37] It is the prevalence and tenacity of the imagery of the inheritance—rather than the inheritance itself—that reasserts itself as the compelling focus of historical study.

# 2

# The Politics of Feasting

*Having maturely weighed and seriously considered the many
disadvantages and inconveniences that arise from intermixing with the
company at the taverns in this town of Plymouth, and apprehending that
a well regulated club will have a tendency to prevent the same, and to
increase not only the pleasure and happiness of the respective members,
but also will conduce to their edification and instruction, [these men] do
hereby incorporate themselves into a society.*
—Records of the Old Colony Club, Plymouth, Massachusetts,
January 13, 1769

**T**HE CONFLICT in American culture between the ethics of work
and the ethics of play tends to overshadow any evidence of clambaking from
the early 1700s. Since the first stages of settlement, the country's founders had
exhibited a consistently negative attitude toward leisure and play, the context
in which the bounteous clambake feast might have been expected to occur.
This "Puritan concept of the evil inherent in any frivolous waste of time,"[1] as
Foster Dulles has described it in his history of American recreation, was
relatively easily maintained during times of hardship and scarcity, which
predominated during the early colonial period.

However, as the struggle for basic survival began to ease, the early populations of the colonies—never wholly Puritan and steadily becoming less so[2]—
started returning to the pastimes and pleasures of their English background.
"Hunting and fishing, the sports associated with farm festivals, shooting
matches and horse-races, country dances, the amusements of the colonial
tavern. . . . These were the characteristic forms of recreation for the colonial
yeomanry during the eighteenth century," according to Dulles. "The sports
and games were largely those which their forefathers, or they themselves, had
once enjoyed in England."[3]

Sporting activities, agrarian festivals, and tavern life also provided the arenas in which food developed a prominent role in colonial recreational culture. Among the well-to-do, in particular, the pre-Revolutionary decades in America were especially rich in toothsome amusements. One example of an aristocratic culinary craze was turtle dinners, and there are reports of Boston society gathering for "turtle feasts," New Yorkers traveling to country estates for this same repast—even "as far as Harlem"—and of turtle banquets being served in Newport during its first rise to social and aristocratic preeminence.[4]

According to food historian William Woys Weaver, inns also purchased exotic and expensive Caribbean green sea turtles and sold tickets to their turtle feasts, which offered status to all who took part in these events and raised money for one political cause or another. Oyster houses apparently functioned in much the same fashion. By the 1790s, ox roasts, which were associated with the major markets' trading seasons, had become another particularly popular form of political fund-raising—or vote-buying, depending on one's point of view.[5] The celebratory void created by the Puritans was steadily being filled by these kinds of public rallies, with food—the seemingly innocuous component—playing a central role.

This merging of politics with public dining during the period surrounding the American Revolution—a time in which, as Hobsbawm has pointed out, "plenty of political institutions, ideological movements and groups . . . were so unprecedented that even historic continuity had to be invented"—proved fertile ground for the development of an array of "entirely new symbols and devices" of nationalistic identity.[6] The search to establish and nurture an indigenous American cultural identity entailed the intentional manipulation of available political, historical, and religious symbols—inventing traditions— and the growing passion for patriotic feasting served as a backdrop against which the clambake and other forms of outdoor eating became imbued with considerable historical significance and value.

Although it oversimplifies the matter slightly, it can be argued that the Yankee clambake had its spiritual—if not its actual—genesis in the 1769 founding of the Old Colony Club at Plymouth. The Old Colony Club was a group of civic-minded, largely Harvard-educated gentlemen whose aim it was to memorialize "the first landing of our worthy ancestors in this place."[7] The group's initiation of a "Forefathers' Day" celebration that first year had at its center a commemorative meal, which, while hardly a clambake itself, established for clam-eating in general a symbolic context and core of meaning which would deepen and intensify in the years that followed.

Invitation to the Forefathers' Day dinner, 1800, engraved for the Colonial Society of Massachusetts from an original in the possession of the Massachusetts Society of Mayflower Descendants; reprinted in *Publications of the Colonial Society of Massachusetts*, vol. 17, *Transactions 1913–1914* (1915).

According to the club's records, the first Forefathers' Day meal consisted of these foods:

1. A large baked Indian whortleberry pudding
2. A dish of sauquetash [succotash; in this case, a soup]
3. A dish of clams
4. A dish of oysters and a dish of codfish
5. A haunch of venison roasted by the first jack brought to the Colony
6. A dish of sea-fowl
7. A ditto of frost-fish and eels
8. An apple pie
9. A course of cranberry tarts, and cheese made in the Old Colony

It was a meal, the records state, "dressed in the plainest manner (all appearances of luxury and extravagance being avoided, in imitation of our worthy ancestors whose memory we shall ever respect)."[8]

The tradition of commemorating American history through the medium of food dates back at least to the centennial celebration of the landing of the Mayflower, when, as noted by theologian, educator, and early Yale president, Ezra Stiles a "century festival" held in Plymouth included a two-part meal—"first a Wooden Dish of Indian Corn and Clams to represent how our Fathers fed in 1620, then an elegant Dinner to shew 1720."[9] In the 1769 presentation of the Forefathers' meal, however, "Corn and Clams" no longer represented dire need but embodied, instead, a positive cultural valence—the merging of indigenous Indian foodstuffs with the technical and culinary skills of the "worthy ancestors" to produce simple but redoubtable nourishment. The Forefathers' Day feast was an "Entertainment," as it was described a few years later, both "plain and elegant,"[10] in which the clam remained a key symbol.

Although its foodstuffs would be kept relatively simple, the Forefathers' Day feast in ensuing years began to show signs of its organizers having drawn from the "well-supplied warehouse of official ritual, symbolism and moral exhortation" which, according to Hobsbawm, every society accumulates from its past.[11] Prominent among these increasingly symbolic elaborations was the appearance of the phrase "Feast of Shells" to refer to the Forefathers' Day meal. Reported first in 1798, it was a term derived from a number of sources.

The uniquely American identity of the term Feast of Shells was widely assumed to be an historical one: as explained by one journalist in a 1806 newspaper account in Boston—where Forefathers' Day had begun to be celebrated in the last years of the eighteenth century—it was "in honor to the ancestors of the country, who were fed with clams, and other bounties of the sea, [that] they called it a *feast of shells*."[12] In his more extensive historical research on behalf of the Colonial Society of Massachusetts, historian and member Albert Matthews traced the expression to a different, European source: "It should be pointed out . . . that the expressions 'the shells of the feast,' 'the shells of joy,' 'the shell of feasts,' 'to rejoice in the shell,' 'the hall of shells,' 'the feast of shells,' occur in the Ossianic poems: Macpherson explaining that *'To rejoice in the shell,* is a phrase for feasting sumptuously, and drinking freely.'"[13] Within the context of invented traditions, this simultaneous referencing of an historic American colonial experience and traditional European "folk" connotations can hardly be viewed as coincidental.

As Matthews has pointed out, shells were being incorporated regularly in physical as well as symbolic form in American commemorative celebrations by the end of the eighteenth century. At the 1799 Forefathers' Day feast in Plymouth, for example, "a shell of uncommon size"—an oyster shell weighing two hundred pounds and capable of holding a bushel's quantity—was "borrowed from the Museum of the Historical Society, [and] adorned the head of the table, containing the *appropriate succatash*, sufficient for the numerous company." Later, at the 1820 bicentennial anniversary celebration of the landing at Plymouth Rock, the shell of the scallop became a kind of official badge of the event when, according to Matthews, "at the ball in the evening some young ladies hung a shell suitably decorated on the breast of Mr. Webster, the orator of the day." The scallop shell appears again on the cornerstone of the canopy over Plymouth Rock, which was constructed in 1869.[14]

For the people of Plymouth, the choice of the scallop shell was hardly random. Its iconography in the Old World context dates back to at least the twelfth century, when it first became associated with the concept of the Christian pilgrimage. According to one scallop symbolist, "The charmed name of '*Coquille St. Jacques*' was given by the pilgrims of the Middle Ages to the scallop shell with which they decorated their mantles when journeying . . . to the tomb of St. James at Santiago de Compostela. Clad in coarse cloth, staff in hand, they threaded their way on foot in long processions, praying and singing hymns, devoutly carrying their shells dedicated to St. James."[15] Matthews's discovery of the simultaneous appearance of "the word Pilgrim, as specifically applied to an early settler" of America—a descendant of earlier religious adventurers—and the phrase "feast of shells" provides convincing evidence for the intertwining of these otherwise seemingly disparate images in American iconography.[16]

St. James dressed as a pilgrim returning
from his shrine at Compostela, Spain; the
scallop shell adorns his hat and purse. Miniature from a fourteenth-century English
manuscript, reprinted in *The New Catholic
Encyclopedia* (1967–79).

Pilgrims, shells, and clam dinners: the associations were so well established
by the early 1800s that they were capable of supporting satire, as this poem
printed in Boston's January 9, 1804, *Independent Chronicle* clearly demonstrates:

> *The modern Clam-Eaters.*
>
> The *Pilgrim's Sons* who dwell on earth,
> God knows from *whom* they claim their birth;
> On some pretence, as rumour tells,
> Each year renew their *feast of shells,*
> At faction-hall, where *tories* meet,
> Apostate *whigs* and *priests* to greet;— . . .
> For there the living act their part,
> And lay the bottle close to heart.

Whilst clams and oysters round are spread,
And wine to rouse some drooping head.
Old Stephen mounted in the chair
Of *federal feasts* and *toasts* lord mayor,
Proclaims again their cause of meeting
Once more his brother tories greeting.[17]

In addition to identifying the political factions then in currency, this ode also demonstrates how overt the connection had become between Forefathers' Day and partisan politics, between politics in general and the eating of clams.

In the years following the Revolution, European culture no longer served as a viable reference for American identity, and, challenged by the status of their unprecedented political institution—the new nation—Americans were forced to reinterpret their identity through the establishment of an acceptable "native" American essence. Organizations like the Old Colony Club, whose very existence was premised on the assertion of "a suitable past," were faced not only with developing concepts of the country's founding fathers as "Pilgrims" but also with interpreting and defining the role of the Indian as the original "native" American.[18]

In such public and self-conscious celebrations as Forefathers' Day, the ongoing political and conceptual tensions concerning Indian heritage were displayed in largely symbolic terms. At the first Forefathers' Day feast in 1769, for example, among the toasts raised to the English settlers, their governors, and their officers was one made "to the memory of Massasoit, our *first and best friend and ally of the natives*" [italics mine].[19] This toast afforded Massasoit, the "sachem," or leader, of the Wampanoags, a stature of equal value to those of the "ancestors," and it testified to the dependency on honorable friends and allies that characterized the still-tenuous status of the pre-Revolutionary colonists.

By 1799, however, an altogether new approach is evident in the Forefathers' Day toast, which was raised to "*the memory of our Ancestors.*—May their ardour inspire and their success encourage their descendants to maintain their birthrights, and may all their *enemies* be converted like Massasoit, or suffer like Phillip [Massasoit's son and defeated leader of King Phillip's War]" [italics mine].[20] Once "first and best friend," Massasoit was now cast as an enemy who had been deftly dealt with; American ancestry and birthright had come to reside solely with its white, non-Indian and non-European, inhabitants. This shift in imagery suggests a sharp redefinition of American boundaries with significant political, moral, and symbolic consequences.

In terms of the clambake itself, this problematic role of the Indians within

American culture had quite specific implications. Although evidence of isolated incidents of Indians serving clam feasts to whites actually exists[21]—and, based on the rapid development of the clambake's appearance during the early part of the 1800s, might, in any case, be inferred—clambaking as a phenomenon within Yankee popular culture appears to have been the product of this process of white cultural synthesis. That is, it arose as an "American" tradition only when the dominant culture had established the necessary symbolic context for it, as one critic puts it, by "altering the cultural icon so that it conforms to the majority population's notions of itself."[22]

Along with the Feast of Shells, another tradition associating the sumptuous eating of "pilgrims" with Indians was also being invented and would lay further iconographic foundations for the clambake to become an American tradition. Drawing together the spontaneous, secular, English-style Harvest Home celebrated by the Pilgrims at Plymouth in 1621 with the religious commemoration of a sign of divine grace held by the Puritans of the Massachusetts Bay Colony in 1623, the celebration of Thanksgiving in the 1700s showed signs of becoming "a fully grown and established institution."[23] Following the Revolution and heightening during the Civil War, the movement to have Thanksgiving recognized as a national holiday evolved in a fashion similar to that of Forefathers' Day, moving from a spontaneous local commemoration to an annual event to the level of political rallying.[24]

The symbolism of Thanksgiving conjoined two major traditions from the European heritage—the annual harvest celebration and the religious commemoration of holy days and special occasions. Pre-Christian in origin, the Harvest Home is generally considered to be among the oldest of European folk celebrations,[25] and this feast of the final harvest was later incorporated into the church calendar as one of the five festivals associated with the Veneration of Mary. The period from mid-August to mid-September, called "Our Lady's Thirty Days," was considered a period of rejoicing, and it was believed that "all food produced during this period is especially wholesome and good, and will remain fresh much longer than at other times of the year." The Feast of the Assumption, celebrated on August 15, included "blessing elements of nature which are the scene of man's labor and the source of human food."[26]

For the Puritans who arrived in the New World, the resanctification of holy days in opposition to the Catholic church was as much at issue as the forging of religious identity distinct from that of the Church of England. In order to

celebrate fasts and feast days as special occasions—the second of Thanksgiving's two components—the Puritans were faced with decisions of symbolic
import. Fast days were celebrated by the Church of England on Friday, a
remnant of the Catholic *dies stationum*, with Wednesday as the second choice;
Monday in England at this time was "fish day." In order not to appear
"popist," then, the nonconformists were inclined to set fasts and feast days on
Tuesday and Thursday.[27] Long after this original rationale was forgotten,
Thursday continued to be the most common day for the celebration of
Thanksgiving throughout New England and later across the nation; and from
the early 1800s on, Thursday was also the day on which clambakes and, as will
be seen, Squantum feasts, were most likely to be held.

Although breaking with the calendar of the Church of England, the
Puritan choice of Thursday for significant food rituals reestablished a connection with a much older Catholic tradition. According to the *Handbook of
Christian Feasts*, "The weekly memory of the Last Supper, with its institution
of the Holy Eucharist, prompted the faithful to accord special honors and
veneration to the Blessed Sacrament on Thursday. This custom, originating in
the early centuries of the second millennium, was accepted and approved in
the reform of Pius V, who inserted the Mass of the Most Blessed Sacrament
among the weekly votive Masses. In many places it was customary (and still is)
in sections of Central Europe."[28] The fact that the nonconformist calendar
merely reinstituted an older Catholic tradition is but one of the many ironies
that can occur when traditions are being invented.

In addition to being days of fasting and feasting, Thursdays were also
associated in Puritan New England with the midweek Lecture Days, which
were set aside for spiritual revival and moral review. From a very early period,
Lecture Days included not only uplifting speeches but a chance for social
intercourse and even the possibility of idle leisure. According to Dulles,
"Toward the close of the period of the Great Migration [to America], the
popularity of the midweek church meeting, known as the Great and Thursday, began keeping many of the people from their work. 'There were so many
lectures now in the country,' John Winthrop wrote in 1639, 'and many poor
persons would usually resort to two or three in a week, to the great neglect of
their affairs, and the damage to the public.'"[29] In this context, the replacement
of the Lecture Day with such good Christian entertainment as a church
clambake would not have represented such a radical disjuncture.

Although why its clambake takes place on Thursday is a mystery to most of
the Allen's Neck residents, Willy Morrison, the unofficial chronicler of the

community's history, offers this explanation: "People say, 'Why is the Clam-bake held on Thursday?' There's a good reason for it. All of the people in those days were country people, and they all had cows and they all had chickens. And in that particular area down there, they all sold eggs to New Bedford, or wherever. They went to town on Wednesdays. And on Wednesdays, they could bring back [for the clambake] your sausage and tripe and the stuff that you just didn't make on the farm. So simple . . . Wednesday was city day. It was still city day when I was growing up."[30] The feasting habits of the Puritans clearly established a pattern of symbolic social engagements on Thursdays and, as this testimony suggests, undoubtedly shaped the establishment of the American marketing schedule as well.

The people at Allen's Neck today will often refer to their clambake as "a kind of Thanksgiving meal," and many of the symbolic elements that were becoming subsumed under the Thanksgiving celebration during the eighteenth and nineteenth centuries are readily apparent in its present structure. In both timing and tenor, in its seasonal and religious imagery, and in a variety of its other calendrical, culinary, and communal themes, the clambake at Allen's Neck bears a striking resemblance to the celebrations of Harvest Home and "holy days" which Thanksgiving came to entail.

"At the new moon of the month of string beans" at "the old celebrated spot" along the rocky shore east of Neponset Bridge, five miles from Boston, celebrants carrying knives and forks (spoons would be fashioned from clam-shells) assembled for a rustic shellfish feast. An Indian woman, dressed in blanket and moccasins, presided over the ceremonies, intoning "in the meta-phorical manner of the Indians." It was the fourth Thursday in August of the year 1812, and the event was the Squantum celebration.[31]

A descendant of the Forefathers' Day celebration and a variant of the Feast of Shells initiated by the Old Colony Club at Plymouth, the Squantum celebration was a highly stylized, participatory pageant, a dramatic interpreta-tion with ideological and political overtones of one aspect of the national history. It celebrated the indigenous American past and identity through images of the noble native American savage—whose roles were filled, sig-nificantly, by whites—while simultaneously asserting a homogeneous white American present and future. In terms of this chronology, the Squantum feast also represents an essential link in the development of the New England clambake as an invented tradition.[32]

According to American glossaries and slang dictionaries—the primary sources documenting its existence—the Squantum feast was particularly popular in Nantucket and around the Boston area, where it became an annual event in the latter part of the eighteenth century or the early years of the nineteenth. Although later taken to mean a rustic picnic or general merrymaking, its earlier connotations were often associated with Indian origins, as the name of a deity, a location, or native clambaking activities.[33] In his *System of Universal Geography* (1832), S. G. Goodrich provided a brief history for the festival, which he described as already on the decline: "*Squantum* was the name of the last Indian female who resided there ["at a rocky point projecting into Boston Bay"]; and when the feast is held with the ancient ceremonies, a person comes forth dressed as Squantum herself, and harangues the people. . . . Some of the ceremonies consisted in brightening the chain of peace, and in burying the tomahawk in a place indicated by the representative of *Squantum*. A sachem too, dressed in blankets and moccasins, would sometimes assume the direction of the feast."[34]

Goodrich's note that "during the late war [the Revolution], when political parties were violent, *the feast of Squantum* was attended by crowds, and in fact both parties had a distinct celebration"[35] suggests its close chronological, geographical, and political connection to the Feast of Shells. But his identification of the personage Squantum as the last Indian inhabitant of the particular site signals an even more telling association. In tracing the use of Indian imagery in American expressive culture, particularly during the early 1800s, Robert F. Berkofer has noted that "perhaps most romantic of all [of the conventions] was the impression of the Indian as rapidly passing away before the onslaught of civilization. . . . The nostalgia and pity aroused by the dying race produced the best kind of romantic sentiment and gave the sense of fleeting time beloved of romantic sensibilities. . . . The tragedy of the dying Indian, especially as represented by *the last living member of the tribe*, became a staple of American literature and art" [italics mine].[36] The enactment of this drama in the form of a feast situates the Squantum within a larger complex of American popular cultural activities that American Indian scholar Rayna Green has termed "playing Indian."[37]

"Just as it has been said that the Europeans could easily ennoble the Indians because of their remoteness from savage warfare," Berkofer has written, "so commentators have pointed out that authors and artists of the eastern United States conceived of the Indian as noble only after that region was no longer subject to Indian conflict."[38] The identification of early American heritage with Indian foodstuffs as evidenced first by the Forefathers' Day banquet, the

*The Last of the Wampa-
noags,* painting by Al-
bert Bierstadt, 1858.
Bierstadt's work is of
Martha Simons of Old
Dartmouth township,
who died in 1859 or
1860. Collections of the
Millicent Library, Fair-
haven, Mass.; courtesy
Spinner Publications,
New Bedford, Mass.

Feast of Shells, Thanksgiving (to a lesser extent), and later the Squantum feast
depended on the current absence of real Indians as much as it did on their
original presence.

Contradictory attitudes toward native Americans and nostalgia for the purity
of colonial experience are recurrent themes perceptible in the rhetoric of these
various commemorative celebrations. The opening of the West extended the
imagery to include new images of both Indians and the wilderness experience.
As early as the 1840s, food historian Weaver has noted, there was a discernible
popular taste developing for "frontier" rusticity in the form of foods associated

with western Indian cuisine, such as buffalo meat and barbecues (to which, in particular, the clambake bears a striking technical resemblance).[39]

*Superior Fishing; or, The Striped Bass, Trout, and Black Bass of the United States,* published in 1865, is but one example of a proliferating sporting genre that dealt with the desire—distinctly masculine in cast—to experience the "real" world, to be nourished by it, and to consume its bounty, simultaneously. Within this context, the clambake, which had by this time already appeared as a commercial entity, garnered additional symbolic attributes. Under the heading "Cookery for Sportsmen"—suggestive enough in its gendering of the outdoor fare—the clambake is presented as a rugged, steaming, juicy, and aboriginal fare, to which "burnt fingers and lips add to the pleasures."[40]

The masculine nature of clambaking deserves further consideration in its own right: rugged in the wild, robust in public, the tradition of clambaking can be seen as embodying the manly image of "the noble savage," the "toughness" of Calvinism, and the macho pride of the American nationalist, all within an evolving discourse on the *body* politic.[41] As Harvey Green has demonstrated in *Fit for America,* the concern with health, which became increasingly serious as the nineteenth century progressed, was clearly focused on threats to virility—both a physical and political matter—and sporting and outdoor dining were among the proposed antidotes.[42]

One particular prescription for the emasculated, neurasthenic, urban middle class was the picnic, which increasingly overlapped with Squantums and clambakes. Appearing in America during the 1830s, the picnic began as a pastime for the wealthy but rapidly reached democratic proportions. In contrast to the sportsmen's rugged adventurings, the picnic was a much more domesticated outing, with baskets and cutlery sets and even groves set aside for its performance. Gentler, more romantic, idyllic—and coeducational—the picnic nonetheless drew on some of the same sources that inspired the gnawing on buffalo meat. "The great charm . . . is to eat, to chat, to lie, to sit, to talk, to walk, with something of the unconstraint of primitive life," wrote one enthusiast in 1869. "We find a fascination in carrying back our civilization to the wilderness."[43]

By the end of the 1800s, as Teddy Roosevelt attempted to demonstrate how the frontier experience could yet be reclaimed through sport and the sporting life, historian Frederick Jackson Turner explained "The Significance of the Frontier in American Life" in terms of its physical curtailment.[44] The closing of the West signaled both the defeat of the Indians and the end of the wilderness. By continuing to provide themselves with rustic menus in outdoor

Fourth of July on Savin Hill, ca. 1863. Dorchester, Mass. Courtesy of the Society for the Preservation of New England Antiquities.

settings, Americans sought in their own ideas about "primitive life" respite and antidote from the very civilization they had wrought.

Hobsbawm has written that the "most difficult to trace" of invented traditions are those that are "partly invented, partly evolved in private groups (where the process is less likely to be bureaucratically recorded), or informally over a period of time."[45] The clambake is certainly of this class. In addition to the intentionally constructed, large-scale political celebrations that valorized shellfish consumption in general, traces begin to appear in the early 1800s of events—which now bear the name "clambakes"—taking place in precisely this manner, "informally over a period of time" among "private groups" of Yankees.

Documentation is partial and sporadic, but it does exist. For instance, according to a newspaper inquiry in 1975, the Hornbine Church in Rhode Island was celebrating the 150th anniversary of its clambake—making its founding the year 1825.[46] According to an account in the Bristol, Rhode Island, *Phoenix*, 1825, this was the same year that local schoolteacher Otis Storrs took a group of students out to Rocky Point on the sloop *William Allen* and, upon discovering that they had no provisions, "invented" the clambake on the spot.[47]

In his 1909 short story, "A Cape Cod Clambake," local author Joe Lincoln wrote of this area's clambaking past, "when the village was peopled with sea captains, who went away on long voyages and came home occasionally to enjoy themselves with their wives and families"; based on the information in Lincoln's work, these Cape Cod clambakes date back to the 1830s, at the very latest.[48] By 1838, according to a local newspaper account, Jared Sherman had introduced, if not actually a clambaking business, then at least "the Indian method of roasting clams" at Sconicut Neck, near New Bedford.[49] And as far away as Philadelphia, the term "Clam Bake" was recognizable in the popular press as early as 1835.[50]

Clambakes seem to have existed in Yankee culture at this time on the level of "the Grange meeting, a social at the local school-house, a country dance, the Fourth of July picnic, the annual county fair, the coming of the circus"— the main events, according to Dulles, of rural American cultural life.[51] In conjunction with the constructing of "appropriate" cultural iconography represented by the Feasts of Shells and the Squantums, these small-scale, relatively private bakes paved the way for the large-scale public and commercial activities which began to appear by midcentury.

Another influence on the development of the tradition was the presence of native American clambaking. Indians in southeastern Massachusetts, particularly on Cape Cod and the islands of Nantucket and Martha's Vineyard, had been feasting on clams in a manner at least related to the nineteenth-century Yankee clambake for some indefinite length of time. And while Forefathers' Day events undoubtedly fostered the public, political identity of the clambake, the Indian practice almost certainly served as the original model for the feast.

Ann Holyoke's 1775 diary reference to having been served "roasted Paqwaws (a sort of clam)" by Indians on Nantucket[52] does not by itself constitute proof of extensive cross-cultural exposure, but the case is strengthened by the fact that the small-scale Yankee clambakes taking place in the early 1800s were centered in seaside communities where there were extant Indian populations, including, for example, the area near Allen's Neck known as "paquachuck."[53] The name is significant. As noted in the 1872 *Americanisms: The English of the New World:* "The common shellfish . . . known as clam . . . is frequently still called by its Indian name *poquauhock.* This word, however, has shared the fate of other long Narragansett terms, and been made to do duty in parts: *pooquaw* being now the name of the Round Clam in Nantucket while *quahog* represents the same shellfish in New York, New Jersey, and Pennsylvania."[54]

Other circumstantial evidence of contact with existing native practices includes the sporadic mentions nineteenth-century authors made to a particular Indian style of clambaking, which, I would conjecture, had their source in firsthand, contemporaneous experience, but which, for reasons of cultural bias, these authors chose not to discuss. For example, John Russell Bartlett, of *Quotations* fame, cites the phrase "Indian bed of clams" for the first time in the 1859 edition of the *Dictionary of Americanisms* as a method in which "the clams are simply placed close together on the ground, with the hinges uppermost, and over them is made a fire of brush." In his 1865 *Superior Fishing,* sportsman Robert Roosevelt described the same technique.[55]

More telling still is Nantucket author Joseph C. Hart's novel, *Miriam Coffin; or, The Whale-Fishermen* (1834). Based on his own ethnohistorical research, Hart's account of island life during the latter part of the 1700s includes this mention of the "'Squantums' of Nantucket":

> Even unto this day, some of the eastern people adopt the same method, to "stap the vitals" of the quohog at their "roast-outs" or forest junketings. As to the peculiar mode of cooking. . . . the quohogs were placed upon the bare ground, side by side, with their mouths biting the dust. The burning coals of the camp-fires . . . were . . . applied plentifully to the backs of the quohogs. In a few minutes after the application of the fire, the cooking was declared to be at an end, and the roasting of quohogs complete. The steam of the savoury liquor, which escaped in part without putting out the fire, preserved the meat in a par–boiled state, and prevented it from scorching, or drying to a cinder, and the whole virtue of the fish from being lost. The ashes of the fire were effectually excluded by the position in which the animal was placed at the beginning; and the heat [h]as completely destroyed the tenacity of the hinge which connected the shells.[56]

In this context, the idea of "roasted" clams, Squantum feasts, and—indirectly—of Indians preparing a bivalve feast within sight of white folks are brought together.

Given the absence of other, documented theories, Nanepashemet's explanation of the white adaptation of an older Indian culinary custom seems convincing. The clambake in Yankee culture, he states originated with the blossoming of tourism in the area; you know, people coming down to the seacoast for their health, or whatever reasons, and getting into the seacoast economy. It's likely, by conjecture, that certain people that lived in the area might have known some of these [clambaking] techniques and done them for themselves, possibly. Certainly, in the native communities that lived near the seacoast, there was still a practice [of clambaking], but people weren't documenting native customs during the seventeen, eighteen hundreds. You know, Indians were no longer a novelty, and they were more considered to be, you know, nothing—just a bunch of poor people that had curious customs and had some Indian ancestry.

But they didn't have Indian customs like those out West, and the Indians out West were more attractive to easterners than the ones that lived right next to them. . . . The easterners were always quick to decry what the westerners were doing to the Indians out there, forgetting what they were doing to the Indians in their own backyard. 'Cause [native] people around here were basically living in poverty and weren't much noticed.

So people become surprised that nowadays that there are still Indians around this area that maintain a lot of customs . . . many people are not aware, because of lack of documentation, that native people did clambakes long ago. And it's just really because some European person didn't write about it. That's one of the problems we have with documentation.

It [the adoption of clambaking] could have been in the 1800s. Even probably lower-income white people that lived near Indian places might have picked it up, and they weren't written about either. They weren't any more fascinating to the public than the Indians were, but they could have been doing clambaking because they learned it as a way of life around that part of the country. Then somebody probably decided, "Hey, I can make money off of this," and so it became noticed.[57]

Nanepashemet's testimony offers an alternative vantage point, the other "voice" in the matter of white and Indian interactions. The vitality of his description of the commercial context of the event, of native experience, and of the dynamics behind their invisibility stand in particularly sharp contrast to the Squantum celebration, which "worked" symbolically for white Americans because it managed to deny the presence and perspective of living Indians.

Like the overtly partisan Feast of Shells, one of the earliest official documentations of a clambake—qua clambake—in Yankee New England is also associated with a political party, affirming the connection between eating American and eating clams for one's political candidate.[58]

In his *Dictionary of Americanisms,* Bartlett recorded that "the greatest feast of the kind that ever took place in New England" was "that of a grand political mass-meeting in favor of General [and subsequently President William Henry] Harrison on the 4th of July, 1840[;] nearly 10,000 people assembled in

Rhode Island . . . [and] a clambake and chowder were prepared."[59] It was, according to available documents, the first bake of such grand proportions, and it established a precedent for mass partisan clambakes in the state of Rhode Island for years to come.[60] In 1860, for example, a large bake was held for presidential candidate Senator Stephen Douglas, and another was held in the 1930s for Calvin Coolidge. Miss Martin, born in 1896 and brought up in Seekonk, Rhode Island, remembers the Coolidge bake: "And they had a clambake in Rehoboth that was a political bake—Coolidge was there one year and everything. And they came from everywhere, and it was really politics on top of it. Now that bake used to serve a thousand, 11 or 12 hundred. . . . And that was held in a big tent."[61]

A report issued by Prussian professor Anton Siegafritz, sent to the United States during the 1880s to look into the feasibility of establishing oyster plantations in Eastern Europe, suggests that political clambakes were occasions of considerable rowdiness.[62] "While I was in America," Siegafritz wrote, "I saw the excitements caused by immoderate indulgence in shell-fish violently illustrated. They have there a sort of political assemblage called a clambake, where speeches and music and songs are interspersed with profuse feasts upon a species of oyster called the clam. Vast crowds attend these celebrations, and no sooner are they gorged with the insidious comestible, than they become full of excitement and furores [sic]; swear themselves away in fealty to the most worthless of demogogues; sing, fight, dance, gouge one another's eyes out and conduct themselves like madmen in a conflagration."[63] His recommendation, overall, was that the proposed oystering venture be abandoned because of the danger of "emotional insanity" caused by too much ingesting of shellfish.

As historical consciousness and collective self-consciousness became an increasingly central aspect of American culture in the nineteenth century, more and more Americans organized themselves into local groups and staged their own "historic" commemorative events on the model of the Colonial Club and the Pilgrim Society. Increasing numbers of towns throughout New England, particularly, celebrated the years of their foundings, their subsequent illustrious histories, and their roles in the larger national story. Where location and season permitted, clambakes were often common commemorative repasts.

The celebration of Old Home Week was another context for "traditional" clambaking throughout New England. Considered these days to be as venerable as the clambake itself, Old Home Week, or Old Home Day can be traced as a local tradition to Portsmouth, New Hampshire, at least as early as 1853. It

Old Home Week celebrations, New Haven, Conn., 1902. From *As New Englanders Played* (1979).

was officially "initiated" by the governor of New Hampshire in 1899, whence it spread rapidly throughout New England, into the Midwest, and into Canada's Atlantic maritime provinces. Introduced as a town reunion, Old Home Week was from its inception an organized, civic affair; it was legalized by several of the New England state legislatures, and funding for it was authorized by popular vote.[64]

In addition to its value as an impetus for reestablishing friendships, this "cultural production"[65] had an essentially economic purpose. An article in a 1906 issue of *New England Magazine* stated, "The practical phrase of Old Home Week, and the one that will do much to keep it a permanent institution, is found in the fact that many of the annual home-comers—the well-to-do class—are beginning to signify their appreciation of the friendly Old-Home Week invitation by sending here and there a substantial check for a new drinking fountain, a statue or memorial window in honor of some deceased worthy, a public park, a tablet for some historic landmark, or the liquidation of some burdensome church debt."[66]

The towns went all out. In addition to the official tours and speeches, activities of every sort—technological, social, recreational, and nationalistic—represented the issues and self-images of the times and places where they were presented. "Hose-reel tests, and pie-eating contests are held for their special edification," the article continued. "There are dramatic performances by local talent, tableaux of old-time scenes or historical events. Old Folks Concerts and 'Deestrick School' performances; yacht races and canoe carnivals; *clambakes* and corn-roasts; exhibits of historic relics, balloon ascensions (perhaps), jolly hayrack rides . . . illustrated lectures, camera club exhibitions, military parades, lawn parties, automobile processions, four-o'clock-teas, family reunions and all manner of things under the canopy, all for the personal and particular benefit of the returned native" [italics mine].[67] In Fairhaven, across the river from New Bedford, Old Home Week in 1903 also featured a children's parade, complete with bicycle squad, police squad, drum corps, and flag bearers, all ending up with "the event of the afternoon," the clambake for five hundred.[68]

By the end of the nineteenth century, the clambake had become solidly embedded within Old Home Week, a miniature version of the grand expositional mode which was itself an expression of the period.[69] Well integrated into the activities and symbols of "authentic" New England traditions, the clambake became a part of the essence of America and of Americana, along with Thanksgiving, the Fourth of July, barbecues, and apple pie.

# 3

# Leisure and Industry

*Clams, a sort of mussel, are largely in demand in the Eastern States, and
a clambake is a famous "feed."*
—W. E. Adams, *Our American Cousins* (1883)

**N**EARLY INVISIBLE at the beginning of the 1800s, clambaking
became by the end of the century a veritable institution in many parts of New
England and an increasingly common metaphor for the region's bounty.
Something had happened to bring about this emergence, and that something
was rooted in the concept of leisure. The same forces that transformed
American society as a whole in the nineteenth century—industrialization,
urbanization, immigration, the explosion of transportation technology, the
accumulation of greater wealth and the growth of the middle class, and
the Civil War[1]—also produced a new context for leisure and recreation in the
country. The growth of tourism; the propagation of public dining, commercial
eating establishments, and popular amusements; and the establishment of
summer resorts and seaside communities that resulted constituted the backdrop against which the clambake reached the apex of its popularity, cap-
tivating both the popular imagination and the public appetite.

Following the religious revival at the end of the 1700s, a renewed Puritan
ethos became evident that, like its earlier manifestation, was generally intol-
erant of leisure and recreation. This rekindled strictness was displayed in,

49

among other places, the revival of Sabbath observances. Dulles has stated, "No sports or games were allowed on the Lord's Day, let alone public amusements. Travel was no longer permitted. . . . Public opinion, if not actual laws, decreed church attendance as the only permissible Sunday activity."[2] In this sense, play impulses and behaviors were not so much outlawed as heavily censured.

The portrayal of Americans by outsiders during this period confirmed, and to some extent reinforced, the impression of severity. As the snobbish Frances Trollope remarked in her 1832 *Domestic Manners of the Americans,* "I never saw a population so totally divested of gayety; there is no trace of this feeling from one end of the Union to the other." This observation was echoed in an 1837 report, *The Americans in Their Moral, Social and Political Relations:* "The Americans are not fond of any kind of public amusement; and are best pleased with an abundance of business. Their pleasure consists in being constantly occupied."[3] Although clearly overstatements, these were the commonly expressed attitudes of Europeans who visited and wrote about America during this period.

With the coming of the Revolution, the days of the highly visible turtle-feasting aristocracy had come to an end. Well-to-do European travelers, blinded by their own aristocratic prejudices, could hardly have been expected to encounter or seek out other levels of American society and contexts for leisure. It is unlikely that they would have been any more favorably impressed by "the social gatherings in New England [which] were more likely to be associated with useful communal work—house-raisings, sheep shearings, log-rollings, or husking bees"[4]—if they had been exposed to them.

As the culture experienced the radical fracturing brought about by industrialization, latter-day Puritans developed a new component to their anti-idleness ardor, later designated by the term "Protestant work ethic."[5] In his *Recreation and Leisure in Modern Society,* historian Richard Kraus has noted that "as industrialization became more widespread, there was a renewed emphasis on the importance of 'honest toil' with a strong antagonism expressed against play. The church fell in with the attitude of the merchant-manufacturing class that idleness led to drinking and vice and that consequently long hours of labor should be maintained for the sake of the wage-earner's moral welfare. Religious leaders supported the twelve- to fourteen-hour factory day, as part of the 'wholesome discipline of factory life.'"[6]

In spite of this Protestant enthusiasm for work, or, perhaps, because of it, the quest for entertainment grew stronger. Different scholars have highlighted a variety of causes and contributing factors to America's interest in leisure, including the shift from "a rural-agrarian to an urban-industrial society" and "a rising standard of living" for a new middle class; "improved land and water transportation"; industrialization itself; and the presence of "foreign-born city dwellers, who brought their own native amusements and above all a European dedication to the active pursuit of pleasure."[7] But all seem to agree that sometime after the middle of the nineteenth century there was a burgeoning of large-scale, public recreations.[8]

Of course, recreation for the well-to-do had been initiated long before the middle class began to enjoy the fruits of their labors and certainly before workers or the foreign-born even hoped to participate. During the early decades of the 1800s, wealthy Philadelphia Quakers were already flocking to Long Branch, New Jersey—purportedly the country's oldest summer resort— some thirty miles south of New York City. A steamboat line making the resort accessible to the New York upper class was instituted in 1829, and some of the nation's first bathing beaches were built along its shoreline in the 1850s and 1860s.[9] Despite the judgment of visiting excursionists in 1876 that "this place will always command the patronage of the aristocracy of wealth," Long Branch had lost much of its exclusivity by the end of the century and had become, instead, a popular destination on weekends for the day-tripping working class.[10]

Having benefited from its role in the Triangular Trade (molasses to rum to slaves), Newport, Rhode Island, was already known for its fashionable opulence in the 1700s. Following a period of "senile decay" after the Revolution, Newport revived in the early part of the nineteenth century due to the influx of "wealthy Southerners," who, according to Richmond Barrett in *Good Old Summer Days,* came "to escape the heat and malaria of South Carolina . . . bringing some of their slaves with them. These aristocrats loved the place, finding in it something of the boasted Charleston savor."[11] According to Dulles, "Until the bitterness aroused over the slavery issue caused them to stay at home . . . some 50 thousand southerners were said to visit the northern states annually."[12]

Activities geared toward making Newport into a resort spot initially appeared in the 1830s: Ocean House, the city's first real hotel, was built in 1846.[13] A real estate boom followed, as did the building of summer "cottages" and the establishment of a cottage colony. Sports and recreations also abounded. In addition to its famed "bathing," the list of amusing activities compiled by an English visitor during an 1870s stay in Newport included horses, sailing,

"On the Beach at Newport, Rhode Island," *Harper's Weekly*, 1869. Drawing by
C. G. Bush. From the collection of the Newport Historical Society, Newport, R.I.

billiards, picnics, dances, croquet, getting engaged, ice cream, lobster salads,
and *clambakes*.[14]

Health was often an early rationale for retreat to the country or seaside in
New England. Invalids seeking rest and cure found lodgings with local
residents in the various healthful environs. It was an arrangement that served
mutual need: as historian William Varrell has noted, "The coastal farmers
quickly accepted the source of their new found cash crop of tourists, with a few
making it a year round business."[15] Boarding in the country was an opportunity soon extended to others. George Makepeace Towle, a British consul to
the United States, noted in his 1870 *American Society* that country towns and
villages were increasingly being frequented by "families who desire to enjoy
the green fields and rural landscapes in the summer, and are not wealthy
enough to have their own country seat."[16]

In no time, the economic potential of summer tourism began to be explored and nurtured on a large scale. The burgeoning transportation industry, in particular, quickly recognized that a natural extension of its business—literally and figuratively—was the resort. Railroad companies were the first to build and operate hotels to attract tourist-travelers; subsequently, as Varrell has noted, trolley companies also "invested heavily in land, built hotels, casinos, and dozens of amusement parks and picnic grounds at every bend of the road. By providing the attractions they also insured passengers, round trip."[17] According to Rollin Hartt in his 1909 *The People at Play* (originally subtitled *Excursions in the Humor and Philosophy of Popular Amusements*), "You could scarcely find a [trolley] company unenterprising enough not to stimulate traffic by opening a grove or a park supplied with alluring bears, irresistible simians, and the enticements of al fresco vaudeville."[18]

Development of amusement facilities hand-in-hand with steamboat, train, and trolley lines occurred throughout nineteenth-century New England, where tourism was definitely thriving. It is still within the memory of people today. Willy Morrison, who tends the general store in Russells Mills (the village of the Allen's Neck area), can elicit from an elderly customer a recollection of the time when the local trolley company issued a Sunday pass for a quarter, which allowed travel all day long: "You could ride wherever you wanted." Willy added:

> When we were kids, the trolley used to run up to Middleboro, and I saw them at Onset, from New Bedford—I don't know how far they might have gone before. And they carried the mail, they carried the papers, on the runs down the Cape. The city was paved with trolley cars, round the center there. It went north, south, and east and west, over the bridge. . . .
> You know why—that was why Lincoln Park [the local amusement park] was built, for people to have a place to go. They didn't have automobiles then, so they could go on a trolley car. Padanaram: you could go uptown to New Bedford and go to Lincoln Park. Fact is, you could go all over the country. And they had clambakes. And the amusements weren't so great, but there'd be a ballgame rather than you'd stay to home. And my grandmother used to take us every summer—and to Fort Phoenix—on the street car.[19]

The necessity to publicize the new facilities, likewise within the bailiwick of the transportation companies, resulted in such multiple-edition brochures as *Popular Resorts and Fashionable Watering Places,* published by the Old Colony Railroad. Printed as early as the 1820s and flourishing particularly in the 1870s and 1880s, these tour guides were so numerously produced and widely read as to constitute a new genre of literature.

*Monohansett* and *Cygnet* ferries at the Old Colony Railroad Steamboat Wharf in New Bedford. Courtesy Spinner Publications, New Bedford, Mass.

Expanded transportation capacities clearly played a role in the democratizing process during the course of the nineteenth century. In the 1820s, travel between New York and Boston had depended upon a combination of steamboat and stagecoaches and was beyond the means of most Americans—the steamer fare alone was a forbidding ten dollars. Within the next few decades, however, between competition within the steamship industry and the establishment of three railway lines emanating from Boston, steamship fare was sometimes as low as fifty cents, well within the range of all but the emptiest of purses.[20] The trolley car, from the beginning conceived as an inexpensive way to link older and more physically limited transportation systems, provided the public extensive access to the resources of their region, as well as to all variety of recreations.

Which is not to say that everyone equally valued this trend, which was decried as often as it was celebrated. As the nineteenth century drew to its close, an antimodernist sentiment predominated which was simultaneously critical and ambivalent—sometimes even fatalistic—about all aspects of modern life.[21] Perhaps precisely because of the growing participation of the lower classes in the pursuit of recreation, questions began to be raised about the proper way for a society to use its "free" time. Speaking to a gathering at Lake Chautauqua in 1880, President James Garfield expressed the breadth of the concern: "We may divide the whole struggle of the human race into two chapters, first, the fight to get leisure; and then the second fight of civilization—what shall we do with our leisure when we get it?"[22]

The Chautauqua Movement itself was but one of many attempts to make leisure time, and the rapid societal changes that had produced it, a more meaningful, less threatening aspect of "modern" life. Indeed, all of the major themes of the Gilded Age—the striving for a health that was both moral and physical, the search for the right balance between work and play, nature and the machine, the national and the international, the upper and lower classes, and between the sexes—were inherently related to the development of leisure, both as causes and effects.[23]

Clambaking appears as an ongoing commercial enterprise in New England in the middle of the nineteenth century. During the same period that the rail-water route was being completed between New York and Boston—the country's two major cities and the source of most of New England's visitors—Rocky Point was established as a resort in Rhode Island.[24] Catering to wealthy tourists steamboating from nearby Providence, Rocky Point became renowned for its clambakes, which soon bore the title, "the genuine Rhode Island shore dinner." *Appleton's Illustrated Handbook of American Travel* from 1860 characterized Rocky Point as "a wonderful summer retreat among shady groves and rocky glens. . . . In the summer-time half a dozen boats ply, each twice a day, on excursion trips down the Bay, charging 25 cents only for the round voyage. Rocky Point is the most favored of all these rural recesses. Hundreds come here early and feast upon delicious clams, just drawn from the water and roasted on the shore, in heated seaweed, upon true and orthodox 'clam bake' principles. Let no visitor to Providence fail to eat clams and chowder at Rocky Point, even if he should never eat again."[25]

Similar accolades appeared in Grieve's 1888 *Picturesque Narragansett: An Illustrated Guide to the Cities, Towns, and Famous Resorts of Rhode Island:* "The largest, most famous and popular resort on the bay is Rocky Point. . . . Rhode Island's great sea-shore celebrity is also a central attraction at Rocky Point, and at the proper season and hour it is served here in excellent style." Noting

Advertisements for Oakland Beach, 1888, which featured "genuine" clambakes and
an early version of the water slide. Reprinted from Robert Grieve, *Picturesque Narragansett* (1888).

the prevalence of clambake facilities at other resorts, such as nearby Oakland Beach—with its "seating capacity for 1,200 persons, which can be readily expanded to accommodate 5,000, if required"—Grieve's guide acknowledged Rocky Point's pavilion and dining hall as "the largest on the bay devoted to the business of catering to the multitude in the matter of shore dinners."[26] So prominent was the role of Rocky Point in the "mass production of clambakes and shore dinners" that it eventually operated its own steamboat, "with a crew of 16 to 20, which set out daily to gather clams for crowds up to 10,000."[27]

Taken in conjunction with the Harrison political bake of 1840, the success of Rocky Point fixed the association of the clambake feast with the state of Rhode Island, and the first mention of a clambake to appear in an American cookbook referred to it as "A Rhode Island Clambake." The author, Mrs. D. A. Lincoln, Fannie Farmer's predecessor at the Boston Cooking-School,

Rocky Point, 1888; the clambake pavilion, which seated thousands of visitors, is to the right of the pier. Reprinted from Robert Grieve, *Picturesque Narragansett* (1888).

noted that "an impromptu clam bake may be had at any time at low tide along the coast where clams are found" and proceeded to tell readers how to "do it yourself."[28] This "shore dinner" continued to be a prominent feature of Rhode Island's summer culture throughout the rest of the nineteenth century, and Rocky Point continued as its reigning star into the twentieth.[29]

"In all great centres of population there must be some resort for recreation," noted the official chronicler of the 1876 Centennial Cruise, a ten-day, fifteen hundred-mile jaunt for a party of seventy-five guests from Albany hosted and underwritten by Commodore John H. Starin, proprietor of the City, River and Harbor Transportation Company of New York City. "New York has its Coney Island, and also its Long Branch, and, by the same rule, Providence and its surrounding towns have Rocky Point."[30] Obviously sparing no expense, the captain of the Centennial Cruise steered a course for Rocky Point and its clambake. According to a local newspaper report, the ship reached its destination in the afternoon, "and then the company of the steamer, headed by the band, formed in line and marched to the time of martial music to the clam-house, where a fierce charge was made upon a real Rhode Island shore dinner." Following the meal, there was bathing (swimming), and, in the evening, the band provided music for a "hop."[31]

The next stop of the Centennial cruise was New Bedford, and there a second clambake was performed at Light House Point. It was "in every respect first-class," according to the *Daily Mercury,* although Centennial travelers found it "rather amusing, too, to observe the mingled courtesy and embarrassment of the light-house keeper and his wife, who were hardly accustomed to such a crowd of visitors."[32] Clearly a nonprofessional establishment at this point, Palmer's Island, on which Light House Point was located, boasted a summer hotel as well as a bowling alley and amusement park by the latter part of the century—no doubt attracting other clambake crowds.[33]

The history of clambaking in New Bedford is less well documented than that at Rocky Point, although it seems to have been spawned by the former's success. An 1899 article in the New Bedford *Evening Standard Times* which attempted to trace the "development of Rhode Island's institution here" credited Otis T. Sisson with having introduced the Rhode Island custom in Massachusetts.[34] Sisson started his business in New Bedford in the early 1870s with a modest building for all-weather eating. By 1877, a much more elaborate Sylvan Grove had come into existence, and an advertisement for the annual clambake of the Young People's Circle of the North Christian Church described Sisson's establishment as "fitted up in the nicest manner, and . . . far

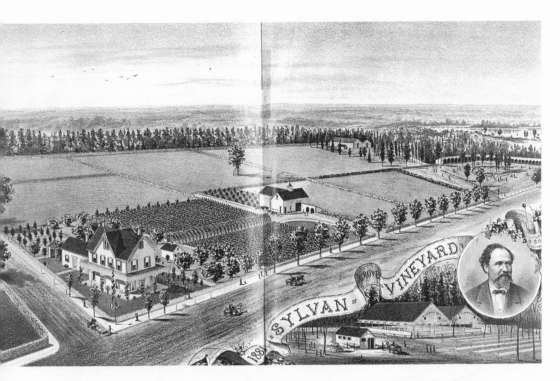

Sylvan Vineyard, 1881, which, along with Sylvan Grove, featured fishing, bowling, and dancing, and clambakes. From *Atlas of the City of New Bedford* (1881); courtesy Spinner Publications, New Bedford, Mass.

superior to anything in this vicinity, and all may be assured a good time. An opportunity which should not be missed will be given to view one of the finest out-door graperies in the world, also one of the prettiest situated ponds in this vicinity, stocked with 150,000 black bass; parties attending the Bake having free use of the pond for fishing. . . . A Quadrille Band has been engaged to enliven the occasion with music." During the same season, Sisson also added a dance hall and bowling alley to his offerings.[35]

The scope of Sisson's clambakes was impressive. One particularly "notable occasion" which took place at Sylvan Grove was the bicentennial celebration of the nearby town of Rochester in 1879, when, according to a later account, "ten thousand people thronged the grounds. A hundred barrels of clams and stacks of green corn, fish and tripe were buried under the steaming seaweed. Those ten thousand numbered a record breaker for Sylvan grove. . . . There were so many people present that the day was altogether too short to feed them all, and when night came a bake 20 feet long, 10 feet wide, and four feet high remained untouched to represent the company unfed."[36]

While Sylvan Grove thrived, New Bedford steadily became a critical crossroad in the transportation system and in the summer tourism industry. From the Civil War on, Martha's Vineyard and Nantucket had increased in popularity as resort areas, which encouraged the growth of local transportation. By 1889, it was fair to say—as the New Bedford Board of Trade in fact did—that "passengers from New York, Boston, Providence, and the vast regions of country that must make these centres their gateways in visiting localities in southeastern Massachusetts, find railway lines arranged with direct reference to New Bedford as a terminal point," with direct connections and "most delightful excursions" to New England's summer resort areas.[37]

This tourist traffic, in conjunction with the many other societal factors already affecting leisure and recreation, helped stimulate competition for Sisson's clambaking establishment, and during the 1880s, a number of professional bakemasters and pavilions made their appearance. From the advertisements and listings in the "Amusements" section of New Bedford's newspaper, it is possible to trace the growth and breadth of clambaking in the area during the latter part of the nineteenth century. The range of groups participating and the facilities turned over to the activity expanded with each season. For example, in 1888, an annual bake for the twelve hundred members of the Bristol County Fruit Growers Association was held at the nearby town of Dighton; Brown's Steamboat Landing announced the completion of its new clambake and picnic grove in the same year; and in 1890, bakes were held at River View Park in Acushnet and at Cadman's Neck in nearby Westport.

By 1899, the numbers of bakes appearing in print had increased exponentially. There was Brooklawn Park and Brooklawn Casino, Tarklin Hill, Perry's, and Davis's; in Padanaram, there were two sites—Laban's Folly on the wharf and Woodhouse's on the corner of Bridge and Elm Streets. Lincoln Park, the amusement center opened in 1893 by the Union Street Railway Company, featured its own clambake pavilion, serving two bakes a week, on Sundays and Wednesdays. A military installation during the Revolutionary War, the War of 1812, and the Civil War, Fort Phoenix—located in the harbor between New Bedford and Fairhaven and "a favorite rendezvous for yachts during the summer"—was first used for picnics and clambakes in 1880. In 1886, the trolley company added a dance hall and, later, public bath houses.[38] From the end of the 1900s until recent decades, Fort Phoenix was associated with two separate clambaking establishments, Whitfield's and Grimshaw's, which served as many as five clambakes a week to hundreds at a sitting.[39]

*Leisure and Industry*

Advertisements for summer clambakes, New Bedford *Evening Standard Times*, August 3, 1899, under the heading "Amusements."

The increasing appearance of weekend clambakes reflected a shift in societal values as much as it did the recreational calendar of the buying public. As Arthur H. Brown noted in New Bedford's *Evening Standard Times* for August 26, 1899, the clambake pavilions in the area "rarely, if ever, until within the last three weeks held a clambake on Sunday," due to conservative city administrations which prohibited such profanation of the Lord's day. But as Puritan restrictions loosened throughout New England, businesses of all kinds were able to cater to the occupational schedules of their potential patrons. Brown's article continued, "Sunday bakes very naturally draw double the crowds which go on a week day, owing in all probability to the fact that more people are able to leave town and go to them than on a week day. It is noticeable moreover that Sunday bakes attract a different element. The week-day bake is participated in, as a rule, by the more well-to-do class of people while the former embraces for the most part a laboring class which is obliged to toil without ceasing through the week and finds Sunday its only day of leisure."[40]

Even the midweek bakes began to be patronized by the working class, as factory owners initiated annual outings for their employees at the many new clambaking establishments throughout the area. The trip to these sites was usually made by specially scheduled "electric cars." A 1919 trolley schedule and route map of the Union Street Railway Company revealed under the heading "HOW MUCH RIDE A NICKEL WILL BUY" how easy it was to go from the center of New Bedford directly to Fort Phoenix and Padanaram, where the major pavilions were located, as well as to the many less formal picnic and clambake groves along the various routes.[41]

Toward the end of the century, "New England" as a conceptual region began to take on a sentimental quality, one that was redolent of the homespun and of quaint historicity.[42] In the explosion of travelogue literature beginning in the third quarter of the nineteenth century and continuing into the first quarter of the twentieth, such titles as *Nooks and Corners of the New England Coast* (1875), *Along New England Roads* (1892), *Old Paths and Legends of New England* (1903), *Historic Summer Haunts* (1915), *Vacation Tramps in New England Highlands* (1919), and *Wayfaring in New England* (1920) suggested New England as a site for sentimental journeys along byways of the past. This was also, of course, the language of tourism.

A general longing for the lost or retreating roots of the American essence was reflected in many popular media. One particularly prominent response

"Seaside Sketches—A Clam-Bake," engraving by Winslow Homer, *Harper's Weekly*, August 23, 1873.

was the art of Winslow Homer, which, according to one art historian, forms "the most genuine pictorial record of rural America in the 1860s and 1870s."[43] Homer celebrated the American folk culture in an accessible graphic form, producing hundreds of illustrations of life on the farm and in seaside communities for the popular journal *Harper's Weekly*. "In a day when most American artists depicted farm life with nostalgic idealization, [Homer's] uncouth figures and homely settings carried the conviction of utter authenticity," claims this critic, "yet underlying his honest naturalism was a strain of pastoral poetry, a love of country life at its simplest and most primitive—life spent close to nature, ruled by the cycle of the seasons. The combination of reserved poetry and unsweetened realism gave Homer's country pictures a flavor unique in the art of the time."[44] His 1873 woodcut of a children's clambake, entitled "Sea-side Sketches—A Clam-Bake," was produced during a summer spent in Gloucester, Massachusetts.[45]

The concerns with naturalism, realism, and authenticity that characterized Homer's art were among the most central issues in both high-culture and low-culture discourse in the late nineteenth and early twentieth centuries. Such themes likewise accrued to the clambake he had pictorially celebrated. Early advertisements for various Rhode Island resorts, for example, offered shore dinners that were termed "authentic," "genuine," and "real," as if in answer to societal questions concerning validity and truth. After the turn of the century, however, the adjectives "traditional" and "old-fashioned" began to appear, suggesting a greater sense of alienation or remove from the past and different questions about history, identity, and change.

The clambake—already connected to the colonial past nostalgically—became a kind of trope. At the same time that increasing numbers of people were gaining access to the commercial pavilions, the clambake began to appear in literary and visual display. In the popular media, clambaking became emblematic of a range of themes—of American origins and originality; of the New England region itself; and of the Yankee temperament, which was genuine and full of vigor, in body as well as spirit.

In literary usage, the clambake appeared increasingly as a symbol of sanctuary from the world gone awry. In his novel *The Clammer* (1906), William John Hopkins employed the clambake to embody an overt antimodernist message. In it, the clambake thematically represents, first, a cynic's refuge from the ills of the world and, finally, his salvation through the love of a good woman and the ensuing acceptance of her father, who is likewise seeking his own release from the constraints of an overly materialistic, industrialized life. At the novel's conclusion, the menfolk are found bonding and being redeemed in the glow of the untainted purity of the bake.[46]

As in all of his short-story reminiscences of the Cape Cod life of his boyhood, Joe Lincoln described clambaking with humor, wistfulness, and nostalgia. Lincoln's 1909 "A Cape Cod Clambake" captured the pleasure and playfulness of a three-generation family outing, though it ended on a somewhat gloomy note:

> Later in the evening you are conscious that your legs and arms are red hot and that witch hazel is good for sunburn. Also that a dyspepsia tablet or two might prove a restful solace for the clams you have eaten. Robinson limps over to say that Brown is in bed, swathed in cotton and vaseline, and that his ankles are beginning to blister. And, please, what is good for a lame back?
>
> But the children, lobster red though they are, went to bed perfectly happy. No dyspepsia there and no regrets, either. In fact, the youngest, who is so burned that

You used to feel that way, too. Now you shudder to think of it. If old Father Time would pause for a while in that everlasting march of his. . . . "Folks don't have the good times they used to have." Well, perhaps that's so.[47]

For Joe Lincoln and many of his readers, the clambake represented a conjunction of losses—of youth, of rural culture, of health, and of humanity.

The sense of loss soon became real as well as imagined. The hurricane of 1938 destroyed most of the clambake establishments along the New England coast, as well as thousands of vacation cottages and resort establishments from Long Island through Buzzard's Bay.[48] A few of the pavilions in the New Bedford area did survive the storm, however, and a 1939 Federal Writers' Project publication on Fairhaven reported that Whitfield's, Grimshaw's, and Brown's were still in operation at Fort Phoenix on Sundays and Wednesdays throughout the summer.[49] Members of the Allen's Neck community in their fifties, sixties, and seventies can add to this list an impressive number of smaller clambake pavilions in the area which they attended after the 1938 hurricane—Remington's, Dan's, Pine Grove, Woodhouse's in Padanaram, Perry's Grove in Dartmouth, Pine Hill Pavilion in Acushnet, Lincoln Park, Acushnet Park, Washburn's in Marion, and Prospect Grove at Faunce's Corner, among others.

But the Depression and the Second World War put most of these establishments out of business, and the Hurricane of 1954 finished off the remaining few. As the clambake receded in physical form, its symbolic imagery also underwent a discernible transformation. The intensely felt yearning for the past associated with the clambake reformed itself into a kind of glorified revival of a seemingly timeless practice. By 1947, the clambake had become the "ancient New England rite" for Llewellyn Howland, a native of the New Bedford and Allen's Neck areas, and the proper attitude toward it was "that of pilgrims to a shrine."

> But from this point on how can I attempt to set down in words, which after all are poor things, the disposal of all these gifts of God, which have been for the most part cooked in the good earth, seasoned by the salts thereof, uncontaminated by the impurities of civilization, fresh as the dawn, and in such abundance that no one has to bolt his first helping to ensure a second, third, or even a fourth—[followed by] a contentment that can come only from the know-how of making the most of Nature's gifts and the satisfaction arising from such knowledge, which has been acquired, not from endowed institutions of learning, but from attendance at that greatest of all universities, the outdoor world.[50]

All of the old clambake pavilions in the New Bedford area are now gone. The only professional clambake business in the region today is Francis Farm in Rehoboth, Massachusetts, which, although close to a century old, has undergone significant changes and now serves clambakes baked over metal ingots heated by gas jets to largely private and corporate groups.[51] In Providence, according to Calvin Trillin, the Squantum Club was continuing to serve clambakes in 1983 as it had for the past century, but only to its exclusive male membership, decked out in coats and ties.[52]

A new phenomenon has arisen to take the place of the old pavilions and the sentimentality associated with clambaking. Today, the name of the game is business. Consulting the Yellow Pages of the Boston telephone book, a would-be clambake consumer can find more than twenty listings of catering businesses specializing in clambakes, often offered along with such other outdoor fare as picnics and barbecues. Although the techniques vary to some degree, for the most part these clambakes consist of steaming a variety of foodstuffs in large, industrial-strength metal woks, with neither rocks nor rockweed in evidence; one company's sales representative explained over the telephone, "Seaweed ruins the taste of a bake."[53]

The most successful companies have been called upon to travel and enter-

A gathering of the Whaleman's Club, Grimshaw's Clambakes, Fort Phoenix, 1928. From the author's collection.

tain celebrities—jetting out to the islands (Martha's Vineyard or Nantucket) or across country to Rodeo Drive in Beverly Hills—or to feed casts of thousands at very special occasions—Lady Liberty's Fourth of July extravaganza on Governors Island and Harvard's 350th anniversary, for example. One company offers a ready-to-cook clambake package which can be shipped anywhere in the United States. This trend toward packaging clambake has appeared elsewhere along the eastern seaboard, wherever the meal has become fashionable business.

In the New Bedford area, the clambake industry has become an avocation for a few men, including Raymond Davoll and Robert Wordell, who, having worked at some bakes and patronized others during their youth, learned the routine from the old-timers and now hire themselves out for a dozen or so events during the summer months, approximately half of which they do for free. Now and again, the two men find themselves bidding against other would-be clambaking enterprises, but the competition is always short-lived. It's too much work for too little money, Raymond grumbles: you have to be a real Yankee to think it's fun.[54]

More than a century's worth of romantic, sentimentalized, and nostalgic notions surrounding the clambake have enabled it to continue as a powerful,

PHOENIX JUNE 27. 1928

The clambake as public and commercial meal: catering companies, fund-raising dinners, banquets, and how-tos. Photograph by Joe Ofria (1991).

multi-faceted symbol into the present day. Clambakes inspire feature articles in *Yankee* Magazine and similar publications. At least one how-to clambake book has been printed, and, in parts of coastal New England, magazines and newspapers are littered throughout the summer with favorite pre-bake chowder recipes or hints on using charcoal and aluminum foil as clambake shortcuts. In 1985, the *New York Times* featured a lead article in the "Living" section on clambaking in Maine, while the *Boston Globe,* in search of even more exotic angles, reported in 1986 on how transplanted New Englanders do clambakes in Texas.[55]

In the current popular media, the clambake, like images of whales and nautical gear, has come to represent New England summertimes in the popular imagination. Photographs of the bounty of the clambake illustrate New England tourist brochures and direct-mail clothing catalogues—the kind

that use healthy, young, blue-eyed models in casual settings to sell "natural,"
all-cotton casual wear. Clambakes have also become the public relations
extravaganza of choice for commemorating annual meetings, anniversaries of
various kinds, and political events—forever political events—all of which
support and expand the market of the clambake producers.

From the prehistoric clambaking of native Americans to clambake pavilions filled with hungry voters, from pictures in old family albums of church
bakes to glossy ad photos of robust Yuppies in 100 percent cotton sweatshirts
steaming shellfish on the beach, the images of the clambake have communi-
cated a wide range of messages about time and place and the role of community therein. The proliferation of these images as well as the continuing
presence of clambakes like that at Allen's Neck have kept clambaking a vital
tradition. There is every reason to believe that in gastronomic as well as
symbolic terms, the history of the clambake is far from over.

## Section Two

# THE ALLEN'S NECK BAKE: AN ETHNOGRAPHY

*In other words, they was born among the shells, you know. They should know how to make a clambake.*
—Ralph Macomber, Clambake day, August 15, 1985

In Don Yoder's seminal article on folk foodways, he asserts that "like all aspects of folk culture[, folk cookery is] related, integrally and functionally, to all other phases of the culture, and in its elaboration, like dress and architecture, [becomes] a work of art."[1] Unquestionably the most elaborate and elaborated of the area's numerous clambakes, the Allen's Neck Clambake is a work of just this kind of cultural art.

To call it "art," however, does not mean advocating that Clambake be removed from its context—to be framed, hung on the wall, and moved away from in order to get a better "view." In fact, part of the whole allure of the anthropological process of analysis—moving from the outsider's impression to the insider's view and ending up, finally, with an informed outsider's interpretation—is that it seeks to avoid this kind of distancing. The notion of the clambake as art seems useful, at least for the moment, because it signals a significant structural and symbolic complexity.

Section Two is the catalogue raisonné for the Allen's Neck Clambake, a description that includes information about its style and dating, its subject matter and iconography, comparable works, and the provenance or history of ownership. Chapter 4 touches on several of these different aspects, sketching out a portrait of the community against which the individual units making up Clambake can be better understood. Chapter 5 is a brief history of the last hundred years of the Allen's Neck Bake and the aesthetic standard which its history has engendered. And Chapter 6 describes in detail many of the pieces that make up today's Bake.

There is no lack of things to analyze, in technical or symbolic terms. The complex of objects and processes entailed by a clambake—its material culture—include natural fuel and raw foodstuffs, a constructed fire and prepared food, and a process of transformations—gathering, preparing, cooking, serving, consuming, and cleaning up. And each of these elements has individual physical, traditional, aesthetic, and narrative dimensions. The number of ways that a clambake can be performed, if not infinite, is at least large enough that the selections Allen's Neck clambakers make and the selection process itself are significant indications of deeper communal values.

When asked to describe the modus operandi of their clambake, the people of Allen's Neck move quickly and smoothly into a larger arena of meaning. What begins as an explanation of "the proper rocks" can suddenly become a commentary on the ethics of work; a simple reference to a squash pie opens deftly into a discourse on childhood and the "old days," into recollections of the textures of everyday life which spill over with affective content and moral and aesthetic judgment. Through stories and anecdotes, the people of Allen's Neck invest Clambake with value and meaning at every turn.

For this reason, the Allen's Neck clambakers tell much of the story in this second section. They speak the language of Clambake; their key words, metaphors, and moods compose the dictionary and grammar upon which it is built. If the clambake is a work of art, then the clambakers are its artists, or artisans, whose opinions and insights should be sought and revered.

The Allen's Neck people show a degree of intentionality, self-awareness, and discernment about the expressive and symbolic activities in which they are participating that should serve as a caveat against casting "the folk" in the role of ingenuous naifs. In the face of the many invented aspects of the clambake, the people of Allen's Neck have managed to keep the central meaning of this event their own. Authenticity, antiquity, and regional or nationalistic identification may be significant attributes to the tourist, ticket-holder, and theoretician, but they are not necessarily what compel this community and nurture them in their experience of the bake.

# 4

# A Portrait of Allen's Neck

*It's something about this square mile. There are a lot of people that really feel right, here. It's really special . . . really different.*
—Julie Brown, August 5, 1985

ALLEN'S NECK is a tiny strip of land along the Atlantic coast in southeastern Massachusetts, just east of the Rhode Island border and southwest of New Bedford. Originally the home of the Wampanoag Indians—a confederacy of Acushnet, Apponegansett, Acoaxet, Sconicut and other tribes—the area began to be settled by English colonists during the 1650s.[1] Many of the earliest English settlers, with such names as Allen, Slocum, Howland, Smith, Tucker, Tripp, and Gifford, were Quakers seeking refuge from the religious persecution of the Puritans of the Plymouth and Massachusetts Bay colonies.[2] Others came from Rhode Island seeking better and larger parcels of land.

Although maps show it as part of the town of Dartmouth, Allen's Neck constitutes a kind of human "ecosystem"[3] including parts of neighboring Westport as well as the nearby village of Russells Mills. This integration of community and physical environment has a temporal as well as spatial dimension: for example, figuring the distance from her farm to Horseneck Beach causes Gram Gifford to recall the amount of time it used to take when she was a girl to travel by buggy from her home on the beach to the Sunday school on

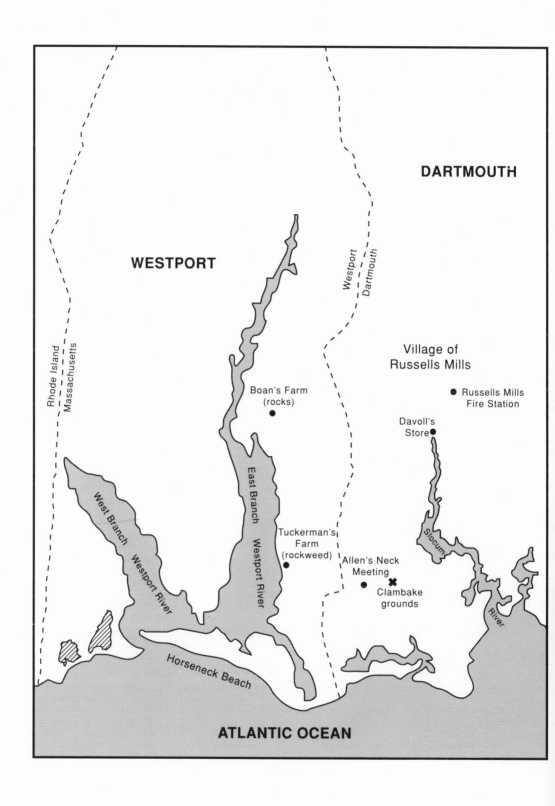

DARTMOUTH

WESTPORT

Westport
Dartmouth

Village of
Russells Mills

Rhode Island
Massachusetts

Boan's Farm
(rocks)

● Russells Mills
Fire Station

Davoll's
Store ●

East Branch

West Branch

Westport River

Westport River

Slocum

Tuckerman's
Farm
(rockweed)

Allen's Neck
Meeting
● ✖ Clambake
grounds

River

Horseneck Beach

ATLANTIC OCEAN

Bald Hill. The route from any-here to any-there almost always involves a series of landmarks no longer visible—the schoolhouse that burned, the old barn, torn down, farmers long since dead, and the fields where Indian arrowheads used to be found.

This conflation of time and space makes getting around for the newcomer fairly difficult. Says Ernie Waite of his own father, "I'll never forget one day down at the shop, some people wanted to have some directions how to get down to the bottom of the road, and he says, 'Just go down to Davoll's Store, take a right there; when you get to Bill Tripp's take a left.' And he says, 'It's the next house after George Lake's.' I says, 'You darned nut! If they don't know how to get to Manny Perry's, how in the heck they going to know where George Lake and Bill Tripp live?' So I went out and told them."[4]

The ecology is defined by the social networks as well. Says Elden Mills, speaking of his nearly seventy years of contact with the community, "I think the main character of the Allen's Neck Friends is their closeness as a community with one another, that their lives are very profoundly intertwined with each other—say, not only their religion but socially and maybe by blood relationship, by a large part, economically. . . . You see, when I was there, there were sixty-five members of the meeting, and thirty-five of them were Giffords."[5]

Davoll's General Store has stood at the mercantile center of Russells Mills since the end of the 1700s; down the road is the fire station, a kind of political core, the center of male bonding. In the symbolic center of the "square mile" of Allen's Neck, however, is Bald Hill, on which stands the Allen's Neck Meetinghouse. When Bald Hill used to be bald, when the hill and the surrounding fields were bare of trees, the white clapboard building served as a beacon for ships at sea. Still white, the meetinghouse, built in 1873, is one of a half-dozen Quaker centers for worship in the immediate area. The Apponegansett Meetinghouse is the oldest of these, having been built in 1699, but meeting for worship took place in private homes—at considerable personal risk—both before and after that date.[6]

In keeping with a general model for Quaker architecture, the Allen's Neck Meetinghouse is simple and relatively unadorned: in the meeting room itself, the rough-hewn wooden floors are painted gray; the benches, purchased from another local church that closed down, are suitably uncomfortable; and the walls are bare, except for two framed pictures and one extremely loud clock. The aesthetic, while "traditionally" Quaker in some respects, is rendered distinctive by local, personalizing influences. During the summer months, for

Allen's Neck Friends Meetinghouse, Bald Hill, Dartmouth, Mass. Photograph by Kathy Neustadt, 1985.

Interior of Allen's Neck Friends Meetinghouse, with flowers. Photograph by Kathy Neustadt, 1987.

example, the meeting room is ablaze with color, the taste of Betty Amaral, a neighbor from down the road, who arrives each weekend with an armful of flowers from her garden and decorates the organ and altar with the brilliant bouquets.

Ila Gonet, the treasurer of the Allen's Neck Meeting, figures the current membership to be about eighty, with about thirty-five or forty "working members." On Sunday mornings in the summertime, however, when the Sunday school is closed, there are many fewer in attendance: a group of about twenty women and less than a dozen men—mostly in their sixties, seventies, and eighties—sit in the unlit room, listening alternately to the words of the minister, the loud ticking of the clock, and the lowing of cows in the adjoining field. Difficult as it is to imagine, this is the core group that generates the loud and boisterous crowd of six hundred-plus that gathers on Clambake day in the stand of oak trees just down the road.

Although the New England Yearly Meeting remained undivided during the Great Separation of 1827–1828[7]—in which the Hicksites separated from the Orthodox Friends—it was not unaffected by the second wave of division between the continuing so-called conservative and liberal tendencies within Quakerism.[8] Along with most of the other meetings in the area, Allen's Neck joined the ranks of the Gurneyites, followers of the British Friend Joseph John Gurney. The effects of the new allegiance were fairly extensive:

> Many of the older customs, such as the plain speech and dress, the emphasis on silence in worship, the habit of rising during prayer, the wearing of men's hats in the meetings, the "plain" names of the days of the week and the month and marriages after the order of Friends were generally discontinued. . . . Other new methods were imported by the revivalists. Singing was introduced because many of the leaders coming from other denominations felt that there could not be a revival without singing, and after some years of hesitation musical instruments were brought into the meeting-houses also.[9]

Today, most of the meetings surrounding Allen's Neck are superficially indistinguishable from other liberal Protestant sects: they have "ministers"—the previous minister at Allen's Neck was actually an Episcopalian—who conduct "church" services, complete with sermons, pastoral prayers, hymn-singing, and an offering. The Meeting members have little sense that there is any other way to be Quaker. Under pressure from some of the younger members during a short-lived "generation gap" in the early 1970s, a time for silent prayer was set aside during the service, but it remains a slightly uncomfortable silence and is regularly broken by requests to sing favorite hymns.

Burney Gifford tells how his grandmother, Gram, a strong-minded woman and a central figure in the Allen's Neck Meeting in her day, leaned over to her family during the newly instituted silent portion of the meeting and "whispered" loudly and with obvious distaste, "Well, what do we do *now?*"[10]

When Elden Mills came from the cornfields of Indiana and an Orthodox Quaker background to become the pastor at Allen's Neck in 1918, he discovered a Quakerism quite different from his own. "The Quaker influence is pretty thin," he noted, "but it's there. Long ago, they kept what they wanted of it and discarded what they didn't want (which good Quakers have been known to do)."[11] For all of the respect that Mills the man clearly felt for his new neighbors—evident particularly in his memoirs—Mills the minister found his new flock somewhat mystifying: "I don't know if they knew what doctrine was. They were Quakers by tradition, and that was good as far as it went."[12]

Raised on Allen's Neck-style Quakerism, Ginny Morrison feels something similar: "I've said that the only reason that I'm a Quaker was because my grandmother went there to that meeting, and she took my mother, and then my mother took me, and I took my kids. But I'm sure that had it been any other kind of church in that neighborhood, transportation being what it was, that's the religion I would have been brought up in."[13]

A "convinced Friend" and member of Allen's Neck Meeting for thirty-odd years, Florence Smith chose Allen's Neck more actively:

> Our kids were little, and we wanted a place for them to go to Sunday school. And I always believed you go to church in the area where you live. . . . There are the silent meetings, and then we wanted a minister, because we were somewhat more liberal, I think, than some of them. But the principles are the same. And I think the work ethic is one of the real things, the motivating things that Quakers have—and the freedom of thought: you live by your conscience, that's the primary thing. And I think people like the idea, and I was very much attracted to it; the fact that they are great educators, and they were the people who pushed education in this part of the world.[14]

The Quaker influence—traditional, nondoctrinal, and vernacular as it certainly appears to be—runs deep and informs many of the simplest aspects of everyday life. The Quaker antipathy to hierarchy and the belief in the essential goodness of human beings and the sacredness of life is discernible in the everyday interactions of the group. For example, there are no courtesy titles in Allen's Neck—no Mr. and Mrs.—and it is common (if striking, to this observer) to see the young people after Sunday school, outside Davoll's Store, or at Clambake engaged in conversation with men and women more than fifty

years their seniors, using first names, talking and laughing, with apparent
mutual respect.

The Friends of Allen's Neck consider theirs to be "a community meeting,"
catering to the needs of local residents, and they are pleased with the great
popularity of their Sunday school, which is attended by many non-Quakers in
their midst. According to some of the birthright Quakers at Allen's Neck—
those whose parents were Quakers before them—the role of the Sunday
school as well as the accessibility of the church itself have been largely
responsible for the size of its membership and support. The clambake is like
the Sunday school in this respect, its ranks of workers being swelled by
friendly but unconverted neighbors. "I think it's very gratifying for our Meeting to know that people care enough to work for us that day," Barbara
Erickson explains. Her brother-in-law, Gordon Parsons, adds, "It's pretty
ecumenical down there—I don't know what we'd do without them."[15]

Fertile soil and easy access to the ocean have greatly shaped the history of the
region. Farmed from the beginning of their settlement, Dartmouth and
Westport continue to make up part of the largest remaining agricultural
region in the Commonwealth. Once largely populated by poultry farms, dairy
farms predominate today.[16] As part of a general move in the direction of
specialization, nursery businesses have begun to develop in Allen's Neck: two
large companies and one moderate but growing newcomer have peppered the
landscape with plastic tunnel "greenhouses." Across the road from each other,
Julie Brown and Ila and Gus Gonet have carried on herb businesses with
slightly different markets; nearby, there is a small nursery that raises mums.

Otherwise, traditional farming for a living is growing steadily more difficult. Families continue to own their farms; a few have grown over the
years through a merging of family holdings, although most have diminished
through necessity or disinterest. But only a few can claim to make an annual
income equal to the price being paid for an acre or two of their now-prime
residential land. Against the larger drama of the demise of small farming in
America, local farmers in this area—or their more urbanized, less tradition-
bound heirs—are yielding to the pressures to sell out. As a result, developments have started to appear, and the building of new homes is constant
throughout the area, as Boston and Providence seem to sprawl ever closer.

Local residents, having watched the devastation uncontrolled development
brought to nearby Smith Mills and reading regularly about similar problems
occurring throughout the New England countryside and vacation areas, have

become more vigilant. One summer, posters appeared on the front of Davoll's Store advertising a picnic fund-raiser, the proceeds of which go to pay the fees of the lawyer who is helping the people of Russells Mills fight off unscrupulous developers. The Lloyd Center for Environmental Studies nearby raises funds for special projects, sponsors lectures, outings, and nature walks, and puts out a newsletter, all geared to protecting the environment of the Buzzards Bay region. And while the Almys have now given some of their marshlands to the Audubon Society for perpetual protection, farm conservancy legislation is being energetically argued over the farm family's dinner table.

Fishing has its own saga. At the time of white settlement of the Allen's Neck area, the well-stocked rivers, streams, bays, and sea made fishing an obvious and rewarding enterprise. But today, between government regulations and man-made pollution, the bounty has greatly diminished. The clams for Clambake, for example, are brought down from Maine, and other bakes nearby have had to get theirs from Nova Scotia: the local supply is neither plentiful enough nor sufficiently safe to meet the need. And mackerel, the traditional fish used in the Allen's Neck Bake from the beginning, no longer live in these waters in any reliable abundance.

The pollution of the water off New Bedford with highly toxic PCBs, among the worst in the country, is only one of the factors affecting the larger patterns of fishing. When Raymond Davoll first started lobstering in the late 1950s and early 1960s, there were four or five boats fishing out of Westport; today there are close to thirty. Offsetting this kind of competition for a diminishing commodity, however, is the rise in prices paid for the catch, which in turn attracts more would-be lobsterers to the sea. Raymond remembers his grandfather's stories of selling lobster off the back of a horse-drawn wagon along Horseneck Beach in the summertime for four cents a pound. When Raymond first began lobstering, he was making closer to forty cents a pound; in the mid-1980s, some twenty-five years later, the price was running above $2.60 a pound.

The whaling industry, which originated on Nantucket and Martha's Vineyard, took hold in the New Bedford area as early as the mid-1700s and continued into the 1920s, albeit in much degenerated form. Mary Davoll's father, Raymond's grandfather, was a whaler around the turn of the century, and like a lot of other men who left the sea, he "retired" to the farm. "As I have understood it," Mary tells, "when he wanted to marry my mother, her father took a dim view of whaling and made him give it up."[17]

The demise of whaling represented the first of several major economic

New Bedford's golden age of maritime activity: the whaling vessel *Catalpa*.
Courtesy Spinner Publications, New Bedford, Mass.

depressions that have plagued New Bedford, the second being the decline of the textile industry in the 1920s. According to some concerned citizens today, the city's growing dependence on the fishing industry as an economic base is capable of bringing on a new one. In recent years, New Bedford has undertaken significant and extensive renovation of its historic downtown area in hopes of developing its tourist market.

Over the years, New Bedford has been a magnet for immigrants from various countries. The Portuguese first came to the area as whaling crew and then settled. In the nineteenth century, the mills of New Bedford and Fall River also attracted large numbers of foreign-born people—Poles and Acadian workers from French Canada, as well as Englishmen, with their long tradition of textile manufacturing. Today's immigrants to the city are from Puerto Rico and Southeast Asia, and the problems they have faced upon arrival are both unique to their situation and common with those of their multinational neighbors who settled earlier.

For the early Portuguese immigrant, in particular, success often meant a second immigration, out of the crowded city into the countryside. "A lot of Portuguese people made their way out to farms," says Allen Gifford. "They were the next ones that took over when the old Yankees petered out on the farms. The Portuguese bought them all, 'cause they were interested in doing that."[18] Many of the stories about the clambake through the years have highlighted the good feelings and generosity of the newer Portuguese residents toward the "birthright" Quakers, including the donations of land to the Meeting by Muriel Silvia and her family, and Manuel Rose Perry's generosity in the matter of the property where the clambake is currently held. The Portuguese brotherhood, which owns the Holy Ghost grounds down the road from the Bake site, has openly invited the Bake to use its covered facility in case of rain; although the Allen's Neck people have only had to take them up on the offer a couple of times, it has been much appreciated.

At the same time, the influx of these particular "outsiders" has not been completely free of tension. Jokes about the "greenhorns," specifically referring to the Portuguese newly arrived in America, are common, if not particularly venomous. Because many of Allen's Neck's oldest families are now mixed in their ethnicity, talk like this is often prefaced by such statements as, "I'm part Port-a-geeze myself, so it's okay." But the public "good humor" isn't always appreciated. For such people as Muriel Silvia, whose mother was English and father Portuguese, the Yankee chauvinism can be a bit overbearing: "See, they all are related to Richard the Lion-Hearted here—'course, he never had any children, they forget that. They've all got the coat of arms, Richard the Lion-Hearted. So one day Elsie [Gifford] and I was talking—she's Portuguese—and she says, 'I'm related to Umberto Madeiras,' and I said, 'Well, I'm related to Magellan.' But they're all related to Richard the Lion-Hearted."[19]

Cathi Rebello (now Gonet), who moved to Dartmouth from Portuguese New Bedford with her family when she was twelve, found it difficult to be accepted into the local community. As Peter Gonet's girlfriend—Peter's family, through his mother, being one of the founding Yankee families—she became aware of this exclusiveness even more pointedly. Laughing, but with a certain amount of bitterness, she comments, "Oh, yeah, there's moments that

they give me the eye, but I don't mind. I figure, 'Well, go ahead, be that way.'
'Cause one day there's going to be no natives left. They're going to turn
around; it's all going to be people moved in from the city. I'm going to go,
'Haw, haw, who's the native now? Gotcha!'"[20]

Still, the influx of the hard-working Portuguese to the area is considered to
have been a good thing overall for the original community, which was "old
Yankee—like this," one native says, extending a clenched fist. Some sixty years
ago, according to Elden Mills's recollection, Nelson Gifford, Jr., expressed a
sentiment, and a self-deprecation, still being echoed today: "'It's the best
thing that's ever happened to us—this infiltration of Portuguese blood. The
old Yankee strain has petered out. Look at us. The Giffords. Five different
branches of the family, all intermarried. It's a wonder we aren't all im-
beciles. . . . It's been going on for years. We need new blood.'"[21]

Another more recent "infiltration," which has been met with a less hospita-
ble reception, is that of the gentrifiers—the people from "the city," who are not
farmers but who want to live in the country. "I find that there are a lot of
people who move into the rural area," says Muriel, reflecting the feelings of
many of the other birthright locals, "and then they want it to be just the way it
was [in the city]. That is kind of too bad because, like, the people who built up
in Russells Mills, right?, they were mad 'cause this guy—the guy had a little
farm there, and his rooster crowed every morning. And they wanted to get rid
of the rooster. They gave him all kinds of trouble, they wrote letters, you
know?—Tough, 'cause the rooster was there first."[22]

The problems can be even more serious than a few muffled roosters,
according to Burney Gifford:

> These people [the newcomers] really raise hell in some places. They've really
> screwed up things in Vermont, you know. They come in, they do their little thing
> and buy a farm, or something, and work it, and just about subsist and like that. But
> boy, when it came time for school . . . Most of these people didn't grow up in
> poverty; I mean, they're middle class, and they had a good education, and they
> want that for their kids. So they come in and start demanding that for their kids in
> these little Vermont communities that always got along fine without spending a
> million dollars on a school or something. And then—that's exactly it—then a lot of
> them just screwed off, and then they're gone, and the poor Vermonters are left with
> this big tax bill and the school is half empty.[23]

Scornful of the organic interests, old BMWs, and "desire to barter," the
old-timers have often made it clear to the newcomers that true membership in
the community might take generations—maybe longer. In this exchange, the

much admired "Yankee spirit" can seem cold and unfriendly. Under the title "Parsimony," one writer for the *Boston Globe* described the attribute this way: "Imagine a lake. Anywhere else in the nation, local authorities in charge of water access would say, 'Hmm, people are going to want to fish here. We'll have to find somewhere for them to park.' In New England the thinking would be different. 'Hmm,' we'd say. 'People are going to want to fish here. We'll have to put up some no-parking signs.' (Overriding philosophy: 'When in doubt, deny.')"[24] In this context, the new welcome sign between Route 88 and Central Village signed "Westport Newcomers' Club" seems at once wry and hopeful.

The substantial summer population in the vicinity creates additional fodder for tension about "membership." The summer colonies, many of them started during the latter part of the last century as products of the leisure revolution, have their own history, and the colonists their own inherited sense of belonging.[25] At fêtes such as the Allen's Neck Clambake, the ticket-holders are sometimes third- and even fourth-generation participants: from their perspective, Clambake is part of *their* heritage. Ila Gonet has a photo in one of her albums of a clambake day from the 1910s or early 1920s which is a composition of contrasts: in the background stands the stark white Quaker Meetinghouse, and in the front, rows of black Model T Fords, the property of the affluent summer residents, appear with an occasional black chauffeur at the side.

The dividing lines between insiders and outsiders have changed with the times. A few years ago, in Westport Point—an area considered by the farmers to be tourist-infested and citified—a disgruntled local posted the sign "Skewks go home" and triggered a short-lived but heated discussion in the local papers of the nature of the "true community." The term "skewk," according to Julie Brown, was understood to be an Indian term (which, of course, makes the critique more authentic): "It was a bird that used to come here from other places, and it would come in and kick out the old birds: not necessarily kick them out, but they'd take all the old nests that the birds had before, and they'd move into the nests for the summer. And they were obnoxious birds, from what the Indians said; the Indians didn't like these birds. And then in the fall, they would head off and leave," to which her husband, Burney, added, "leaving everything a shit house."[26]

Feelings are as varied and complex about the term "skewks" as they are about the presence of the people incurring the name and the larger issues of tourism and "progress." Many of the older people around Allen's Neck are

Old Bald Hill Road (now Horseneck Road), Dartmouth, Mass., early 1900s. The farm on the left (with a series of small chicken houses) currently belongs to Ila and Gus Gonet; the Howland-Gifford farm, on the right, is where Hettie Tripp and Mary Davoll were born, and where Al and Elsie and Burney Gifford live today. Courtesy Alice Macomber and Hettie Tripp.

uncomfortable with this expression of animosity and with the suggestion that such a rift exists within the community. The older they are, the greater their tolerance of change seems to be. What's a few more outsiders, a few more retail stores, to a woman such as Mary Davoll, who, at eighty-five, has seen her world altered in ways almost inconceivable to her younger neighbors? "Well, of course, traffic we have now is unbelievable. I can remember when I first came up here to live, that road there, Rock O'Dundee, was a dirt road, and there wasn't much of anyone down there—and now, there's so many houses been built down there. And there was a man down there named Ed Smith, I think. He used to come up on Fridays, I think, and get, well, a few groceries maybe, and some horse feed. Well, that was about all the traffic there was down there. I came here when I was married; I've lived here since 1924. Well, we've changed it quite a bit."[27]

The next generation tends to be quite matter-of-fact about the future, unsentimental about the existing way of life being threatened. To Allen Gifford, in his sixties, the influx of people and the developments are inevitable, even logical:

> You have to stop and consider: we have twice the number of people that we had forty or fifty years ago; we're still on the upswing. You have to do something with them. That's what bugs me about the environmental people: they get all shook up because, what are you going to do?, have it like it was when the Indians were here, with a few thousand people in the whole United States? We've got two hundred twenty million people: you going to send them back now, or what? You just have to do the best you can with them. You can't make it all like wilderness, for God's sake. That's what some of them want to do . . . You get two hundred twenty million people, there's a few problems around.[28]

It tends to be the younger people, particularly those who hope to inherit the family farms and continue to be farmers, who are less tolerant and accepting of such changes.

Perhaps in reaction to the lack of control over what will happen to farming in the future, a number of people in the community are active students of the farming culture of the past. When Allen and Elsie Gifford or Muriel Silvia talk about the Shakers and the Amish, for example, they display a depth of knowledge that reflects the extensive reading they have done on these groups and the pilgrimages they have made to their farms and communities. There is passion to the interest, as well. Says Willy Morrison of the Amish country, "We went up there once, but I keep saying I would love to go back. Not on Sunday or a holiday but just a plain working day. . . . I said, 'God, would I like to get up there when they're working the horses and plowing.' . . . I said, 'We've got to make it a point either this fall or sometime for a few days to go up there while they're still farming.' "[29]

There is a growing sense among the old-timers of Allen's Neck that they themselves might already be the proprietors of a form of rural culture that is nearly gone. Ralph Macomber and Willy Morrison, both sons of blacksmiths—the traditional jack-of-all-fix-it, rework-it, and recreate-it trades—have visited historical museums where they've needed to educate curators about tools in their collections. When Ralph went to Holyoke for the restaging of the Massachusetts part of the Smithsonian's folklife festival, he was the one who suggested that in addition to clambaking he bring along some of his old tools, maybe make some old-fashioned cedar shakes, and generally "tell the people what I know."

On the Howland-Gifford farm, Allen has been informally gathering "old stuff" together for some time—old machines, old tools, odd containers and "junk": his family calls it, with considerable amusement, "the chicken museum." Cliff Allen, Al's cousin, has his own collection of poultry paraphernalia at his house in the village, and, mixed in with the carpentry tools of his father and grandfather out in the workshop, he has stored old wrought-iron gate hinges, old latches and handles—"things too good to throw out." It's part of a Yankee tendency, he admits, to hold on to nearly everything, because "you never know when it might be serviceable."

In the shed at Ralph Macomber's place, there's a working model of an overshot water wheel which he built from diagrams in books and what he remembers from his youth: he's put it on display at the Acushnet town festival. In the kitchen, in which until only recently a wringer washing machine resided and old magazines are piled atop an old wood-burning stove, Marjorie, Ralph's wife—also Cliff Allen's sister—makes her brown bread and pies with the tools that her mother used. The Macombers' house, like many around Allen's Neck, is filled not only with old "stuff" but with books that explain the origins of all the stuff.

This phenomenon led Elden Mills, after nearly seven decades of association with the community, to characterize the people by their "erudition" despite a general lack of advanced formal education. People know their local history—the older ones at least—and talk easily and freely about it, connecting current goings-on with what came before. They read all of the books written about them and by authors in their midst and integrate the information rapidly into local lore.

*Turtle Rock Tales* (1975), J. T. Smith's privately published booklet of reminiscences, can be found in many neighboring households, and his daughters, Barbara Erickson and Jean Parsons, are still giving copies away. Everyone seems to own—and to have read—the *Allen's Neck Friends Meeting Cookbook*, the fund-raising publication with an introduction by Gram (Gladys) Gifford and Marjorie Macomber on the history of Clambake. People know Milton Travers's work on the Wampanoag and go to hear him lecture at the Westport Historical Society. And the older generation has read Joe Lincoln and Llewellyn Howland, who wrote about "the old days" on Cape Cod in ways that evoke their own local past.

The Allen's Neck Meeting library is a substantial historical resource overseen by Ginny Morrison, a professional librarian now retired. Already one graduate student has culled the minutes of the Meeting for his dissertation on the famous Quaker philosopher and teacher Rufus Jones; another pokes around asking questions about Clambake. Among other unofficial duties, Ginny keeps files of the many articles that have appeared over the years about Clambake, articles that are also saved in many of the other households throughout Allen's Neck.

*The Christian Science Monitor* has published a couple of pieces, and the New Bedford *Standard Times* regularly sends a reporter to capture the local color of the clambaking season. An article by Raymond Sokolov in *Natural History Magazine* in 1978 was later reprinted as a chapter in his 1981 book, *Fading Feasts: A Compendium of Disappearing American Regional Foods,* which featured a picture of the opening of the steamy, clam-filled Allen's Neck Clambake on its cover. Because they've read about themselves so often, the people of Allen's Neck have become critical readers and have ready opinions on where the authors have gone astray. They have also come to realize what good copy their clambake makes.

The sojourn of the Allen's Neck tribe at the Smithsonian's 1988 Festival of American Folklife produced additional press, memorabilia, and self-awareness of all sorts. The Meeting's newsletter carried vignettes about the experience in Washington, and sojourners displayed their photographs of the capital in the front hall of the meetinghouse. In addition, six hours' worth of fieldwork videotapes, taken by Smithsonian art director Daphne Shuttleworth during the summer of 1987 now reside in the Allen's Neck Friends library; and many members of the Meeting have borrowed them, to watch themselves or to show to visiting guests and relations.

The future of Allen's Neck is hard to project. How well will the residents be able to hold back the floodgates of development and change—and will they even want to? Which farms will be sold and which will be held onto, and for how long? Will marine life continue to inhabit the area waters, and will it be fit for people to eat? Who will stay and who will go, and what will they each remember about "the past," once the elder members of the group alive today are all gone? The fate of the clambake will depend to a great extent on the answers to these kinds of questions.

# 5

# One Hundred Years of Clambaking

*Every year in Meeting, we have to decide if we want to have a clambake, to go into our minutes. We'll say, 'Clambake Committee: the same as last year.' According to our minutes, you don't even know who's on the Committee.*
—Ila Gonet, July 17, 1985

UNTIL VERY RECENTLY, the only "official" history of the Allen's Neck Clambake appeared in the introductory essay of the *Allen's Neck Friends Cookbook*. This was the source from which most everyone in the community derived the general outlines of the bake—that it was started as a Sunday school activity, that it was opened up to nonmembers for a price, and that it moved off the beach to up near the meetinghouse around the turn of the century and then to its present site some sixty years later.

The first Allen's Neck Clambake, held at Horseneck Beach, was really an outing for the Sunday School, only. It was held in the pines, in the south end and west side of what was Reed Road (now State Road).

Early on that August morning, a few of our menfolk sailed out on Buzzard's Bay for fresh fish—one of our members owned a catboat—others dug clams—not to forget the women who prepared many goodies that go with a bake.

Soon "outsiders" wanted to come and at first were charged 50¢ for the privilege. . . .

According to records, a picnic was substituted in 1910, but apparently didn't quite "fill the bill," because a bake was resumed in 1911.

And for that year, the advertisement in the newspaper reads:

"Clambake, Allen's Neck
Sunday School
will hold their
Annual Clambake,
Thursday, August 24th
in the grove at Church.
Bake opens at 1 P.M.
Tickets 75¢
Children under 12 years 50¢
Pie, Cake and Coffee served at Dinner.
If stormy, next day.
Please bring knife, fork and napkins."

The last bake at Horseneck was held in 1903. From 1904–1960 they were held in the grove across from the Meeting House, on land loaned to us. . . .

In 1959, the Meeting purchased the present site, using a legacy from a devoted member. The cook house is bigger and walking around certainly is better.[1]

Besides the 1910 picnic fiasco, the other hiatus in Clambake was during World War II, when for a couple of years it wasn't held: "Some of the men were gone," explains Elsie Gifford. "It was hard to get things."[2]

An earlier historical account also exists, a couple of pages written by Elden Mills on the anniversary of the fiftieth clambake in 1938. At that time the pastor of the West Hartford (Connecticut) Congregational Church, Mills filled his short history with bits of information he'd garnered from the old minutes of the Meeting and records of the Sunday school. Much of what he recorded was about social matters:

*Famous Locally*

The Allen's Neck clambake is famous locally and is known to many people at a considerable distance. A distinguished New York surgeon often drives up to the bake; one year as he finished a remarkably ample dinner the bench gave way beneath him. Several people, among them Ben Cummings and Isaac Ashlay, have a standing order for tickets from one year to the next.

In 1908 the school voted "that we extend invitation to James Allen, William Collins and George Gifford to free dinner showing an appreciation for their having fixed the driveway into the churchyard. Elihu Gifford agreed to get the clams." In the early years the clams were dug and the fish caught as a part of the committee's preparatory work. Today only pies, cakes and brown breads are donated. . . . A distinctive feature of Allen's Neck bake is the table of the Missionary Society, where the year's labors of [the] society are sold.

In addition to the textural quality Mills's account provides, it also highlights one particular aspect of the Allen's Neck Clambake that has grown in importance over the years, a theme that lies very much at the center of this study of

the clambake as a tradition. "On my first Summer there, in 1918," Mills wrote,
"there were some heated remarks when plans were being agitated because in
the motion proposing the clambake were the words 'and have the same
committee as last year.' It was with considerable pleasure that I found in the
Sunday School record of Aug. 4, 1889, this minute: 'The school voted to have
the clambake the last week of the month; voted to elect the same committee as
last year.'"[3] It can be confusing, Florence Smith points out: "They call,
'meeting of the Clambake Committee.' Okay, you're not sure you've ever been
on a committee, but you go. . . . just go and do what needs to be done. . . . it's as
simple as that."[4]

According to Ila Gonet, the minutes of today's Meeting read the same as in
1889: "same as last year." It is the clambake refrain. But what it meant in 1889,
the first time it even *could* have been said—or in 1918, after some thirty
repetitions—and what it means now, a century of "sames" later, has surely
changed. For example, where it seems to have caused consternation to members
of the 1918 congregation, for today's population, it is a source of pride and
gratitude: we're still able to do it "same as last year."

The annual pre-bake preparations—the outdoor chores the men and the
young attend to, and the older women's work on the baked goods—are
handled in the same "continuous" fashion. As Karl Erickson's eldest granddaughter gets ready to salt and pepper the fish, one of her cousins seeks advice
on the size of the pieces he's supposed to cut:

"You remember last year?" he asks. "The same?"

"If you've cut them before," she answers, "keep them the same size."[5]

Norma Judson's example of being solicited to bring pies for the bake is also
typical: "It's like, I haven't been to Meeting in a couple of weeks because I've
been ill, and Hettie called, and she says, 'I've been looking for you.' I said, 'I
know. I'll do what you're going to ask me.' She says, 'Will you do the same?' I
says, 'Yup.' And she says, 'Okay, that's it.' Will you do the same?"[6]

The traditionalizing impulse has grown stronger since Elden Mills wrote
his tribute to the fiftieth clambake, which is no surprise. For one thing, in the
time frame of this young country, the number 100 has an authority-granting,
sanctifying power all its own. But the community also fully endorses the
themes of repetition and continuity: yes, they declare in one voice, this is the
way it has always been done. Changes that have occurred, innovations that
have been made—things *not* the "same as last year"—have tended to be
obscured, forgotten, or relegated to the personal voice, the individual's accounting of private memories.

In comparing Allen's Neck with other bakes around, Imelda Waite concludes, "They've had their bakes already a hundred years, so I think they want to stick to the old tradition. They don't want to change, no matter what." Providing an unintentionally wry insight into the nature of traditionality, she adds that since the clambake has received publicity from the likes of *Yankee* Magazine, "they *wouldn't dare,* I don't think, change it. And I don't think they ever will either" [italics mine].[7] When asked whether the menu has changed over a hundred years, another woman answers, "Not allowed to." This is part of the same pull toward the consensual voice and of the perception among insiders that they don't have the power to effect changes because the bake is immutable, fixed by tradition, by reputation, and by the expectations of its consumers, the ones who buy the tickets or read *Yankee* Magazine.

Every now and then, someone gets concerned about the pieces of the picture that start to get lost. Willy Morrison is more interested than most in preserving the whole story of Clambake, in its numerous details.

> There's also one more thing, and I dwelled on it when we were having a little problem one time: the whole thing [the clambake] comes out of the Sunday school. There's a little thing there that nobody thinks of. . . . These kids—like if you had grown up here and gone here [to Sunday school] and gone away—why did you come back to it [Clambake]? Because you used to go to Sunday school and . . . you come back hoping to see the ones that you went to Sunday school with or you grew up with, and like that. . . . You'd better believe it, that's why you see them once a year, the ones that moved away and can get back.[8]

Ila Gonet confirms Willy's claim. "Years ago," she says, "there was one table set aside for the old Sunday school members that couldn't work and the small children that couldn't work. A special table was set for them to eat at when the rest ate. But that—we did away with that as times changed."[9] Times *have* changed, and although the Sunday school is officially in charge of the sale of sodas at Clambake (with Willy at the helm), there is almost no trace of its once central role—and just barely more memory that it ever was like that to begin with.

There have been some attempts to innovate over the years, not simply to adapt—as, for example, when mackerel was replaced on the menu with an easier-to-obtain, more locally abundant fish—but blatant change usually has not fared well. For example, there was one attempt, spearheaded by Elden Mills, to resurrect the original insiders-only clambake: "I remember one summer down there I engineered—much to the disgust of Charles T. Gifford—I engineered another bake for the church only and it was not a success. Or it was not as successful as it should have been because I did not know

Setting up tables and benches in the Allen's Neck clambake grove (Barbie Gonet Schultz and Al Gifford). Photograph by Kathy Neustadt, 1985.

enough to get salt water on those clams and let them drool into the hot stones. See, it's the hot stones that makes the steam."[10] It was an experiment that was never repeated.

Some changes have fared better, such as the move to the new clambake grounds in 1960 from land the Meeting didn't own. "It didn't belong to us," Florence Smith explains. "And then when the man bought it from Palmer Scott who had had it for all those years—Palmer Scott was a boat builder, and Isaacs bought it—he didn't say we couldn't go there, but he planted grass over where we had the fire, and no one mowed it, so we took the hint."[11]

When the Meeting bought the new site down the road, it was possible to increase the seating from three hundred to five hundred; but more than that, it was possible to sink roots. The purchase of the new clambake grove had been made possible by a bequest from a loyal member of the Meeting; another, more recent bequest has sparked talk about putting in a parking area behind the grove to handle the clambake traffic. "With all those cars along the road, it's gotten quite dangerous," argue some; "all that expense for one day a year!," say others. The decision is not likely to be made quickly.

One change instituted in the recent past turned out to have some disastrous effects. In Norma Judson's recounting, "We had new arm bands made, and the purpose of the arm band was originally to let people know, I guess, if anyone had an arm band on, that that is a person that would help you, serve you. That really was, I think, the only reason. Then a few years ago, that arm band took on another dimension, and that was unless you have an arm band on, you're not working. And if you're not working, you're not eating. Now, that sounds like a very efficient way of running things, but that proved to be very disturbing, and, ultimately, it was thrown out."[12] but not before a number of people got into arguments over the "rules," became disaffected, and withdrew from Clambake altogether.

Among other details, Elden Mills's fiftieth-anniversary article contains information about Clambake's fund-raising capacity, which is today considered one of its major functions.

| year | money made |
|------|-----------|
| 1902 | $28.87 |
| 1903 | $45.00 |
| 1904* | −$5.75 |
| 1905 | $38.00 |
| 1910 (picnic) | $1.03 |
| 1915 | $150 |
| 1925 | $554.54 |

*after the clambake moved from Horseneck Beach

Between 1900 and 1938, according to Mills's rough figures, the clambake raised $6,700. The figures are interlaced with additional bits of information. For instance, Mills wrote, "An interesting minute in 1905 after proceeds of $38 were reported read, 'Voted, the Sunday School purchase the dishes which they have been using free of charge for the last six years also purchase a new boiler.'" To this, he later added, "For many years the money was used to pay for the 'barge' which transported children to the Sunday School from distances too far to walk."[13]

The price of a ticket to Clambake in 1911 was seventy-five cents, according to Mills's account; in 1936, the cost was raised to $1.25. Dorothy Gifford remembers, "It caused great anguish because people were sure that people wouldn't pay a dollar and a quarter to come to a clambake."[14] According to an October 5, 1975, article in *The Christian Science Monitor,* tickets were seven dollars in 1975; by 1985, the price had risen to fifteen dollars, and the committee

# *The* Allen's Neck Sunday School Clambake

## will be held in the grove opposite the Meeting House
### THURSDAY, AUGUST 20, 1936

The bake will be opened at 1 o'clock. Tickets should be ordered in advance. Price $1.25.

Please bring knife, fork, spoon, and napkin.

Kindly tell all your friends.

If stormy, bake will be held next fair day.

For the Committee,

(Miss) Dorothy W. Gifford,

Telephone—Westport 24-21                    South Westport, Mass.

Ticket from 1936 clambake. Courtesy Virginia Morrison.

in recent years, with the same sense of anguish Dorothy reported, has raised the price from fifteen, to sixteen, to eighteen, and, most recently, to twenty dollars apiece.

With tickets now costing substantially more than three bits, it is not surprising that today's revenues are also larger, amounting to about three thousand dollars in ticket sales, with close to another one thousand dollars each from the bake sale and handicrafts tables. In the last few years, the five hundred available tickets for Clambake sold out within a matter of days after the announcement of Clambake went out in late June or early July; in 1985, at least, while Florence Smith and Kate Gifford were still handling ticket sales, there were more than two hundred names on the waiting list.

No one seems to know whether there was a bakemaster when Clambake was held on the beach, but, according to Mills's memoirs, the "chairman" of the bake from 1902 until 1936 was his friend Ed Gifford. From there on, Willy Morrison relates the line of succession of bakemasters: "I can go way back as a kid to Charles T. Gifford and Gardner Gifford. And then Ralph Gifford had it for a long time, and I used to work with Ralph."[15] Charles T. Gifford, it turns out, has the dubious distinction of being the only bakemaster to turn out a bad bake at Allen's Neck. "I remember one year," recalls Ila Gifford Gonet, "oh, I guess maybe when I was in my twenties [this would have been sometime during the 1930s]: for some reason or other, the bake didn't get done, and when they took the bake off, a lot of the stuff was raw. Not done. And my Uncle Charles—Gifford—was superintendent and also head of the bake then. He made the announcement, and he says, 'You may come and get your money back. You can eat what is good and then you can come and get your money back from your ticket.' Only one person asked for their [money] back. So you see the spirit."[16] "The only thing that they could find out," says Willy Morrison about the disaster, "was the rockweed we used that year hadn't been up to par on moisture. There wasn't enough steam."[17]

Norman Waite, who, according to his son Ernie, had served his apprenticeship working the huge clambake at the Old Stone Church in Adamsville, Rhode Island, was the next bakemaster after Ralph Gifford. In addition to the Allen's Neck Clambake, Norman also put on bakes of his own—with the help of his family—to make extra money by catering these feasts for some of the wealthier Westport residents. "But then," Ernie says, "my father got the idea to sell tickets and put them on at home, when we lived next door down there. And I don't remember now, but it seems to me that we fed one hundred fifty people. So for a few years we put on a few of those. . . . It was one thing he tried to get an extra dollar, and he liked doing it, but he used to get so nervous. . . ."[18]

J. T. Smith, Waite's successor, acknowledged the training he received from Waite in his published recollections, *Turtle Rock Tales,* but added that his mother "used to put on bakes at Sunnyside Farm. She served about forty paid guests and I cooked the bake, so I was no greenhorn."[19] J. T. was something of a legend as bakemaster, in part because he held the position for about twenty years, far into his seniority, but also because he brought his own flair to the job. "J. T. Smith was the darnedest," Willy laughs. "He'd get [the clambake] all put together, and then he'd go and play horseshoes. He'd go across the street to the church and play horseshoes. I was never able to relax that much."[20]

J. T.'s son-in-law, Karl Erickson, took over for a few years, and then Willy Morrison held the job for another half-dozen years. "Karl quit," explains Willy, "because he couldn't stand the racket. And he and I had been doing it for quite a few years. Then I got it, and my family got after me and says, 'It's time for you to change. Too much to it.' And it can get quite tough."[21] Willy passed the torch to Peter Gonet in 1984: "I gave Peter the go-ahead last year. When we had the meeting, we got all set up, and I says to Peter—I'd been after him—I says, 'Are you ready to take it?' He says—I never will forget it—he will never forget it—'Aw, if you say so.' And Sonny [Raymond] Davoll is sitting

Peter Gonet, Allen's Neck bakemaster, standing next to the constructed bake. Photograph by Kathy Neustadt, 1989.

right next to the side of me, and he says, 'Peter, you've said too much.' He got it. So, of course, we all worked with him, but he was the boss."[22]

Peter's talent and experience—he's been working on the clambake, by his own accounting, since he was about six or seven—clearly qualify him to be bakemaster. But it's his youth—he's only in his thirties now—that makes the community as a whole breathe its deepest sigh of relief at his induction. In the affirmation of Barbara Erickson, a communal hope is clearly expressed: "he's gonna last fifty years."[23]

Over the course of years, along with the development of a history of "sameness" and of revenues and personnel, a clambake aesthetic has also been taking shape. It's not something people discuss, but it's embedded in what they say. However varied the personal takes, there's a general notion within the group of what constitutes a "proper bake." The phrases "real one," "traditional kind," and "old-fashioned" are also mentioned, but "proper" is the term people use again and again.

Of course, like most other clambakers—and most people, in general—the people at Allen's Neck tend to think that their way of clambaking is the best, and when they talk about "the right way," what they usually mean is "how *we* do it." But "proper" is something else again: when people use the word, they seem to be struggling toward a more elevated basis for judgment, more external and abstract. For example, pit bakes aren't "improper" just because they involve digging in the sand while bakes at Allen's Neck are built off the beach and up from the ground. Pit baking is totally legitimate: it's a matter of taste and the result of place. Pits are "old-fashioned" and traditional; pits are definitely "proper."[24]

But not just any kind of pit is proper. What about the kind written up in *The New England Cookbook*, which involves digging a hole on the beach and then sinking a barrel into it? These bakes take rocks from a wood fire, put them into the barrel, alternate layers of salt hay and food, and cover the whole thing over with a tarp and more sand.[25] Someone put on a clambake like this at a local country club a few years ago: that was the word around town, anyway. "Some fool" had outbid the local bake-for-hire people and was using hay. Wordell went over to check it out, but, he said, it was a real mess; he couldn't figure out what the hell was going on.

The men who tend the bake list the three bare essential ingredients for a "proper" bake: there's the *wood* for the fire, the *rocks* that it heats, and the *rockweed*, which makes steam and flavor and separates the food from the heat. Without these three, it's not a real clambake. The barrel bake didn't use rockweed; the method that places a wash boiler full of rockweed and food over a pit with a fire in it doesn't include rocks.[26] And one catered bake put on to benefit the Lloyd Center for Environmental Studies—which cost, they say, fifty dollars a head—used charcoal instead of wood.

Of course, the biggest distinction is between a clambake and a clamboil. "Clamboil" generally refers to a method of preparing clams and the rest of the meal by steaming them in a pot. The term is used as a general category for what is "not-clambake," but it is apparently not quite broad enough to encompass the use of salt hay and charcoal. Some clambakers use the term "clamboil," never actually a derogatory term, as a shorthand way to dismiss someone else's bake style, but it can also be used more positively. Willy

Morrison says, "There's nothing wrong with it: it's good eating, there's no problem there. And it's a lot less messy, I'll tell you that."[27]

Everyone has a different idea about how to discern a bake from a boil, and the fact that the distinguishing features are never both necessary *and* sufficient seems to bother no one. For Hettie Tripp, for instance, it's about taste: "You can have a clamboil in a kettle and about the same things, but 'tis nothing like the same. It's the rockweed that gives you the flavor, of course."[28] Interestingly enough, Leona Ashton uses the same reason for putting rockweed in her clamboil—for the flavor.

> We have a thing, if you want to try it [a steaming pot]. You put your clams in the bottom. We used to go get a little seaweed, rockweed: you can get that easy. Put that in the bottom. [Husband John adds: "Or you can do the same thing with salt water, to get that flavor."] Then your clams. And then we put everything—you know those bags we used to put penny candy in? We put our sausages in them. You wet them first so they don't stick—and then put all that on top. Clams first, then your tripe, sausage, fish, and then your potatoes on top. This makes it nice for six people. Then we cook our dressing and onions separate. And when the potatoes are done, your bake is done. It makes a delicious boil.[29]

Bake, boil: they don't seem so terribly different sometimes, at least to some people. Willy Morrison suggests that the foods may make the difference: "If you have a clamboil today, you'll put in hot dogs and *linguiça* and probably stuffed quahogs and a whole lot of other stuff, and you may call it a clambake. Well, the old-timers will say, 'That's no clambake, that's a clamboil.' If you want to cook a lobster, that's all right, but this bake never has them—that's been one of its traditions: it's strictly the same bake it's always been. We keep it that way on purpose. But a lot of people have these small clamboils and things, and they put everything into them."[30]

Although Allen's Neck Bake doesn't do it, the Fire Station Bake in Russells Mills uses *linguiça*—Portuguese sausage—and some bakes serve *chouriço* as well. To Willy Morrison and others, these additions seem to be okay—not the way "we" do it, but okay—but clambakes that serve mussels and chicken, even hard-boiled eggs, are hardly what Morrison would call "proper."

A lot of people around Allen's Neck actually prefer a boil to a bake. The Ashtons like it because it is practical: it's easier and quicker, with less mess—and they should know, because they both used to work some of the local catered bakes when they were younger. As Nanepashemet points out, there's the matter of cost, too: "Since it's an expensive deal, not too many people can afford a clambake." When he was growing up in New Bedford, his family had clamboils for family gatherings as "the easy way to do a clambake"; it would have been tough, too, to have that big a fire in a city backyard.[31] In terms of expense, labor, and tools, the clamboil is a creative alternative.

Dave Ramos, the postman who delivers the mail to Russells Mills, has never been to an "old-fashioned" clambake and can't begin to imagine what they do at Allen's Neck on a Thursday morning. In his house, it's always been strictly clamboils. And clamboils with red pepper: that's what makes it taste right (there are old Yankees turning in their graves!). How much pepper depends on which part of the family he's feeding: his Portuguese parents, their relatives, who come from different parts of Portugal, or his wife's family, who are of English descent.[32]

Though they are not as old as the clambake, clamboils have been around for a long while, long enough for Imelda Waite to remember "the olden days" when her family used to use copper kettles for their boil. Boils were popular during the Second World War. Willy Morrison recalls one put on by the Continental Screw Company, where he worked.

> Every Sunday after Labor Day weekend, they used to take all of the people, the police and the first aid, the whole shebang, all down to the Boy's Camp, and Audrey Coon, who was a caterer, would put on a clambake. Now here you go: he would take regular galvanized trash barrels and he had—of course, he was used to this—he had these square metal things, and he would fill them full of charcoal, and he would light them, and when they got going, he would set the whole barrel right on top. Now, he would have the clams on the bottom, of course. Now what he had was a clamboil. They would call it a clambake, but we never called it a clambake unless you used the hot rocks.[33]

There was enough call for clamboiling during the 1940s that Ernie Waite made some extra money fashioning a special container.

> I had a welding shop down at Russells Mills for thirty-three years, and I used to make out of a barrel . . . so they'd get the smoky flavor. . . . It was a simple thing. You just drilled some holes in the side of it to give the fire a draft down at the bottom, you know, and then you drilled some holes so you could push a couple of rods through it after you got the thing ready to put your food in, and after your rockweed and everything goes on. Then they used to just drop a grate on top of it; then you would throw the clams in and everything on top of it, put the cover on— that way you don't need no canvases or nothing. So they said that worked well. . . . In them days maybe it used to cost them six or eight dollars to make [the cooker], if they brought the barrel.[34]

Other people would deliver a finished clamboil, just cooked and still warm, in a fifty-five-gallon drum.[35]

COPYRIGHT, 1902, BY DODD, MEAD & COMPANY

| | |
|---|---|
| 1  AMERICAN HARD CLAM OR QUOHOG-(VENUS MERCENARIA) | 5  PIDDOCK OR DATE-FISH-(PHOLAS DACTYLUS) |
| 2  AMERICAN SOFT OR LONG CLAM-(MYA ARENARIA) SEE FIG.4. | 6  RAZOR-CLAM,-(SOLEN ENSIS) |
| 3  EDIBLE MUSSEL-(MYTILUS EDULIS) | 7  SCALLOP - (PECTEN IRRADIANS) |
| 4  BRITISH SOFT OR GAPER ,CLAM - (MYA TRUNCATA) | 8  COCKLE - (CARDIUM EDULE) |
| SHOWING EXTENDED SIPHONS | 9  PULLET - (TAPES PULLASTRA) |

The "proper" clam for the Allen's Neck Bake is number 2 at bottom right, *Mya arena-ria*, the soft-shelled clam. Reprinted from *The New International Encyclopedia* (1902).

As long as a boil is called a boil and not a clambake, most people in Allen's Neck find nothing wrong with it. But even if it uses a fire, rocks, and rockweed, a clambake can still fail as a clambake. According to Mary Davoll, mother of Allen's Neck's recognized clambaking expert, Raymond, "It must be cooked thoroughly. That's really important. And, of course, the clams have to be good."[36] Thorough cooking may seem obvious, but it is a part of the consciousness that informs the aesthetic: "I heard their bake wasn't even cooked," someone will say about a neighboring clambake.

At one recent Smith Neck bake the meal was an hour and a half late because the regular clam supplier was short and a second retailer was waiting for a delivery from Nova Scotia. It was bad form to be late, but not "improper," and people at Allen's Neck are careful not to blame bakers for their suppliers' mistakes and the larger constraints of distribution. They place such problems more in the category of there-but-for-the-grace-of-God: they are grateful that they haven't happened at Allen's Neck yet. It is a frightening thought— not just late clams, but no clams at all, a time when they will have run out of "up norths" for their molluscan supply.

Late clams can be forgiven, but bad clams cannot. Raymond describes a particularly frustrating experience he had at a clambake he once worked on: "They took the clams down, ten crates of clams, and all they did was sit them in the water, and nobody went through 'em, so we had to pick 'em . . . We started dumpin' 'em in the racks; you hear this, rattle, rattle, rattle—Christ, here's one there has the guts are runnin' out of it, and one thing and another. So it looks to me as if they don't give a damn—why should I?"[37]

Ultimately, this critique may constitute the community's underlying standard for judging the propriety and authenticity of a clambake—the attitude with which it is performed. A proper bake, it would seem, requires attention to details and a healthy respect for the vicissitudes of nature. Carelessness— such as reported by Raymond—overly romantic notions, an addiction to novelty: each of these dispositions can lead to an improper, even an unsuccessful, bake. Like listening for the sound of a dead clam, proper clambaking requires an awareness that infuses both thinking and action.

# 6

# How They Do It at Allen's Neck

*I think we have a pretty good reputation: not a reputation for being the cheapest, but maybe the best, you know?*
—Burney Gifford, July 30, 1985

**A**sk the Allen's Neck locals to explain how they put on their clambake, and they can provide a pretty quick rundown of the structure they build with wood and rocks, the rake-out and the rockweed, and maybe some details about what's done to the food before it gets stacked in racks on the weed and is covered over with tarpaulins. They might not give all the details, though, the first time; a person would have to ask a lot of questions before being able to put on a bake alone.

Ask a folklorist how they do the bake at Allen's Neck and, for better or worse, a very different story emerges. For one thing, because the folklorist's impulse is to examine all of the pieces of the bake in the context of its "material culture," it is hard to keep the thing simple. The way the fire works, the way the food is prepared, how the food is arranged and presented and consumed—all of these components have distinctive character and form, and what doesn't readily meet the eye or isn't mentioned directly is often the most interesting part. This is certainly true on the technical level, and the rule-bound complexity that sets the Allen's Neck Bake apart from most other clambakes begs analysis. Add to that the desire to discover the symbolic import of the event, which is rarely addressed directly by the participants themselves, and the task appears anything but straightforward.

Although this would make for a most cumbersome set of how-to instructions, the preparation of the clambake can be divided into two major categories—the fire and the food, that which cooks and that which is cooked. Each of these can be divided further into the smaller units of objects and processes they involve. This division seems justified, if a bit static, because the two components involve different raw materials, tools, and techniques; they take place in separate, if overlapping, time and space; and, until serving time, most people tend to participate in one or the other, but not both, of the arenas.

The very term "clambake"—or "bake"—includes a number of different meanings that also fall into these two major categories. A "bake" can refer to the fire or to the food; it can also indicate the process of preparing the meal and the event taken as a whole—as in, "that's a hot *bake*," "the *bake* was good," "I'll be there to help with the *bake*," and "the *bake* was over at three o'clock." The "bake" is also the site of the culinary metamorphosis, which exists before, during, and after the food is cooked but in different structural and functional forms. First, the bake is a carefully or loosely constructed piling of rocks and wood; next, it is a blazing bonfire; then, a bed of hot rocks; and, finally, an oven full of food.

It is not even clear whether the "bake" stops here. There is a period of time after the guests at Allen's Neck have been served when the "bake" becomes a warming oven for the food that the workers will eat. And even after the rocks and rockweed have been scooped up off the cement slab by the bulldozer, loaded into the back of Al Gifford's truck, and driven off to the dump or the field behind his chicken houses, this pile of debris, as it smokes and cools over the next couple of days, may still, perhaps, legitimately be referred to as a "bake."

This multiplicity of meanings demonstrates how much information has been packed into the technical details of the Allen's Neck Clambake, how many personal and communal experiences are embedded in its materials and operations. This loading on of significance, of course, means that any of the parts of Clambake has the potential to evoke a wealth of memories for individuals and the ability to invoke corporate values. This explains to a great extent why there is such emphasis on putting on a "proper" clambake: the bake is more than a meal—it's a microcosm of the community.

## The Fire

The basic ingredients of the Allen's Neck fire are the wood, the rocks, and the rockweed. Mirroring these essential elements are the concrete slab, the various wooden containers for the food, and the canvas covers. Although the fire inhabits only a small portion of the grove, it plays a primary role in the overall clambake event and is at the center of most of the dramatic action. Traditionally attended to exclusively by men—this has changed in recent years—the fire is the site of a good deal of enculturation for the boys, the bonding of young men, and the awarding of emeritus status to the male elders.

*The Wood.* It takes a lot of wood to feed a clambake fire. Clambakes for three hundred and up require roughly six feet of wood, or three-quarters of a cord (stacked four by four by eight feet), or ninety-six cubic feet. In addition to the cordwood, sometimes referred to as "four-footers," an Allen's Neck Bake also uses kindling or "trash wood" to get the fire started and a number of large pieces for the side of the structure, called "stringers" or "runners."

Most of the four-footers have been put aside sometime earlier, with different people taking on the burden of the work at various times. "I didn't do any of the wood this year," Burney Gifford explains, "but usually—one year I did the wood because Raymond screwed up his back. You've got to: that was unasked, you know; he didn't ask me to go up and split his wood, but you know, if you're going to work with him, you know—help him out."[1] Sometimes the stringers are trees from the clambake grove that have died over the winter and been taken down a couple of days before the bake, but mostly they come out of Raymond Davoll's wood lot. The kindling can be any kind of small branches or twigs, but if there is construction going on in the area, it will often be shims and leftover shakes.

To begin the construction of the bake, two eight-foot stringers are laid down on the concrete slab somewhat less than four feet apart, and the space between them is filled with paper and kindling. The four-footers are laid across the stringers with a log-size piece on each end and two more stringers along the sides to create a crib, which is then filled up with rocks. Another layer is built on top of that, and another, and another, until there are four tiers of wood and rocks.

The cross pieces are usually hardwood, because it burns longer and hotter than softwood. Burney explains, "The top layer's the smallest, and we'll mix in some pine so it catches well and burns hot. If you used all pine, it'd burn too

Collecting stringers from Raymond's woodlot. Photograph by Kathy Neustadt, 1985.

fast, and it wouldn't make much coals either. We don't want a lot, but you want some to keep things hot."[2] For the stringers, Raymond explains, "you should use oak for the upper ones. The bottom one, that can be about anything, 'cause they hardly ever burn out anyway, because all your heat is up. But your stringers, from the bottom on up, should be oak or maple. Pretty good size, 'cause that's what holds the whole thing together. And then when the middle burns out and the rocks fall down, you've still got the stringers there to kind of hold it together."[3]

*The Rocks.* A bake also takes a lot of rocks, which, like the wood, are not reusable. "You take a pickup truck body, there, that's four feet wide by eight feet long," Raymond explains. "You can figure out how big a bake you're going to build, load her up with rocks accordingly [three or four rocks deep]. I always keep a few extra ones under the tree in case we run short, but you know, you can figure it pretty well."[4] After the wood burns away, a pile of hot rocks should remain, "maybe like two deep, I guess I'd call it, or one and a half deep—about like that," Burney says, holding his hands apart ten to twelve inches. "You can't look through and see the ground, except maybe along the edge . . . Maybe twelve inches, some places more, some places less."[5]

A small crew of men—usually Allen and Burney Gifford, Peter Gonet, and Jim Acheson—gets rocks from the quarry at Boan's farm every couple of years. The quarry is an eerie place made more eerie because, in its barrenness, it bears no resemblance to the green, vegetative world above. Rivulets run down the side of the sundered earth, exposing the sought-after rocks within. The sounds of the rocks hitting the metal side of the dump truck echo in the man-made valley, and dark birds fly overhead. The men stay away from rocks with a greenish cast that, experience tells them, tend to crack and explode. They look for rocks the same size, "like a melon," "the size of your head," they all say, before they plunge into what is clearly annual "melon head" humor.

A couple of hours after the fire is lit, the rocks will drop through the burning wood to the concrete slab below; rake-out will clear away the ashes and cinders and leave the rocks as the only source of heat for cooking the food. The whole purpose of the fire, Raymond explains, is to get the rocks good and hot, "'cause if you don't heat enough rocks, you're stuck before you start. It's

The construction of the bake: passing rocks to fill the wooden "cribs." Photograph by Kathy Neustadt, 1985.

Burney and Al Gifford col-
lecting rocks at the quarry at
Boan's Farm. Photograph by
Kathy Neustadt, 1985.

not going to cook, that's all."[6] In fact, the rocks get so hot that they often split in the fire; afterwards they're brittle and chalky, their chemical makeup changed; they can't be used again.

According to Ralph Macomber, the sawyer from Acushnet who married into the Allen's Neck Clambake some fifty years ago, the fire at Allen's Neck is too hot—hotter than it needs to be—and the proof is in the rocks:

> I go by the look of the stones more than anything—go for the looks of the stone. If there's black ones in there, you don't have the heat. 'Cause the black is the soot from the fire, the soot has got to burn off. In other words, if you watch a stone, a stone will get black to begin with because of the smoke and everything around it. Gradually that will whiten out and go back to its natural state when we—we pulled

red ones out of there, out of the middle of these: there was red stones. And, of course, a red stone will break, it'll disintegrate. And you shovel that one back, it won't hold together. You don't want so much heat.[7]

At one bake at the Russells Mills Fire Station, where they make a fire the size of the one at Allen's Neck, one of the firemen stepped out of the rake-out circle when the visor of his helmet started to melt. That's how hot it is.

*The Rockweed.* It's all right to make the mistake of calling rockweed "seaweed," but only if you are an outsider, and only once. "You know the difference now between seaweed and rockweed?" Willy asks. "Well, rockweed has those little blister-like things, yeah. So many people will say 'seaweed,' and I say, 'No, you make it with seaweed, and you'll really be in trouble, 'cause there's no water—nothing to hold the water.' It wouldn't be enough moisture for a bake. You might get away with it in a little small thing, if you make it just for yourself or a few people—if the clams were good and full of water; covered it up good and tight, you know—you might get away with it."[8]

According to Ralph, rockweed is a fairly recent innovation. "The seaweed we was using had some kind of blight—just died out, couldn't get it any more—so we turned to the rockweed and it does the trick, oh, yes, it does it nicely,"[9] but no one else seems to remember that event. Nowadays, a few weeks before the bake, Gus Gonet pays a visit to the coastline at Tuckerman's farm, to make sure that the supply of rockweed there hasn't died out. "As long as the water's warm," his son Peter explains, "it just keeps growing. It depends on the winter. The worst part of it is the winter; if it's got a lot of thick ice on it, it tears it up and it's not too good. But if it's a nice easy winter, it's thick; it grows beautiful. And I've seen steers eating it, too; I don't know why."[10]

Gordon Parsons remembers a year when they couldn't find rockweed at Tuckerman's farm.

> So we went somewhere else. Are you familiar with Gooseberry Neck? Well, it's a neck that runs out from Horseneck, and it was tough because they had to go out quite a ways to get it. And one of those baskets wringing wet weighs a good fifty pounds, and you have to lug it and then throw it up on a truck. You see, the rookies always get that job. I was a rookie, so I can tell you all about it.
>
> I remember the night we had to go down, and Ernie let us take his flatbed, which was good, but you still had to carry it. But the guys that are out there in the water—up to here, usually—a lot of them have sickles, and they'll cut the thing off the rocks, and you have to watch out 'cause the barnacles are on there . . . cut it away from the rocks.
>
> And I was doing the lugging. . . . Jeez, I carried about eighty million of those

A crew collects rockweed the day before the clambake along the shoreline at Tuckerman's farm. Photograph by Kathy Neustadt, 1985.

baskets that night. Because the guys that are out there don't want to come in every time they get a basketful. They just float it in towards shore, and somebody else picks it up.

You have to watch the tide, too, for the rockweed. In other words, you can only get the rockweed at low tide. So, it depends—if you're lucky, a low tide might be at six or seven o'clock the night before [the bake]. That's great, because everybody goes down that night and gets the rockweed. Then you cover it over with canvas and wet it down, and it stays wet. Swell. See, the salty flavor of the water that you want is inside the bubble. Then of course, if you have any excess rockweed, what you do is dump it on the outside and it helps seal.[11]

These three essential elements of a proper bake—the wood, the rocks, and the rockweed—together lend an air of naturalness, untainted by things artificial. Only a few basic tools, mostly weathered farm instruments, are enlisted to manipulate these elements for the specialized tasks of Clambake—sickles for severing the rockweed from its stony roots; rakes, shovels, and pitchforks for separating rocks from the burnt wood and embers. Some of these tools are stored year after year in the cookshack, some are brought in to be used that one day, and some are loaned and borrowed among the local clambaking groups. Like silverware at the dinner table, they appear to render service and disappear nearly unnoticed.

More prominent than the tools, an additional group of man-made objects completes the complex of materials involved in the fire—the wooden racks, the concrete slab, and the canvas covers. They are viewed as practical additions, but not essential, and are valued only while they are serviceable. In addition, people remember when their functions were handled by different means.

*The Wooden Racks.* "Fat Mac [Ralph Macomber] built them, I think," Willy offers. "Now, Sonny [Raymond Davoll] has probably built his own, 'cause he's a carpenter. But he probably got stuff from the same place. I know Mac used to say, 'Come on up, and I'll give you some more stuff'—when they're sawing, they can get certain stuff out of certain things that they can't get much else out of, but they can saw them out. Not only do these trays make putting the food on the fire easier—they stack beautifully, 'cause they go one on top of the other—but they help in the unpacking. Fat Mac has always said this: 'You can grab a wooden tray right out of the fire'—that is, right out of the steam."[12]

Not all of the food has always been put into trays: "clam bags" were once part of the system. Peter Gonet learned about clam bags from his mother, Ila: "We used to put all the clams in white bags, like pillow cases almost, but now we haven't used those in years. Sometimes we put any extra corn that we have—if we run out of racks—we put the corn in the bags."[13] One of the photographs that accompanied the 1958 *Christian Science Monitor* article on the Allen's Neck Bake shows the clams being emptied into strawberry baskets from burlap bags.

"The reason they used the burlap was it was the thing fit the thing perfect to start with," Ernie Waite explains. "Burlap was the best to use because they're so coarse-woven that the steam could pass through them and go right up through the trays [of vegetables]. . . . Well, see having everything in trays wouldn't be as convenient because they're so darn hot when you start taking them off, as you'll notice. And then there's a good chance that the clams would get spilled."[14] Whether it was a better system than working with all racks or not, burlap bags disappeared some time ago; farm feed and the like now come in woven plastic bags—not exactly the appropriate material for clambaking.

Wooden trays and canvas tarps for the clambake. Photograph by Kathy Neustadt, 1985.

At the Fire Station Clambake and some of the other bakes that Raymond puts on where the amount of serving help is limited, the string bag—the kind used on hams—has recently come into use. While the clams, fish, sausage, and tripe are still cooked in racks, the vegetables are bundled together as individual servings—the white potato, sweet potato, corn, and onions. This means one server can take the place of four. A couple of years ago, Peter Gonet hinted that as bakemaster, he was going to get the Allen's Neck group to use string bags, but nothing has come of it and probably won't any time soon.

"Actually, it's much more efficient," says Ginny Morrison of the string bags. "Everything arrives hot, you have everything warm on your plate all at once, but as I explained to you before . . . it depends on what you want; it's that you can have ten people going down like this, this, this, or two people, one carrying a big container and the other one going plop, plop. It all depends: do you want mail service or do you want old country store service?"[15]

Certain other types of trays have been built over the years, baskets that are not put in the fire but that are used for serving the food as it comes out of the bake. "We use these old-fashioned things. If you go to this [clambake], you'll see something old-fashioned: they made a little tray basket with a hoop handle that holds just so many baskets of clams. The old-timers built them years and years ago, and, you know, those foolish things are still going." The thought makes Willy Morrison laugh. "Every once in a while one will start to go backwards on you. So, you know the trays that soda cans come in? I take a whole mess of them from the store, and I'll drop 'em in the trays when they want to put in stuff."[16]

*The Concrete Slab.* The concrete slab used at Allen's Neck for many years is a good example of a practical solution to a specific clambaking problem. Raymond, who has the broadest experience with a range of bake conditions, points out the practical considerations: "If you build [a clambake] just on the ground, just on the gravel, like we've done in some places, well, first thing you know you've got a hole there. Then you've got to fill it in. Concrete slab is easy to clean the stuff right off, stick it back on, and that's the end of it. And then you've got to figure out how big you're going to make the thing. If you've got a concrete pad, there it is, right in front of you, and you build it accordingly."[17]

However, the concrete creates problems as well as solves them. "We never use gasoline on the fire, we use kerosene," Burney says, "and you've got to be careful when you put the kerosene on . . . you don't want to have it running down on the slab, because that taste will get in there."[18] The concrete slab at the Fire Station Bake is newer than the one at Allen's Neck, but it's been a headache from the start: it would "blow up," be rebuilt, and then blow up again. "It's really bad because it will blow off parts, like shrapnel," explains Burney. "It's not fun. Raymond and I had one or two of the damn things in there go off—it was awful."[19]

Speculation on why the slab was exploding and how to make it stop was a major topic of conversation at the fire station while the bake was cooking: talk about pea stones and air expansion and uncured concrete, of inserting steel rods and removing steel rods and starting over, abounded. For several days after the Fire Station Bake, almost no comment could be made, in almost any company, without triggering a report on how and why the slab was in trouble. A few years ago, clambakers there dug the slab up and now do the bake on gravel.

Covering the bake: the parade of canvas (John Smith and Jim Murphy). Photograph by Kathy Neustadt, 1985.

*The Canvas Covers.* "A real old clambake, years ago, that you might make for yourself down on the shore, you'd cover it all up with rockweed and hope you'd have one canvas to put on top of the whole works," Willy Morrison recalls.[20] Now, for big clambakes, canvas coverings are considered a necessity. Canvas is expensive, despite the fact that it is manufactured locally for the nautical market, so covers are kept for a long time. The Allen's Neck tarps generally spend the winter in Willy's chicken house; Peter Gonet says, "They store beautifully there." Most of them are pieces of old tents from the nearby tent company where some of the local men pick up extra summer work.

The parade of canvases begins after the fire has been swiftly and deftly raked out and the rockweed and food have been put in place. The first cover on is special. "We have a cover—just might as well say it's like a table cloth—that's mostly just for looks: that white sheet, yeah," Willy says. "Over the

years, it'll get rotten and they'll get another one and so forth. It just looks nice,
it makes it look clean, but actually it doesn't amount to a darned thing because
everything's covered up already—everything's in a bag or everything's in a
something. So it looks better because the canvases get to look pretty crummy
after awhile." After all, as his wife, Ginny, adds, "There *are* people who've
come from New York, and these people from Pennsylvania."[21]

Then come the tarps—the bigger pieces first, which will cover the Bake
mound, the extra yardage folded back again. Smaller pieces, with rips and
tears, are laid this way and that, to cover. Some of the canvases have holes
where rocks have burned through in past years because the rockweed wasn't
piled thick enough; steam sought its escape through other holes. It's possible
to manage without canvas at all, people say, but you'd need a lot more
rockweed to seal the bake and keep the steam inside. Before they are put away
for another year, the tarps are spread out to dry: odd pieces of canvas draped
over fences and stone walls are a telltale sign in the Allen's Neck area that
someone has just had a clambake.

## The Food

The other major complex of the clambake's material culture is the food, which
is prepared and stored at a distance from the fire and overseen largely by
women. Like the components of the clambake's fire, the foodstuffs reflect the
area's environmental resources—goods from local farms and from the sea. Like
the fire, too, there appears to be a kind of primary and secondary grouping of
items. In the primary category are the raw materials from the water, the clams
and the fish. The secondary category includes the vegetables and, occupying
some kind of interstitial position, the goods from the butcher's store.

*The Clams.* When the clambake was a Sunday school picnic on Horseneck
Beach, the clams were dug right there. By 1918, when Elden Mills was
minister of the Meeting, the clams arrived in barrels, having been shipped
overnight from Cape Cod. There were still clams to be had then around
Allen's Neck, however, and Raymond remembers some twenty years later
"going down here, eight or nine years old, and digging a bushel. But you
couldn't do it now; I don't think there's a bushel in the whole river."[22] Too
polluted and overfished, everyone agrees. Today, the clams tend to come from
Maine, and, when that supply is low, from Nova Scotia.

They are clams, not quahogs. Quahogs do show up at New England clambakes, but usually only in the chowder. At the Old Stone Church Clambake in Adamsville, part of the town's Old Home Day and served to thousands, chowder always started the meal. "And that was made right there, too," Ernie Waite recalls. "And like I say, this big cauldron, cast-iron kettle . . . gosh, I can see old Billy Case there now, stirring that with a big paddle, there, looks something like a canoe paddle. When the bake was getting ready, they'd serve you chowder, a whole bowl of chowder. They used to be bigger bowls than they'd give you in a restaurant, and I guess one of the things was so you'd eat less clams and less everything else. Maybe there was a gimmick there, too, but I guess it was traditional there, you know. . . . But you could go if you wanted and just buy chowder—you didn't have to buy the bake."[23]

But at Allen's Neck, it is strictly *Mya arenaria*, the soft-shell clam, that holds the center stage. No chowder, no quahogs, and no lobster either—there never has been. "They're New England clams, you know, the coastal clams," explains Gordon Parsons. "The only time they ever had any real problem— remember that red tide? Do you remember when that was? Well, it was some kind of disease that was along the Maine coast, and they couldn't . . . we bought our clams from Maryland somewhere. They had big long necks sticking out: they were edible, but not like the Ipswich clam or the Maine clams."[24]

In the 1980s, the cost of clams rose at a frightening rate: in 1985, a bushel cost seventy dollars; by 1988, it was eighty-five dollars; in 1990, it was more than one hundred dollars. The clambake uses about twenty-six bushels of clams, and the summer's highest price always seems to be during the third week in August. "I don't know," says Burney Gifford, "they always used to say that a lot of people in Maine who dig clams . . . go off to go blueberry picking at that time. They make more money at that, so . . . so, the kind of people doing that to make a living, you know, they have to go when they can. So that drives up the prices."[25]

Raymond Davoll picks up the clams in New Bedford and drives them down to Horseneck Beach, where a waiting group of helpers empties the crates into the two skiffs they've filled with water. "You've gotta let them sit and get a drink, gotta let them open up," explains Raymond. That one last drink of water is what makes extra steam. The time on the beach in midmorning gives the clam crew socializing time they don't usually have. Cliff Allen and Al Gifford are cousins and lifelong buddies; Gus Gonet used to build houses with Cliff and lives across the road from Al. They sit down together for clam cleaning and take time to joke and chat.

Clam cleaning in an old skiff on the beach in Westport. Photograph by Kathy Neustadt, 1985.

"Company" from Ila Gonet's house—cousins from around the country, family "from away"—form another whole crew. "I think there must have been a secret society that came down here, and women weren't allowed," says one of the out-of-town Gifford women. "This is fun."[26] Kneeling in the sand around the boats, arms in water up to their elbows, people find the job of separating living clams from dead ones a pleasant pastime. Compared to the bustle and noise of the bake grounds, it is soothing and calm. Sometimes, when the work is all done, Cam Gifford will get out his bagpipes and play a couple of tunes.

According to Elden Mills, only two things make or break a clambake: the first is the proper advance preparations, the second is the clams. "As the Giffords all told me the first time I was at the Clambake: one dead clam will spoil the Bake. Enough water is put on to ensure that all the clams can gobble up all the water they want. And that does a number of things: in the first place, it tells you how many clams are dead—a dead clam will float. I learned to stir them up so that they would be free, not to be held down by anything. That guarantees, if you're alert, that you will have live clams to begin with. Plus, the fact of drinking in gobs of water as they do, that dribbles down as they cook and makes steam, which cooks the bake."[27]

The pros, Gus and Cliff and Al and Raymond, can hear one dead clam in a whole rack full of live ones. As Gus describes it and demonstrates, it's a hollow, rattling sound. A lot of dead clams is obviously a problem. "We don't like to get short on things," notes Ila, "but you can't tell: sometimes the clams aren't too good. When you're picking over them, you have to discard a lot. One year they had to go and buy another bushel, they were so poor."[28] The clams are considered to be especially clean, well picked through, and scrumptious at the Allen's Neck Bake. Every year, as the guests painstakingly rise and attempt to walk away from the table, they say things like, "Oh, my, the clams were the best ever this year!"

*The Fish.* Another central part of the menu is the fish, which is cut into pieces, seasoned with salt and pepper, and steamed in the penny-candy, brown paper bags. Today, the fish could be anything not too fishy—turbot or haddock, for example—but it always used to be mackerel, easily caught in the fish traps on Horseneck Beach. "Years ago, the mackerel were all over the place," explains Willy. "Different times of year you could catch different kinds of fish—what's running. Now it seemed that mackerel would be a predominantly timed fish. Timed fish, it is, at that time of year, the month of August. Certain times of year, you go down off New Jersey to get 'em, but this time of year, you can catch them up here. Simple. Yup. So, you see, it was a homegrown product."[29] "That was one of the specialties of the bake," Ila Gonet points out. "But we can't get mackerel now—it's impossible to get that amount of mackerel. So we had to go to whitefish—though we don't like it."[30] Peter has looked in to getting mackerel for the clambake, but without success.

It isn't just the taste or the texture of mackerel that makes the seventy-year-old cohort of Allen's Neck get caught up in the topic of fish. For Ila, for instance, the fish is significant in her personal history: it evokes the memory of her mother and her mother's memory.

Well, as you can read in that history [the introduction to the *Allen's Neck Meeting Cookbook*], the men went out fishing that morning, in the beginning. And I've heard my mother tell that one time the women were all down there, and they'd got all their food, and the bake was all ready to put on—they were down at Horseneck. And the men were still—my father and somebody else—were still off the beach trying to catch fish enough. And she says, "We stood on the beach and we watched and watched and watched and they didn't seem to get fish. And finally," she says, "we saw them pull up anchor and start to row in." And she says, "They got there and they got—the men got all busy and dressed the fish and they got it [the bake] on. So," she says, "We did have fish in our bake that year." But they thought they were going to have to do without fish that year.[31]

In Ila's youth, mackerel for the bake meant an additional special occasion, a pre-bake kind of get-together at the Giffords'. "I can remember years ago when my father was living—and he died in '27—there used to be a barn out here and the fish always came the afternoon of the evening before [the bake]. And the men would gather out in the barn, on sawhorses, sitting on sawhorses, and dress that mackerel, and ice it down in the barrels."[32]

Ila's sister-in-law Billy Gifford remembers this custom, too. A tomboy Quaker girl from Maine, Billy was in her teens when she first met Ila's brother Lincoln at Moses Brown, the Quaker boarding school in Providence, and started staying in the Gifford house during the summers. Clambake and clambake preparations were all a part of her courting days and the height of her generation's social life in the late 1920s.

> They cut the mackerel up in the barn, put a couple of [saw]horses, maybe three, and put boards across—standing on both sides somehow, some of them cutting here and there on these old mackerel. You had to cut the heads off, cut 'em up. . . . It was a gang out there, that's what I remember. Dad was out there—Grandpa Gifford—and I suppose Ralph and Linc and even maybe Uncle Warren was over here, I don't know. I can't remember. And then, there was always lots of men around because you had a hired man living over here [pointing]—the house isn't even there—and he would be around. And all the boy cousins, Peter and Clarence and . . . would be over there. And they always were running back and forth [between the two houses]. And then there were all the people down at Uncle Ed's, Dorothy and Richard and Eleanor. I don't remember the Manchester boys: that was Grammy's sister, Aunt Lil—they were down there; they were twin boys. Grammy was a Gifford, a Gifford married a Gifford, but it was her sister that married a Manchester.[33]

*The "Fruits" of the Land.* Onions were also prepared at Giffords', only instead of a few teenaged girls scurrying among the men, it was a whole group of women doing the work. "The first time I remember being here," says Billy, "we were peeling the onions ourselves out here, under the tree—the tree is gone. But we were sitting around outside, out there peeling I don't know how many bushels of onions. Well, and then they put them in a big iron kettle in the crib out here and cooked them. They used a big old iron kettle they used to cook chicken feed or something in. That would have to be the day before, they had to warm them up. But whether they warmed them up here and took 'em up—see the bake was right across the road from the church: it was closer—but they really cooked them out here."[34]

When the bake grew to serve more than six hundred people, the amount of onions went up to one hundred pounds—too many to peel by hand. So women no longer prepare the onions at Giffords'. Women aren't around home the way they used to be, on hand for chores like these. "It was beginning to get too difficult for us to handle," says Ila. "Of course, we would've preferred not to, but it was a case of couldn't find anyone to peel the onions, and that's a lot of work the day before. So we had to go into canned goods. It services."[35]

Onions are the one thing Raymond doesn't think the Allen's Neck Clambake handles properly: "I wish they'd put the onions in the thing. I think it gives it some flavor."[36] Peter, who has largely been "trained up" by Raymond, agrees: "I've been trying to talk them into it for years, to put [the onions] on the bake, and the committee's a little stubborn. They think it gives it an oniony flavor, and they don't like it."[37] So for the forseeable future, the onions will probably continue to be heated over a small charcoal fire, off to the side of the fire, their flavor unmingled with that of the other food.

In addition to the onions, the bake also includes corn, sweet potatoes, and watermelon. According to Florence Smith, Andy Perry used to plant a whole field of corn just for the Allen's Neck Clambake; these days, Peter Gonet or his wife, Cathi, drive to Tiverton at nine o'clock for seventy-five dozen ears. It has to be picked the morning of the bake—"come right in, husk it, otherwise it isn't any good," Gordon Parsons says; "you lose your sugar."[38]

The sweet potatoes are bought at the grocery store because it's too early in the season to find them locally. Some bakes in the area use only white potatoes; some use both. Allen's Neck used to serve only sweet potatoes. Ila Gonet says, "There was, at one time, somebody said, 'Ah, I don't like sweet potatoes: we should have white potatoes, too.' So we did for a couple of years, we had white potatoes. Nobody wanted them after we got them, so we said, 'Well, we're not going to bother with them.'"[39]

Although supply has sometimes been the mother of invention at Clambake, her innovations seem not to have lasted. Records from this century as well as the last indicate that watermelon has traditionally been the clambake dessert, but, Ila remembers, "One year, we couldn't get watermelon. I don't know why. That's a long, long time ago. We couldn't get watermelon, so we got pears

The food crew husking corn. Photograph by Kathy Neustadt, 1986.

instead of watermelon. I just thought of it—I don't believe anybody else remembers that. They were delicious: great big yellow pears."[40] Ernie Waite recalls that his father served grapes at at least one of his bakes because Ernie remembers being amazed that the senior Davolls—Raymond's father and grandfather—could eat so many after the enormous meal they'd consumed. Raymond's father was once observed to eat fifty-seven sausages.

*The Sausage.* The sausage comes from Herbie Davidson's butchery in the south end of New Bedford, "a good old company, as you've probably heard," says Florence Smith.[41] "See, the reason I get the sausage over in New Bedford—see, in the first place I think he makes the best sausage there is," Gordon Parsons explains.

> I drove a truck for him one summer when I was out of school, and I know how that stuff is made, and it's really good. Well, we used to buy . . . I think we started out buying fifty pounds; now we're up to two hundred. And it used to come in those great big, long links, but you have to cut 'em into twos, to put in the penny candy

bags, and twist 'em, you know? . . . What a pain it was: you'd come home that night and—if you had those little scissors?—all the skin [on your fingers] would be gone.

So I went in one day, eight or ten years ago, so I says, "Herbie, gee what a pain it is cutting up."

"Oh," he says, "you want 'em cut up?"

I said, "You mean you cut 'em?"

He says, "How many you want in a box?" So he's got a machine that goes wock, wock, wock, wock, and they all come out all cut, so it's a little easier.[42]

Sausage is a popular item on the menu, always one of the first foods to run out: for this reason it has become the center of some tension. The problem that the disastrous arm band system was meant to address, according to Muriel, was one of petty thievery: "Kids would come that weren't supposed to be there, and eat all the sausages and stuff up. And they weren't even supposed to be working there: they'd just come there, you know. Show up, so to speak. Nobody knew from where. And we'd be falling all over the kids all of the time, and they weren't doing anything but eating up all of the pies and the sausages . . . so consequently a lot of the people on the bake didn't get any food."[43]

You don't have to be an outsider to risk the wrath of the sausage protectors, however; if a particularly strict head-of-table catches a waiter or waitress trying to sneak a sausage before the ticket-holders at their table have been sated, there is often hell to pay. What gets talked about at the clambake meeting after the bake is over? "Any problems," answers Muriel. "Anybody they see eating too many of the sausages."[44]

*The Tripe.* Tripe is a completely different story. "You either eat it or you hate it," says Gordon.

Now, see, I was brought up in an English household at home, and we had tripe all the time. First tripe, and then you put your own vinegar on it, and ate it—liked it. If you don't like it, you hate it; and when you tell somebody that it's the cow's stomach, they nearly toss their cookies right out there. . . . 'Course, New Bedford used to be, especially the south end of New Bedford, was basically English. They were weavers, mill people. But now, I'd say . . . 'course, the city is now predominantly Portuguese, and they're not tripe eaters. You used to be able to go into any meat market in the south end and buy tripe by the pound.[45]

A number of the women in the community are less than taken with tripe. "We have no use for it, but yet, we can't give it up because it's part of the clambake," Ila says.[46] If the women don't love it, they nonetheless have grown up preparing it. In general, the men tend to like it, although, as Willy Morrison points out, apparently even tripe is changing.

The food crew bagging fish, sausage, and tripe. Photograph by Kathy Neustadt, 1986.

[Herbie Davidson, the butcher] says, all us old-timers are used to the old-fashioned pickled tripe—guess it was almost indestructible besides. He says they don't do it that way anymore. Today you get so many laws about a lot of things that's killing you, so you can't do it this way or that way. . . . When I was a kid, I loved pickled tripe right from the butcher cart. In the old days, the different stores and butchers used to go around the country, even with horses. Now, there was one particular guy that across the back of his truck was this box that was water-tight. In it would be corn beef and tripe. As a kid, I didn't want mine cooked. I wanted a piece right out of the vinegar. Now, today you get it in the clambake and it's . . . it's, to put it bluntly, it's slimy. Yup. I got so that I didn't take any the other day; I think I've had enough. If I could get ahold of real tripe, I'd enjoy it, but not this stuff.[47]

If the quality of the tripe has declined over the years, its quantity in the clambake has increased, and its presence provides an endless source of amusement. The guests sitting at the table will either wave it off brusquely or wolf it down, but for the young people preparing it in the morning, the "flavor" of tripe lingers deliciously long. This rapid-fire banter among a group of a dozen Erickson and Parsons cousins, playful and graceful and communally constructed, is typical of tripe talk.

"What's the name of the stomach that this—ret . . . ?"
"Reticulum."
"Reticulum, that's right."
"Watch where you walk there."
"This is the last bucket of tripe."
"Drain it off some before you . . ."
"I am, I'm pouring it off right."
"Come on."
"I want to see a happy tripe cutter."
"Ain't no such thing."
"What other ways do they prepare tripe?"
"I've had it in, like, a tomato sauce. I'm not sure whether it was pickled or raw—probably pickled."
"Think of all the cows that had to die for this."
"They had to kill them for hamburg anyway."
"How much is this a pound, anyway?"
"A dollar thirty-nine."
"That's pretty steep."
"They ought to pay you to take this stuff."
"Really."
"Don't say that; my grandfather used to make a living selling this stuff."
"Unless you want tripe every night for the rest of your life, you won't say anything."
"They had a triper who used to drive around from door to door—'Tripe!'"
"Back in the old days, they used to have the milk man and the tripe man."
"Was tripe always part of this meal?"
"I think so."
"Well, I know the work crew never eats it."
"A certain amount of people actually eat it."
"I try a piece every year."
"They change every year, because they don't live long after eating it." . . .
"I wonder how tripe got started as a part of a clambake?"
"Sick humor."
"Someone sat down and said, 'Oh, we need corn, fish, clams—oh, tripe. Let's not forget tripe. We needed something with a 't.'"
". . . something really squishy and disgusting—cooked honeycombs."
"We need breaking music while we do this."
"Do you work your way up to the honor of doing tripe?"
"Actually, we're doing penance. We did some real bad things."
"It depends on what you did at Clambake the year before—then you get punished. Remember when you dropped that ear of corn on that lady's blouse?" . . .

Zachary Smith (right) contemplates his first gastronomic encounter with raw tripe (left, Josh Trainor). Photograph by Kathy Neustadt, 1985.

"There's somebody . . . we've got to figure out who eats it raw."

"My Aunt Charlotte eats it raw whenever she comes."

"It's better raw than cooked."

"I've heard you're supposed to try it."

"Yeah, it's tradition."

"It's a law, if you want to come back next year."

"You won't eat anything for the rest of your life."

"It's not bad, actually."

"It's terrible cooked. When it's on the bake, I can't stand it." . . .

"Are you going to taste it?"

"Yeah, just take a bite. You can always spit it out, Zach. I mean, you won't throw up."

"Try it."

"Do you like pickles? That's what it tastes like, only mushier—soggy pickles."

"Zach—that's what it smells like."

"Well, it's just pickle juice. It's not that bad—you can always spit it out."
"I want to see somebody try it. It takes real guts."
"Well, yeah. If you want to see somebody try it, why don't you?"
"He already has."
"That takes care of the bulk of this. The messy part is over."
"It's not all that bad, really—It's not all that good."[48]

*The Dressing.* Just as a subset of man-made materials exists in the realm of the fire, so a subset of woman-made items exists in the realm of the food. The dressing is the only one of these foods that is actually put into the bake, and it goes on the very top, its aluminum foil covering gleaming through the billowing steam. Until a few years ago, in their houses across the street from each other in the center of Russells Mills, Mary Davoll and her sister Hettie Tripp made all the dressing between them. In her eighty-ninth year, Mary turned over her job to Marcia Medeiros, Florence Smith's daughter.

"We use about twenty loaves of, suppose they call it, 'day-old bread'—it comes cheaper that way—and about fourteen pounds of crackers," says Mary.

> Now Priscilla [Mary's daughter-in-law] said yesterday that she uses all crackers. . . .
> Well, we used to use common crackers. Now those are—do you know?—there's no salt, and they're about this big and round, and they're hard. Yes, hard and no salt. My husband was the kind of person that if you did things, you kept on doing it, and I think since he's not been living, I don't think that we've bothered with common crackers. We've just gotten some crackers, you know what I mean?
> Now this [list of ingredients] says, "fourteen pounds Royal Lunch"—they're kind of solid, and not much salt, not like saltines or like that—"and three pounds of salt pork." Of course, I break up the bread and the crackers. Well, my niece has something, some kind of a contraption, which will crunch them all to pieces, which is very helpful, and she generally does it. And then the salt pork: well, I have to hand-grind it, that's all I have to do it with. I imagine some may have something more modern, I don't know. But you put that, and cook the onions and the salt pork together. Now, let me see. I do that Wednesday. Let's see, Clambake's Thursday. I do that the afternoon before, and then I put the onions in salt pork.
> Well, then, in the morning—Clambake morning—well, maybe you'd like to see. I was going to show you what I use—come look. [An enormous square tub hangs in the closet]. That's almost full. And that's half of it; my sister does the other half. . . . And, oh, and I always put—of course you put salt and pepper—I always put poultry seasoning [laughs]. It doesn't seem to get anywhere with it, but I always put I guess a package or so. I don't know that anyone would notice if I didn't. You couldn't imagine how much water it takes: seems sometimes as if I put in water and put in water. And I generally have that tub put on two chairs. I generally get it pretty moist before I add the onions.

Mary Davoll, at age eighty-five, with the galvanized pan she fills with bread-and-cracker dressing. Photograph by Kathy Neustadt, 1985.

Then we put it . . . well, we have some pans that are this long and this wide, and some are round. We generally have about twenty-six pans, and these days we cover them with foil. I can remember when we used to have to put pieces of old sheet over and a piece of string, and all the pans went this way, and the piece of string came down, you know, this way. Now we just put foil right over the top. 'Course, it wants to be . . . 'bout all it needs is to be heated through.

I can remember many years ago, everybody brought a pan of dressing. Well, some of it was just some crackers and salt and pepper, I think [laughs], and some water. And I think some of it was so poor, maybe, that that's how we came to be doing it ourselves—I don't remember. I've done it a long time.[49]

*The Brown Bread.* Brown bread was once a popular New England dish, but it isn't common these days, except at clambakes, and maybe at baked-bean suppers. "Brown bread," says Ernie, "is an old standby on bakes, too. I never knew a bake that served any other kind of bread."[50] "I think we like it," says Marjorie, "'cause we grew up with it, and it was part of . . . if you had baked beans on Saturday night, well, you're supposed to have brown bread along with it. So that's why we've done it that way, I guess."[51]

"Well, there are many different recipes," Mary points out.

'Course, they use Rhode Island meal. Now, you don't know what Rhode Island meal is? I can show you Rhode Island meal, I think [returns from kitchen with a sack from Gray's Grist Mill in Adamsville]. The funny part of it is, it's traditional around here, but it's become quite expensive. 'Course, they used to raise what they called johnnycake corn. It's different. . . . It's a hard white corn, and maybe somebody could tell you better than I. . . . Well, you planted that separate, johnnycake corn.

Now, I can remember, my father—now this is a long time ago—well, he would shell the corn and call up the miller and say, "I'm coming up." Maybe he was even going with a horse, I don't know. And they would grind the meal, and he'd bring it home. And I think my mother used to sift it before she—and we kept it in a wooden barrel. And of course, people ate—well, now this is expensive—but people ate johnnycakes about six days a week, I guess. Well, of course, the men got up in the morning and went out and had their morning chores to do, and when they came back in the house, they were ready for a good meal. And most—a great many people—had johnnycakes in the morning . . . and bacon and something like that.[52]

Brown bread, full of johnnycake meal and molasses, is steamed on the top of the stove for three hours. "We always used to say, 'When the water boils out, there's a storm coming,'" recalls Marjorie. "I don't know whether that's true or not, but some days you have to watch it, some days you have to put in more water." Marjorie knows the brown bread is done by "just that they've been in there three hours, and that's time enough. You can take them out in two and a half, and they're done; I don't know whoever set the time for three hours, but I mean, you just take it, hit-or-miss time."[53]

Marjorie Macomber is one of the few women around who still makes brown bread on any kind of regular basis—"most people don't stay home that long. My mother saw to it that I learned to cook right, 'cause that was the thing to do. Nowadays, I don't think the girls care that much about all this stuff. I don't think their mothers, most of them, don't have time—they're working—don't have time to teach the kids how to cook."[54] Billy Gifford sees the same trend: "They're getting away from brown bread, the younger ones, I think. You go to baked bean suppers in Maine, and you seldom get brown bread at those—they serve hot biscuits. No, I'd rather have the brown bread."[55]

*The Pies.* "They claim that one of the big draws to the clambake is the homemade pies: sounds ridiculous, doesn't it?," asks Muriel.[56] "Well, there's an old joke that New Englanders had pie for breakfast—have you ever heard that?" Mary adds. "I don't think they do now."[57] "No, we don't eat it for breakfast," says Marjorie.

> I've heard that, but I guess that was before our day. Anybody my age or older—like some of the folks that you'll see out at the clambake—were born and brought up on pie. You don't always change just because customs change; you don't always change what you've been brought up to. And, as I say, my husband's fond of pie, and every once in a while, "Gee, Marj, aren't you going to make a pie?" "Well, yeah, when I get around to it." But there's always something else. And in the summer time, particularly, who wants to warm an oven to bake pie, just one pie? Unless you've got some other cooking to do and you can put it in with that.
>
> My husband would have pie every day. I don't want to make it every day, but anyhow.[58]

Pie-making is strictly women's domain, and the women express their dominion by fussing and joking about the whole business of serving pies at Clambake. "Some of us women would like to take that idea and throw it out the window," says Elsie Gifford, with false indignation. "But it seems to always—people like it; they like the pies even though some of them are deadly looking. I swear, one year I saw a pie there made of some old squash—ugh."[59]

Mixed in with a concern that there are too many pies ("we had some left over . . . it seemed a shame") and that it would be simpler with fewer kinds to serve, an undercurrent of aesthetic judgments about the quality of the pies persists. Usually, however, a woman directs critical comments at herself. When people from the Smithsonian were on her farm in the summer of 1987, Elsie Gifford offered to let them film her making an "old-fashioned pie" for

Dessert at the Allen's Neck Clambake: a wide selection of homemade pies. Photograph by Kathy Neustadt, 1985.

Clambake: chuckling, she held up a box of pie crust mix and a can of lemon meringue filling to the video camera's lens. Even Hettie Tripp, whose pies are always homemade, queries with wry innocence whether anyone will die from eating a pie crust she has made a day in advance.

The subject of pies is richest for the older women of the group. Images and words flow easily about cooking and menus and meals. "We always felt like, I guess, that we had to have something for dessert," explains Hettie, "so we've always had pie or pudding. Of course, when you live on a farm, you don't just have dinner at night and a lunch, you have three big meals. You had fried eggs and bacon and johnnycakes for breakfast, and then dinner's a big meal, and supper was a big meal, and we always had pies or puddings for dessert for dinner, and lots of times at supper time—well, when fruit or anything like that was around, we'd make hot biscuits and have fruit."[60] "We always had pies, and puddings," Billy Gifford concurs. "Of course, when I was growing up, we always had some sort of dessert at night, even if it was just stewed fruit, only we'd call it 'sauce.' It could be blueberries, it could be strawberries, it could be canned fruit or applesauce. Dad had an orchard, so we always had plenty of applesauce."[61]

When Mary Davoll mentions the squash pie she is making for the clambake, it triggers another set of sensory and culinary associations, which give texture to a wholly different way of living in what seems like a wholly different time.

> I've often thought how self-sufficient we were. Well, of course, my father had lots of hens, but he was one of those kind that kept—I think he liked to grow things. And he always had squashes, and of course we had all kinds of garden things in the summertime. And we didn't freeze anything, you know: there was no such thing. 'Course, there was a deep cellar under that house, with a dirt floor. So, when the squashes began to—well, they would only keep a short while after Christmas—and then we would have to can squash.
>
> And then in the summertime, we had plenty of milk and cracked eggs. And mother made these lovely pies, and all we needed to buy was sugar and flour. I've often thought of it. It was canned squash, eggs, milk, and that's all you needed. And they used to make huge squash pies. They were good.[62]

Each year, when Ila and Hettie call the twenty women on their lists to ask them to bake pies and brown bread for the clambake—"same as last year," they'll say—they set into motion this complex of revery and reminiscence.

These, then, are the basic elements of the Allen's Neck Clambake: it's the way they do it and the way they think it should be done. Although most of the people involved with the bake are unaware of all of its components—few have ever seen the clams being cleaned, for example; even fewer know anything about the rock collecting; and who *does* mow the clambake grounds?—they sense that their own participation and skills, and the "stuff" that they work with, are part of a larger, integrated, seamless whole. For the people of Allen's Neck, their clambake is not only "proper," but it makes sense.

# Section Three

# CLAMBAKES AND MEANING

*Although anthropologists, like painters, lend their bodies to the world, we tend to allow our senses to penetrate the other's world rather than letting our senses be penetrated by the world of the other. The result of this tendency is that we represent the other's world in a generally turgid discourse which often bears little resemblance to the world we are attempting to describe.*
—Paul Stoller, *The Taste of Ethnographic Things* (1989)

Beyond the specifics of the Allen's Neck Clambake is a form, a series of rudimentary acts and aesthetics that have been systematized and ritualized to provide meaningfulness for the individuals who participate in it and for the group as a whole. To prove useful at all, anthropological theory must help explain the cultural significance of the clambake—its structure, function, and meaning—as well as the dynamic relationship between the community and the particulars of the feast itself.

Three perspectives on the Allen's Neck Clambake fit readily into analytical categories already developed by folklorists, anthropologists, and other cultural specialists—the clambake as food, the clambake as ritual feast, and the clambake as festival. An approach to the clambake as food takes into consideration the unique combination of foodstuffs and preparation techniques entailed in relation to the structure of the culture that produces the meal. The clambake as a ritual feast involves its traditionalized, highly elaborated, and "sacramentalized" aspects. And to look at the clambake as a festival suggests how the event is marked off in time and space within the community's celebratory calendar. Although not yet a well-defined area of research, the interrelationship of these three—food, ritual, and festivity—is another possible direction for theoretical consideration.

Each of the theoretical approaches currently popular in cultural studies has some value in teasing out meaning from the Allen's Neck Clambake, but each also suffers from serious limitations that make it incomplete. One prominent difficulty arises when anthropological theories based on tribal, premodern data are transposed to such complex, modern and postmodern events as the Allen's Neck Bake. The contemporary presence of agrarian culture on American soil, for example, is not well reflected in the theoretical literature. Similarly, Protestant American rituals—to the extent that they are acknowledged as legitimately celebratory at all—tend to be largely underestimated and even somewhat denigrated.

More central still to the theoretical deficiency is the currently popular tendency to value festivals over rituals. In the terminology of structuralism, still evident in cultural studies, a "semantic field" of binary oppositions associates ritual with religious, traditional, and obligational aspects of culture, while festival is associated with choice, revolution, and transformation. Within a related political idiom, rituals can be understood to constitute "the right" and festivals to constitute "the left." These dichotomies appear repeatedly:

| festival | / | ritual |
|---|---|---|
| reversal | / | reification |
| transformational | / | confirmational |
| liminoid | / | liminal |
| revolutionary | / | conservative |
| disorder | / | order |
| optative | / | obligational |
| modern | / | traditional |
| urban | / | agricultural |
| profane | / | religious |
| Catholic | / | Protestant |
| play | / | work |
| weekend | / | weekday[1] |

In their enthusiasm for studying festivals, scholars have tended to become desensitized to the complexity and richness of such rituals as communal

eating. Consequently, their theories exhibit a remarkably limited applicability
to these events. Theorists who focus on food have generally failed to see it as a
dynamic, historical, and multivocal part of a larger cultural context; those who
focus on the larger, symbolic patterning of culture tend to lose sight of the very
tangible, pragmatic nature of food as food. A synthesis of these elements is far
from having been worked out. Currently prominent theories do not reveal as
much about the clambake at Allen's Neck—as the central, highly elaborated,
ritualized, festive foodways event, both sacred and confirmational in nature, of
a group of Quaker farmers—as they might.

In addition, the western intellectual tradition that dichotomizes body and
mind has made dealing with the sensual world—particularly the sensual world
of others—especially problematic for scholars, and they have largely tended to
avoid it. In my own struggle to make sense of the clambake, I have found
myself increasingly compelled to seek answers in the physical rather than the
intellectual realm, as I have been powerfully drawn toward the *experience* of
clam juice rather than its image or metaphoric reflection.

The particulars of the Allen's Neck Clambake—and the perspective of its
participants—are too important to be permitted to drown in (or be totally
excluded through) a preponderance of multisyllabic, "multivocal," and "poly-
semic" jargon. If the search for meaning required only common sense, then
there would be little need for theory—with its specialized and often obtuse
language—and even less for academic training. Theory has the capacity to
shed light on aspects of life so familiar to us that they go largely unnoticed. In
the case of the clambake, this quality of familiarity constitutes at least the
initial indications that the event is inherently cultural.

Although still nascent and rough, my own quasi-theoretical take on ethnographic truth is unequivocally body-oriented.[2] Although I hardly expect to
answer every objection to or anticipate all of the implications of such a stance,
I have at least tried to make my own perspective as clear as possible. I hope
that it will be of some value to others traveling along similar paths.

# 7

# Food, Ritual, and Festivity

*Theory is the imaginative contemplation of reality.*
—Source unknown

**F**OOD IS A particularly fine example of something so common and everyday as to have gone largely uninvestigated, even by scholars. Beginning in the nineteenth century, anthropologists considered the significance of food almost completely in terms of its appearance within the context of exotic primitive religious rituals. Even in the early twentieth century, when Freud proposed additional psychosexual aspects of consumption, the study of food still fell almost exclusively under the study of primitive religions.[1]

It was not until the subsequent development of functionalism within anthropology—an approach that, roughly speaking, equated an object's meaning with its purpose—that emphasis shifted from the sacred significance of food to its social value. At this point, in sharp contrast to her predecessors, anthropologist Audrey Richards stated that "the most important motive in the life of the community and in the interests of the individual is food." To Richards, hunger—the need for and the acquisition of food—was "the chief determinant of human relationships, initially within the family, but later in wider social groups."[2]

The work of anthropologist Mary Douglas elaborated upon this notion that food is emotionally and socially significant by suggesting that food communicates about society itself. "If food is treated as a code," Douglas wrote in "Deciphering a Meal," "the message it encodes will be found in the pattern of social relations being expressed. The message is about different degrees of hierarchy, inclusion and exclusion, boundaries and transactions across boundaries." Using the Mosaic dietary laws as her example, Douglas asserted that the ordering of a meal is related in what she called "a system of repeated analogies" to all other forms of social ordering, from which it thereby gains symbolic power and a sense of inviolability.[3]

Douglas's idea of food as a code and an encoding process has been widely embraced. In addition to its sociological implications—connecting the structuring of food with the structuring of society—her work proposed that a relationship exists between any one meal and all other meals within a given culture's food repertoire. Like the genetic coding of an individual cell, "the smallest, meanest meal metonomically figures the structure of the grandest," or the overall organism, "and each unit of the grand meal figures again the whole meal—or the meanest meal. The perspective created by these repetitive analogies," Douglas maintained, "invests the individual meal with additional meaning."[4]

Clambake is clearly the "grandest" meal of the Allen's Neck culture, but its relationship to the "meanest meal" is somewhat less than straightforward. For the most part, the people of the Allen's Neck community do not actually eat the foods of Clambake in their daily lives—not in the same quantities, not in the same prepared state, not in these combinations, and sometimes not at all. In fact, the foods of the clambake menu are, generally speaking, foods of the past and not the present, art forms of the grandmothers, or specialty foods largely unobtainable today. "Metonymic" connections—the establishment of equivalencies through association—cannot be demonstrated unless theory allows for a temporal depth and the active maintenance of the "old ways" by the present community.

When the clambake began in 1888, there probably was more resonance between it and the everyday meal; those in attendance would have been able to derive analogies between the two realms. The farm vegetables, the "meat" from the sea and the barnyard, the baked goods were all customary fare, part of the regular repertoire of foods. On the day of the clambake, being brought together all at once, in greater abundance than usual and from all categories simultaneously, these foods would have been made special, thereby intensifying the meaning of the meal as a celebration.

The patterns of brown bread, cut and displayed by Paula Waterman. Photograph by Kathy Neustadt, 1985.

Seen in this light, the terms "analogy" and "metonymy," with their literary connotations, appear considerably less valuable than "continuity" and "contiguity," which imply physical and temporal properties. When brown bread, for example, remains on the clambake menu even when it no longer appears in the home diet, something has happened that entails more than an abstract, disembodied "equivalence." A closer investigation of the role of brown bread would undoubtedly lead to a number of explanations involving specific personalities, specific practical matters, and specific societal patterning.

Douglas's concept of the "selection principle," the structuring of analogies that "allows the part to recall the whole" and that makes the relationship between food and society meaningful, is also not as applicable to the Allen's Neck Clambake as one might wish.[5] Even in the early years of the bake, certain traditional foodstuffs, preparation techniques, and combinations of foods that might have been drawn upon and "selected" for associative power in the clambake meal were not. For example, baked beans cooked in a pot over slow heat were regular Saturday night fare; like the steaming of the clams themselves, baked beans shared a rudimentary technology associated with a native American past. But beans did not make their way into the menu; cracker and bread stuffing did. Similarly, eel, another common element of the traditional "mean" meal, was excluded from the bake while mackerel was included.

It is not enough to focus on food as symbol and code without recognizing that food also involves a myriad of practical, technical, historical, and personal issues. The direct correlation Douglas has proposed between the shape of "the meal"—which in this instance includes stuffing (but not beans) and mackerel (but not eel)—and the shape of the society is undermined by the seeming arbitrariness of the selection process. To say that the menu as it exists can be read symbolically is one thing; to say that the menu is *equivalent* to the social structure—that it "encodes" social relations—is a form of tautology if it does not include an explanation of the origins and process required of such correspondence.

Anthropologist Jack Goody has suggested that a more profitable approach to the significance of food would include an analysis within a particular context and within a temporal dimension that takes into account the politics and economy of production and distribution as well as the aesthetic and symbolic dimensions of preparation and consumption.[6] Douglas's assertion that "the recent popularity of barbecues and of more elaborately structured cocktail events . . . act as bridges between intimacy and distance"[7] is worth investigating, not only because it suggests the greater specificity that Goody recommends, but also because the Allen's Neck Clambake appears to function in a similar way to such events, drawing in the larger community yet, through the structuring of its meal, maintaining a distance between "insider" and "outsider." But functional explication alone will not explain the clambake, nor will it ascribe the meaning of the event.

The other major modern theorist who has isolated food as a significant component in human experience, Claude Lévi-Strauss, has observed, "It has never been sufficiently emphasized [that cooking] is with language a truly universal form of human activity: if there is no society without language, nor is there any which does not cook in some manner at least some of its food."[8] Like Douglas, Lévi-Strauss has argued that it is possible to "discover for each specific case how the cooking of a society is a language in which it uncon-

sciously translates its structure."[9] Unlike Douglas, however, who has connected by "analogies" the structure of the meal to the structure of the social
system, Lévi-Strauss has posited an equivalence through "homologies" between the structure of cooking and the structure of the human mind—even
thought itself. Douglas has termed this approach, in criticism, a search for the
"precoded, panhuman message in the language of food."[10]

Designating the use of fire as "marking the emergence of humanity,"[11]
Lévi-Strauss represented the transformative cultural power of cooking by a
"culinary triangle" in which three cardinal points—the raw, the cooked, and
the rotten—delimit the "semantic field" [see diagram 1]. Raw food is transformed by natural forces into a rotted state, but through cultural elaboration it
can be transformed instead into the "cooked" (similar to what Douglas has
called "the meal"), which then also undergoes the natural process of rotting.
Lévi-Strauss posited the culinary triangle as universal, but with each group
evolving its own culturally specific techniques of cooking in order to demonstrate additional interpretations of the relationship between nature and culture
and the tension between them. To Lévi-Strauss, what is articulated in cooking, just as in myth, is "nothing other than an effort to correct or hide [the]
inherent dissymmetry" between the two.[12]

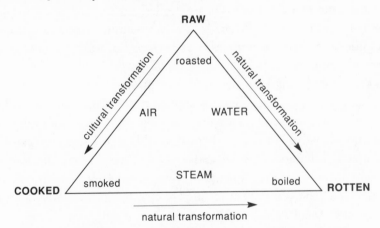

Diagram 1. The culinary triangle: a process of transformations.
Adapted from Jack Goody, *Cooking, Cuisine and Class* (1982), after
Claude Lévi-Strauss's original model.

The concept of the culinary triangle—particularly in its vocabulary and
geometry—has provocative value for thinking about the Allen's Neck Clambake as an event that juggles the issues of nature and culture through the

transformation of food. In particular, Lévi-Strauss's categories of "endo-cuisine" (what is "prepared for domestic use," aligned with boiled) and "exo-cuisine" ("that which one offers to guests," aligned with roasted) provide interesting insights into regional New England cuisine. Particularly in combination with Lévi-Strauss's further assertion that the boiled is associated with women, frugality, and the plebeian, the "New England boiled dinner"—traditionally a home-cooked, home-served, economical meal—is a perfect example of endo-cuisine. The clambake, on the other hand, as a roast, represents the larger, more public food events in which outsiders are invited to participate—it is exo-cuisine. The additional association of the roasted with men, prodigality, and aristocracy is borne out in the case of the New England clambake by the fact that it has historically been a purchased, and often costly, meal; performed by men, and, to a high degree, attended by men.[13]

The actual technology of the clambake, however, is not roasting but steaming, and herein lies a major difficulty with the culinary triangle. Lévi-Strauss has located steaming along the cooked to rotted axis, between the smoked and the boiled, which puts the clambake at considerable distance from exo-cuisine, where it rightly belongs; in light of the clambake evidence, this placement seems arbitrary, at best. When rendered unworkable on the particular level, the model becomes nearly useless on the universal, and Lévi-Strauss's offer to reshape the triangle as a tetrahedron in order to accommodate additional culinary techniques does nothing but exacerbate the sense of the system's arbitrariness.[14]

On the other hand, Lévi-Strauss's perception of utensils as objects of culture has particular value when it is applied to the clambake. As a culinary technique, the clambake requires very few tools. Historical interpretation of the traditional native American clambake holds that it involved collecting natural materials found on a beach and cooking and eating a meal without the use of accoutrements; the Squantum feast, for instance, used a shell for spooning. The historical evidence related to clambaking similarly identifies it as an "organic" event *in nature,* if not a wholly natural event.

It has always been the custom at Allen's Neck—and at other bakes in the area, past and present—for those who eat clambake to bring their own flatware, that is, their own *utensils.* This custom no doubt originated in pragmatic considerations—supplying flatware was costly and washing it afterwards time-consuming—but the presentation of food without utensils suggests a larger association with nature, with the raw. Until recently, an entire supply of ceramic plates and mugs used only for Clambake was stored in the

basement of the Allen's Neck Meetinghouse; each year, the dishes were
brought out and washed, used, and washed again before being put back into
storage. Today, the bake uses only paper products, which disappear after the
meal and return to ashes, or at least to the town dump.[15] In this way, the
clambake would seem to be moving even closer to a representation of raw and
unmitigated nature.

The Allen's Neck's grove setting itself, now unique among the area clambakes, further reinforces this impression of cooking and eating in nature,
unencumbered by societal and cultural constraints. One need only observe the
manner in which the meal is consumed to sense a commonly held desire for
unrestrained experience: to eat as much as possible as quickly as possible
appears to be the goal, with very little attention given to the finer amenities of
savoring the experience or sharing it with one's neighbors. The behavior of
diners at the clambake differs markedly from their behavior at other times,
when it is constrained by their social breeding and socioeconomically coded
appearances. As Elden Mills recounted from his first clambake as pastor of
Allen's Neck in 1918, "I was shocked my first summer . . . I had never seen a
picnic, as it was, in which everybody was dressed up. . . . It was repugnant to
me—the number of women who had diamonds sparkling from all the fingers
they could load on both hands—and clam juice all over."[16] Diamond rings
dripping with clam juice is as radical a juxtaposition of culture and nature as
one could wish for.

It is likewise significant that the cultural elements of the bake—the tools
and utensils—are housed on the opposite side of the grove from where the
food is cooked. The cookshack, as the building is called, only really exists in
community consciousness two days a year—the day of Clambake and the
Tuesday evening before, when the wood planks are pulled out to set up the
tables and benches. In contrast to other food preparations performed out in
the open, certain "civilized" activities are hidden away in the cookshack on the
day of Clambake—the melting of the butter and brewing of the coffee among
them. At the end of the meal, clean-up also takes place at the cookshack. Pots
and pans are washed and put away—clearly an activity borne of culture and not
nature.

For Lévi-Strauss, Goody has observed, "the language of cuisine, unlike the
language of ordinary life, translates *unconsciously.* . . . It is not used to
communicate between men as much as to *express* a structure."[17] From this
perspective, the clambake is a symbolic act most meaningful in abstracted
form, through the abstract analysis of its structure, not so much as its partici-

Old crockery and new coffee urns in the cookshack. Photograph by Kathy Neustadt, 1985.

pants live and experience it. But this approach, like Douglas's, overlooks the very influences that shape the structure in the first place: historical "actors" responding to specific conditions in particular times and places in ways that are meant, precisely, to "communicate between men." Moreover, this tendency to ascribe unconsciousness as a quality of the "Other"—in contrast to the implication of one's own full consciousness—is equally problematic.[18]

One of the paradoxes in ethnology is that the theoretical models applied to experience are borne of literacy, yet they are most often applied to nonliterate and aliterate peoples. Such terms as "analogy," "homology," and "metonyms" as "codes," "communications," and "translations" are, after all, linguistic ones that show the preponderant bias toward literacy. The increasingly popular rhetoric of "life-as-text"—as "systems of signs which refer only and endlessly to other signs"[19]—also suggests the strong literary predisposition of anthropo-

logical studies. Such events as the clambake, however, include a range of
sensory experiences involving the mouth, the tongue, and the taste buds,
among other body parts; they are made of different "stuff," to be known by
other means, and they may not reveal themselves fully when subjected to this
linguistics-based analysis.

In addition to being a meal with historic dimensions, the Allen's Neck Clambake is also a seasonal rite of passage. The people of Allen's Neck often say
that Clambake marks the end of summer; that this should be true of a move-
able feast—which can fall anywhere between the fifteenth and the twenty-first
of August—suggests that they are viewing summer in general, rather than
specific, terms of season. The work of Victor Turner, both central and seminal
in the field of myth and ritual studies, also suggests that the clambake is a
seasonal ceremony, like those found in tribal and agrarian cultures.

Turner's discussion of rituals—which he set within a larger concept of
"comparative symbology"—began with the assertion that "society is a process
rather than an abstract system."[20] Although dependent on structure, society—
as well as symbols, rituals, festivities, and other "cultural performances"—
is nevertheless under constant negotiation for meaning, in process rather
than fixed. Turner's approach redressed much of what was problematic in
structural theories on food: the negotiation process—the "communication
between men"—became of central importance, and not the expression of
structural homologies and analogies.

Rituals accrue to occasions of status change, in natural as well as social
relations. People who take part in a calendrical or seasonal ritual, Turner has
argued, "have been ritually prepared for a whole series of changes in the nature
of the cultural and ecological activities to be undertaken and of the relationships they will then have with others—all these holding good for a specific
quadrant of the annual productive cycle." In addition, Turner observed that
among tribal and agrarian cultures, seasonal rites tended to "elevate those of
low status transiently before returning them to their permanent humble-
ness."[21]

To view the clambake as a ritual preparation for "cultural and ecological
change" seems to make particular sense. Consider the activities that Clambake preparations entail: in order to get what they need to put on a clambake,
people have to go out to the woods (or the woodpile), out to the fields, into the
water, and into their larders; they can hardly help but see the changes taking
place in nature and the forces impacting their environment. Likewise, by

The Erickson and Parsons extended family gathers for a family reunion photograph. Photograph by Kathy Neustadt, 1986.

pulling people together to get these chores done, by drawing in the larger
community of their neighbors, relatives, and the summer residents, the clambakers are able to take stock of the current human population and make and
renew social bonds. They can store up on sociability for the upcoming, more
reclusive season of the year, "prepared for," as Turner put it, "the relationships
they will then have with others." Given the fact that much of the hardest work
of the farming and fishing occupational calendar is nearly over and the relative
harshness of the winter season just ahead, it makes perfect sense that members
of the Allen's Neck community have chosen to celebrate most fully at the end
of the summer season.

It can also be argued that the clambakers of Allen's Neck do achieve a kind
of status elevation. People clearly enjoy the notoriety that their clambake has
achieved in newspapers, at the Smithsonian festival, even through this study.
They like the fact that tickets are considered dear and that the waiting lists are

long, because it confirms their own sense of pride in the bake they produce. Relatives go away pleased—carrying stories of the great rite across the country—and return again next year with possibly a friend or a fiancée in tow, to introduce them to the mysteries of Clambake. Although as farming and fishing families the people of Allen's Neck have traditionally had commercial interactions with the summer residents,[22] on the day of Clambake, the relationship shifts, with the Allen's Neck group holding the limelight.

At the same time, the clambakers of Allen's Neck also show a certain amount of resistance to aspects of this status elevation. The presence of flash bulbs, video cameras, and reporters can make some of the participants uncomfortable; they make comments to the effect that the publicity is out of hand or even unappreciated. Running out of space and tickets and having to turn people away also creates an uncomfortable feeling, certainly for the ticket sellers, but for others as well. Ultimately, Clambake may really not be about status at all—at least not in terms of a hierarchy that includes outsiders. For the people of Allen's Neck, it may rather be an internal striving to elevate themselves as clambakers or, perhaps, to achieve greater perfection as a community.

Turner's focus on the concept of the "liminal," the transitional phase of ritual passage in which reality can be inverted through various manners of status change—through "effacement," ambiguity, and play[23]—has proved extremely valuable in understanding rituals of all kinds. Through defamiliarizing the familiar, Turner asserted—by making the everyday appear mysterious and novel—liminal rituals produce a kind of self-awareness that leads to new thinking and social action, with either conservative or subversive results for the society as a whole. Liminality, in essence, becomes a major source of cultural creativity and social change.

Turner sought to develop a theory that could explain rituals in the modern world as well (the Industrial Revolution being the "watershed division" in history between simple and complex societies). The "liminoid," which Turner proposed, resembled the "liminal" but emphasized the individual, freedom of choice, inversion, subversion, and playfulness.[24] In place of the relationship between humans and God and humans and nature brought into "liminal" play during seasonal rites, for example, "liminoid" cultural expressions in complex societies—art, literature, sport, theater, clowning—provided society with the energy needed "in order to live, to breathe, and to generate novelty"[25]—with the last, innovation, being the new primary value.

Having defined work, play, and leisure as key concepts for understanding the difference between simple and complex societies, Turner affirmed sociologist Joffré Dumazedier's characterization of preindustrial agrarian society as one in which work and play were conflated. "The working year," Turner wrote, quoting from Dumazedier, "followed a timetable written in the very passage of the days and seasons; in good weather work was hard, in bad weather it slackened off. Work of this kind had a natural rhythm to it, punctuated by rests, games, and ceremonies; it was synonymous with the daily round, and in some regions began at sunrise, to finish only at sunset. . . . Feast days, however, were often occasions for a great investment of energy (not to mention food) and constituted the obverse or opposite of everyday life." Turner noted in addition that feast days were "often characterized by symbolic inversion and status reversals."[26]

Despite the fact that Turner himself seemed to find the notion of a modern-day agrarian culture a contradiction in terms, Dumazedier's portrait bears important resemblance to the present-day culture of Allen's Neck. Although by no means universal—and arguably growing less so—a seasonal sensitivity continues to exist in this community in such occupational activities as lobstering, raising chickens, and growing herbs, and indirectly, too, in the rhythm of such domestic activities as baking, making jams and jellies, and running the general store. An internalized biozoological rhythm persists in Allen's Neck and is evident in the way the calendar is punctuated with celebrations that, like the clambake, still involve work and play.

Yet the clambake bears greater evidence of continuity and contiguity than of inversion and opposition. If it looked more like Mardi Gras or Carnival—if the men were dressed up in women's clothing or the tourists donned old work garb and served the farmers a meal—the clambake would fit Turner's ideas about symbolic inversion and status reversal. As it is, a day of laboring over local foodstuffs using familiar occupational tools in order to serve people who have long been consumers of these products in the marketplace as well as in the clambake grove suggests a different dynamic at work.

It may rather be the case that rituals like Clambake invariably *reflect* social relationships at the same time that they *shape* cultural ideas, as anthropologists Sally Moore and Barbara Myerhoff have suggested. Where Turner tended to see the important rituals as surrounding personal, communal, natural, social, and seasonal changes in status, Moore and Myerhoff began with the idea that "*any aspect* of social life and aspect of behavior or ideology may lend itself to ritualization" [italics mine].[27] "Collective ritual," they have contended, is the "dramatic attempt to bring some particular part of life firmly and definitely

The work of the clambake continues long after the guests have gone home (left, Raymond Davoll; right, Willy Morrison). Photograph by Kathy Neustadt, 1984.

into orderly control. It belongs to the structuring side of the cultural/historical process, . . . [the] attempt to structure the way people think about social life."[28]

In addition to their ability to reflect and shape culture, rituals also serve as a kind of "traditionalizing instrument," capable simultaneously of creating a sense of natural process, legitimating the social group and its values, commanding attention, and asserting a cultural reality. Moore and Myerhoff suggested that the effectiveness of rituals can be accounted for by certain formalistic traits—among them, repetition, acting, stylization, order, evocative style, and a collective dimension.[29] For example, the Allen's Neck Clambake is a highly ordered and stylized structuring of cooking. It involves careful ordering of foods and choreography of movements; it orders the various roles that participants can fill; and its use of materials, tools, and techniques is highly repetitive.

Rituals also interact with ideology, the officially professed values and aspirations of a group. According to Moore and Myerhoff, secular culture itself represents a specific cultural/historical process in western society, a shift away from the once-dominant religious ideology: secular rites are therefore apt to bear the burden of modernization. "Indeed, there may be more rather than less elaboration of ritual in secular circumstance, precisely because more presentation and persuasion, more communication of information, is needed when ideology is scanty or fragmentary, and context not reliable as when background and presumptions of shared belief and comprehension are limited."[30]

For example, the 1888 clambake on the beach was a much simpler affair than it is today: held exclusively for the Sunday school, it was more casual, less stylized, and much, much smaller. Nothing needed to be elaborated upon ritually because the symbols and values underlying them were commonly understood. When the clambake was opened to outsiders—to non-Quakers and to strangers—it was done so at the cost of shared ideology, and today's ritual extravaganza, from this perspective, is an overt expression of the degree to which that common understanding has been lost.

At the nearby Fire Station Bake in the village of Russells Mills—where the bakemaster is also a major player at the Allen's Neck Bake and the technical procedures are nearly identical—the ritual aspects of the clambake are much less in evidence, hidden behind the building, where the curious must choose to go in order to observe its inner workings. Even in the communal eating scene inside the firehouse, there are few signs of the formalistic ritual traits Moore and Myerhoff enumerated. This would seem to make sense, since the Fire Station Bake is made up of a strictly local, more socioeconomically and occupationally homogeneous population, one in which shared ideology might be assumed to exist, at least to a greater degree than it does at the Allen's Neck Bake, which caters to a broader clientele—summer people, visiting relatives and friends, as well as the local crew.

This lack of ritual elaboration may also testify to the fact that there is considerably less at stake at the Fire Station Bake, less need to "structure the way people think" than there is at Allen's Neck. For one thing, the group gathered in the fire station—however homogeneous it may be on some levels— also tends to include a number of fairly recent arrivals, for whom fire station activities represent an opportunity to integrate and gain acceptance in the village community. Surrounded by recently built homes and a population of young families, the fire station and the technology and personnel upon which it depends not only accept change and novelty but require it.

In contrast, at the Allen's Neck Clambake, the cornfield in which it is nestled, the old-time crafts, the traditional foods, even the participants themselves, are all potentially in danger of extinction. As a result, the rituals can be seen to "communicate the very things which are most in doubt,"[31] the air of precariousness creating a poignancy and power of its own. The Fire Station *Food, Ritual,* Clambake, although possessing a special and distinctive flavor, demonstrates a *and Festivity* much more limited symbolic scope.

Moore and Myerhoff make additional distinctions between secular rituals, which are situationally specific, and religious rituals, which tend to offer total explanation. The less elaborated bake at the fire station is clearly a "secular" event; it is also what Moore and Myerhoff's would term "mundane." The Allen's Neck Bake, on the other hand—if not directly "religious"—has a "sacred" nature as well as a profane one, and the elaboration of its ritual allows it to evoke and communicate some of the community's sacred values.[32] Responding to numerous internal and external factors, the Allen's Neck Clambake emerges in this perspective as a creative cultural product, a celebration of life's meaning and of its meaningfulness.

How would the Allen's Neck Clambake "feast" be distinguished from Clambake as a "ritual"? How is a "feast" related to a "ceremony" or a "festival," and how are these terms related to the various aspects of Clambake day—the preparations of the fire and the food, the commercial exchanges at the baked goods and handicrafts tables, the social interactions among the various groups, the dramatic performance of the rake-out, and the distribution and consumption of the meal? Little exists within festival theory that answers these questions.

One recent attempt to construct a coherent morphology for festival posits *rites* and *ritual acts* as its "building blocks." These minimal units, according to folklorist Alessandro Falassi, include the rites of valorization that initiate the festival, rites of purification, rites of passage, rites of reversal, rites of conspicuous display, rites of conspicuous consumption, ritual dramas, rites of exchange, rites of competition, and, at the end, rites of devalorization.[33] No one festival contains all of these ritual elements, according to Falassi; instead, they are dispersed throughout the festive calendar. Such dispersion is particularly evident in the modern world, where "older festivals" are broken down into smaller, more focused units, which are most often celebrated at the family level.

This facet of Falassi's morphology has obvious representation in the American festive calendar. For example, Thanksgiving is composed almost exclusively of rites of conspicuous consumption, which, as Falassi has observed, "usually involve food and drink . . . prepared in abundance and even excess,

Rites of conspicuous consumption: the clambake meal. Photograph by Kathy
Neustadt, 1986.

made generously available, and *solemnly* consumed in various forms of feasts
[and] banquets" [italics mine].[34] The configuration of Christmas, on the other
hand, although it likewise involves conspicuous consumption, is also formed
by the ritual elements of conspicuous display and exchange.

The Allen's Neck Clambake, overall, can be seen as a fragment of an older,
larger festival, particularly if its lineage is extended to include the European
tradition of harvest homes and feast and fast days. And because Allen's Neck
residents celebrate all of the major American holidays—a "complete festival
morphology"—they do seem to be participating in the "complete festive

activities that make up the festival calendar at Allen's Neck—the church suppers, auctions, flea markets, and end-of-the-Sunday-school-year activi- ties—not all of the ritual elements within Falassi's morphology are accounted for. Rites of reversal and rites of competition—which Turner and his followers have associated most closely with the ritual status inversion and role reversal in human culture—are noticeably absent.

In a related vein, Falassi has attempted to go beyond the building blocks of festival to define it by its two functions, the announcing and renouncing of culture. Festival achieves these functions, Falassi explained, through a quartet of intertwined symbolic means, what he terms the "basic behavioral modali- ties of daily social life"—reversal, intensification, trespassing, and abstinence.[35] Particularly in light of the scholarly enthusiasm for this position, the question arises, in what sense does the Allen's Neck Clambake renounce culture?

Following from Lévi-Strauss, one answer is that through the clambake, the presence of cultural processes are obscured—if not exactly renounced—by the assertion of natural ones. By getting people out in the woods (at least into a cleared grove) to eat foods untouched by culture and cuisine and cooked without utensils, the clambake celebrates nature and denies culture—that is, renounces it. Yet the event includes all manner of food produced by culture (pies, brown bread, canned onions) as well as tools (the rakes and racks) that are preserved for future bakes. In addition, to the people at Allen's Neck, this way of cooking and this kind of food represent a "natural" reality which they see as inherently connected, rather than in contrast, to their "culture." They view the clambake as part of their history—whether as a tradition of local indigenous peoples, early American colonists, or members of the Meeting a hundred years ago—and for them it embodies the roots and the success of civilization, not its negation. The dynamic tension required by Lévi-Strauss's nature-culture dichotomy, Turner's liminality as dialectical process, and the paradoxical functions of Falassi's festival simply do not exist in the Allen's Neck Bake.

Within this capacity of festival to announce and renounce culture, theorists have tended to focus almost entirely on renouncement—inversion, reversal, negation. For example, in *Reversible Worlds,* Barbara Babcock argued initially that "the social interaction system involves both the conventional means of articulating orders and rules *and* the counteractive patterns by which those very conventions may be profitably and recognizably transformed." Designat- ing this polarity by the larger categories "reversible" and "irreversible," Bab- cock elaborated that "these two world views may also be related to 'metaphoric' (substitutional, reversible) and 'metonymic' (sequential, irreversible) patterns."[36] But it is ultimately the reversible realm—which she argued had been overlooked and even avoided[37]—that became her focus.

Following in the footsteps of Moore and Myerhoff, Frank Manning has emphasized "how cultural performances *reflect, interpret, and influence* their society," the "leitmotif" of such performances being "the relationship between celebrations and the social realities of those who experience it."[38] According to Manning, celebrations have two modes, ritual and play, which exist within traditional societies as "let us believe" and "let us make believe" statements.[39] Unfortunately, in his view, modern Protestant society is almost wholly ritual-istic—"metonymical," a closed structure—and lacks the "ludic," play aspects that give rise to creative forms and ideology in the form of reversals and inversion. Modern rituals can only "affirm, unify, and *soberly* reinforce a broad field of conceptual and emotional significance" [italics mine], Manning has argued. "Ritualistic celebration thus conveys a version of the social order that is meant to be believed, or at least acknowledged and adhered to, and over which the society exerts control."[40] Celebration—even an event like the Allen's Neck Clambake—is thus for Manning inherently political and not generative.

In his view, the major source of public secular rituals is Protestantism, a term clearly associated with capitalism, as well as a kind of literalism and literary predisposition. "Protestantism's major influence was to rationalize action and thought," Manning has written, "a moral thrust that exerted relentless asceti-cism and methodological, productive work and that also refocused religious expression from liturgical elaboration to literal study of the Bible, deemed the only source of truth . . . [;] where Protestant cultural influences predominate, the playful mode is muted and the ritual mode emphasized."[41]

The sobriety of rationalized action and the political implications of the work ethic which Manning attributes to modern rituals rejects the possibility both that a Protestant ritual might have positive, playful qualities and that an agrarian culture could conflate work with play. Despite this, the good humor and resounding laughter woven through the day of the Allen's Neck Bake continue to be heard, and to the extent that they are muted, it is less by Protestantism than by a theory that sacrifices the reality of the insiders—the "emic" vision—to a political statement about the subversiveness of the work ethic and crassness of materialism.[42]

Events such as the Allen's Neck Clambake are not encompassed—nor even, apparently, meant to be encompassed—by most current theories on festival in

The clambake crew at play, 1986; left to right, Ralph Macomber, Peter Gonet, Cathi Rebello (now Gonet), Raymond Davoll, Burney Gifford, and Julie Brown. Photograph by Kathy Neustadt, 1986.

folklore studies and cultural anthropology. The role of food in ritual and celebrations is still largely overlooked. Community celebrations, and particularly American Protestant and agrarian community celebrations, tend to elicit apologies rather than interpretations. Considering Victor Turner's enormous influence in the field, it is appropriate that a critique of his work should contain promising insights and theoretical redress of this situation.

In her essentially feminist critique of Turner's contribution to the study of religious symbols and rituals, Caroline Walker Bynum has observed that "Turner's ideas described the stories and symbols of men better than those of women," which led her to conclude that Turner had failed "to stand *with* the women," to understand the nature of their liminality and marginality as it was experienced in the ongoing, everyday structuring of society.[43] Indeed, as

Bynum has suggested, "Liminality itself—as fully elaborated by Turner—may be less a universal moment of meaning needed by human beings as they move through social dramas than an escape for those who bear the burdens and reap the benefits of a high place in the social structure."[44]

The communities of religious medieval women that Bynum studied were examples of "institutionalized liminality in Turner's sense," but that liminality was "imaged as *continuity with,* not as reversal of, the women's ordinary experience" [italics mine]. When the women represented themselves symbolically, what they chose were images that were either feminine or androgynous, but definitely not masculine.[45] Moreover, Bynum has argued, the women's images and stories represented "neither reversal nor elevation but *continuity*"; women became more themselves through ritual expression, "more *continuous* with their sense of social and biological self; women's images are most profoundly *deepenings,* not inversions, of what 'woman' is; women's symbols express contradiction and opposition less than *synthesis* and *paradox*" [italics mine].[46] In this same manner, it is possible to argue that the Allen's Neck Clambake, whether the focus is on its food, ritual, or festive aspects, or even on its Protestantism as a kind of latter-day nonconformism, is more involved with a deepening and intensification of identity than with inversion and reversal, "contradiction and opposition."

The theories of folklorist Roger Abrahams, Falassi, and Dumazedier support this view of the clambake. Abrahams has argued that "festivals and rites still seem part of the same human impulse to *intensify* time and space within the community and to reveal mysteries while being engaged in revels. Cultural objects and actions become the foci of community actions carried out in common, when the deepest values of the group are simultaneously revealed and made mysterious" [italics mine].[47] Falassi also mentions intensification as one of the four "modalities of quotidian behavior"—the everyday activities—that make festival possible.[48] And Dumazedier's use of the word "obverse" to describe the relationship between feast days and everyday life in agrarian societies would suggest that an occasion such as the clambake complements society's image of itself, "deepening" it, making it more complete and more perfect. In addition, in the sense that "obverse" identifies the aspect that "faces the observer," what is made visible, what is publicly displayed in symbolic form, not only allows outsiders to get a better perspective on the whole but also involves a process of growing self-awareness in which the community itself turns outward, faces its audience, and reveals—and mystifies—itself. Participants in the Allen's Neck Clambake, both guests and hosts, come away

Women cleaning up after the bake (Marcia Madeiros, Betty Amaral, and Debby Smith). Photograph by Kathy Neustadt, 1986.

with the sense of having experienced something "real," which is neither obvious nor simple.

The idea of obversion can tease out additional messages embedded in the clambake. "Obverse" means "the counterpart of a proposition obtained by exchanging the affirmative for the negative quality of the whole proposition and then negating the predicate." The obverse form of "every day we work hard" would be "on no day do we not work hard." "Many bonds hold our community together" becomes "few bonds cannot hold our community together"; "everyone is invited to our feast" is, in its obverse, "no one is not invited to our feast." By doubling the negative, the end result is positive; theories predicated on opposition and single negation do not fit the clambake as well.[49] Within Bynum's theory, obversion is a mode of ritual intensification that involves the *synthesis* of positives with negatives—in the clambake, the tradition maintains a connection with the past even while nothing is constant—and the *paradox* of double negativity—"we will always be here" becomes "none of us will ever not be here," a kind of mystical affirmation.

The Allen's Neck Clambake is not a festival in which culture is renounced and the world turned upside down—which points always beyond itself in a metaphorical way and is associated with rites of reversal and "agonistic," competitive, gaming activities. Nor is it a ritual defined as serious and orderly (Babcock), confirmational and authoritative (Abrahams), no longer agrarian (Turner), but modern, rationalized, tautological, ideological, Protestant, and capitalistic (Manning). Clambake is much more a form of symbolic intensification of the group's identity, in which a communal activity communicates through its process the everyday experience of the group—replete with playfulness as well as seriousness, order as well as disorder, reality as well as ideology, an awareness of change as well as continuity.

More than three hundred years ago, Quakers journeyed to the shores of America compelled by a Protestant desire to live their lives without rituals. Today, in Allen's Neck, their descendants have evolved a highly elaborated clambake tradition that at least one participant has called a "sacrament." In light of this history, it should be no surprise to find that social scientists, as a different variety of Pilgrims, have pursued a Protestant, rationalized study of human society, only to become enamored of the mystical. As middle-class, postmodern Americans, bereft of their own meaningful rituals and aware only of the parades and public ceremonies of popular culture, social scientists must search for the exotic and the radical at the margins of their own consciousness and experience.

In Carnival in Rio de Janeiro, Victor Turner found a "Dionysiac abandonment I have never experienced before or since."[50] Anthropologists are showing such strong interest in the baroque, the mysterious, the mystical, and the non- or anti-rational perhaps because of the academic liminality in which they themselves are engaged, which allows for the elevation of their status and grants them re-entry to the scholarly community only after they have ventured out among the Trobriand Islanders or the revelers of Carnival, where they lose themselves. Their categories become scrambled, their systems lose structure; the reality of others confuses their own way of knowing.

The critique of modern anthropological theory has taken to task the implied desire of predominantly male scholars to merge with the primitive,

The structure and forms of food on the Allen's Neck food table. Photograph by Kathy Neustadt, 1985.

exotic, erotic Other. It questions whether social scientists see their subject as Bynum suggested the male mystics experienced their ceremonies—as "an escape for those who bear the burdens and reap the benefits of a high place in the social structure."[51] Recent feminist scholarship questions just such power structuring and asserts the possibility of a radically different perspective, often centered in the body.[52] In turn, the body-centered perspective also questions the linguistic bias of structural analysis. From this position it can be argued, for example, that the clambake is *not* a language, *not* a grammar, *not* a literary construction, and *not* defined by a series of binary oppositions—that its deepest meanings are not encompassed by these theories.

Social scientists who embrace the analytical tools of linguistics—the terminology of metaphor and metonym, paradigm and syntagm—move away from the body, away from the constraints of the everyday and the traditional, away from anything requiring such mundane energy as digestion. When food, for example, is taken to be a language, its "grammar" is preeminent; its tangible, physical, and sensory qualities are brushed aside. There are no cooks, no eating, no occasion: there are only structures, forms, and systems of signs. Continuity, unlike metaphor, implies contiguity, tangible connection, even physical contact, and it directs the analytical focus inward, rather than outward, toward the site of the "deepenings." Where the "impacted zones" of communal life—the times and places of celebration—are perceived as seamlessly connected with the everyday, participants, instead of seeking out "Dionysiac abandonment," are also directed inward, to dip into the pool of their identity and to gaze deeply into its mirror.

Narratives of any kind involve a separation from events in themselves, and abstract, theoretical narratives simply may not "tell" enough about real experiences. Indeed, the time may have come to stop "defining rather than experiencing the reality of things,"[53] as Paul Stoller puts it, and to construct from these experiences explanations that resonate better with the materials, behaviors, and performances of everyday life. It may also be time to tackle seriously some of the issues that the clambake and related events embody.

The Allen's Neck Clambake highlights questions about the nature of agrarian culture and its presence on American soil as part of a larger challenge to interpret traditional culture in modern life as an ongoing process rather than as an accumulation of remnants. It demonstrates a discernible need for an integration of popular culture, high culture, and traditional culture, and it forces an acknowledgment of the role that "the marketplace" plays in this continuum. The effects of Protestantism on American culture also require further investigation, in terms of its role in everyday life, in the symbolic repertoire, and in its contributions to and constraints on the production of social science theory. The nature of sectarianism—of Quakerism, in particular—as it relates to all of these issues is also worth additional research.

As long as abstraction is not taken to be the *only* truth, or even the *greater* truth, searching for meaning through the application of theory can be just as dynamic and creative as the process that creates the events themselves. There is much to learn. In fact, that the Allen's Neck Clambake, in all of its this-worldly focus, should not only entail transformational potential for its community through the intensification of identity but also theoretical challenges for its analysts is a resounding affirmation of the nature of folklore and the viability of folklore studies.

# 8

# Concluding Thoughts: Clam Juice and Melted Butter

*We might have been a company of ancient Greeks going to celebrate a victory, or to worship the gods of harvests, in the grove above. It was strangely moving to see this and to [be] part of it. The sky, the sea, have watched poor humanity at its rites so long; we were no more a New England family celebrating its own existence and simple progress; we carried the tokens and inheritance of all such households from which this had descended, and were only the latest of our line. We possessed the instincts of a far, forgotten childhood; I found myself thinking that we ought to be carrying green branches and singing as we went.*
—Sarah Orne Jewett, *The Country of the Pointed Firs* (1896)

THE PEOPLE OF Allen's Neck rarely talk about the "symbols" and "significance" of their bake. For the most part, the meaning for them is embedded in the event, in the doing, in the enactment. It also exists in their memory of past performances and in the power of the bake's sensory experiences to evoke these memories. Any larger "truth" about the clambake probably lies somewhere between the inside and the outside, between insiders and outsiders, at an interface fleetingly and even precariously effected and maintained for just such interpretive purposes. This interface is not only the place where identity as a process of negotiated exchange might be discovered—between self and other, between microcosm and macrocosm—but it may also prove to be where practice and theory find some common ground.

In most of their talk about Clambake, the people of Allen's Neck tend to take a pragmatic view. If people want to pay money to come and eat, that's good: the Allen's Neck Yankees will take the money and use it well—"handling money," notes Lewis Cole; "they're geniuses at money"[1]—and give a meal worth more than dollars in exchange. If people want to make a fuss about the bake, that's fine, too: the Allen's Neck people are proud of their clambake, sure of its specialness, aware of its history, and conscious of its nostalgic appeal. Not everyone knows what a clambake is, it seems; not everyone stays in one place long enough to have a tradition like this; and not everyone understands the farming world and the fishermen's lot, the old-fashioned way of life—they might get something out of it, say the Friends of Allen's Neck.

This is not to say that the participants are unaware of Clambake's other meanings. "We are going through a type of ritual that we look forward to and live for from one clambake to the next," says Norma Judson. "I think the ritual of Clambake sustains that tradition. And it's a wonderful feeling, because I know that on the third Thursday of every August through eternity, I am going to have a child there [at Clambake], a grandchild there, or a great-grandchild there, and on, and on, and on. And it's an unspoken thing—I've never really said this before—but I would dare say that everyone would agree with me." At other clambakes she has attended, Norma notes, "the tradition isn't there, the ritual, the meaning, the family ties, all the important things. I mean, it's just food: you pay your money and you get your food. . . . But this, this is like a holy day. . . . Without sounding ridiculous, it is perhaps our most holy day. You know, in some families, it's the only shred of tradition that's really left. In this day and age, there's a diminishing of traditions—it's very nice to have [Clambake] part of your life: it's meaningful. It's practically the only one in mine other than Christmas."[2]

The clambake is decidedly the most prominent tradition of the Allen's Neck community, and it may well be, as Norma indicates, its most mystical one.[3] What the people there say is that their clambake is "old-fashioned," "the way we've always done it," "not allowed to change," even as they acknowledge and make way for change. To Hettie, a tradition is "one of those kind of things like my father used to say, 'Don't think for a minute that things won't go on the same without you.' But I always finish by saying—Ila's mother, that's his sister, said—'Things will go along, but not just the same.' I think that softened it."[4]

Tradition, according to current theoretical discourse, requires a choice, requires willful participation, no matter how automatic and inviolable the "same as last year" makes continuance appear. Traditions are self-maintaining only as long as the group values age and interprets survival as positive, as worthy of respect: perpetuation has to be recognized, allowed, and encouraged. Anthropologist Richard Handler has argued that tradition also involves translation, interpretation, reinterpretation, and participatory action.[5] Each year the clambakers do, indeed, *decide* to hold their Clambake, *agree* to participate, *accede* to the anticipation of others, and *choose* to reinvest in the symbolic process.

But the clambaking group at Allen's Neck community is constantly, and consciously, seeking to find a balance between the old and the new, between what *feels* traditional and what is "serviceable" or necessary: having defined the "proper bake," their responsibility is to follow its standards. The old pie rack is still being dragged out, even though plastic milk crates actually hold the pie slices; on the other hand, using string bags to hold the contents of the meal has not yet achieved the legitimacy necessary to force a substitution. Ticket prices are raised hesitantly, nervously, because market value is only one of the factors being taken into consideration. The issue of putting in a parking lot is debated, not simply because it involves expense, but because it represents change of an aesthetic nature: is it too radical? does it change the "feel" of the day? does it alter too much the appearance of the environment?

In order for an event to survive in a "traditional" role, a dynamic equilibrium between internal and external forces is also required. When there is too much emphasis in any direction—toward individual personalities, practicalities, or past methods—the system, like an organism, will seek to right itself. J. T. played horseshoes while the bake cooked, but not every bakemaster can do this; mackerel was the fish of choice, but others will "service"; wooden crates are a definite improvement over burlap bags. Wearing armbands came to be seen as a misstep, even a mistake, and so it was allowed to die out, to be largely buried through the consensus of group consciousness about "how it has always been done."

The important question about the Allen's Neck Clambake—with the magic one hundred years already under its temporal belt and a rusticity so photogenic that it's a folklorist's dream—is not *whether* it is a tradition but *why* it is one. Why does the community continue to hold the clambake? Why do people choose to designate clambaking their oldest and most celebrated tradition? The clambake, after all, is time-consuming and labor-intensive, a lot of work for a lot of people. Until recently, the economic rewards were modest. And why feed a bunch of skewks, outsiders, people "from away"?

It's fun, a chorus of voices responds. It's a chance to see people you only see once a year and a chance to get "the family" together. It's a day off from work in the middle of the week. And it's good eating, too: you wouldn't put on a clambake for yourself, for your own family, or even for the Meeting members—a clamboil, maybe, but not the *real* thing, not a full-fledged, old-fashioned clambake.

All of these explanations are true, but behind them is something larger, something more compelling and propelling. The clambake is, I would argue, about identity. Its power and perpetuation emanate from its ability to act as a mirror for Allen's Neck, wherein the community sees itself and simultaneously projects an image to the outside world. The clambake represents, as Caroline Bynum puts it, "neither reversal nor [status] elevation but continuity" with everyday life and experience.[6] It is an indigenous foodways event "related, integrally and functionally, to all other phases of . . . [a] culture,"[7] as folklorist Don Yoder has argued, an affirmation rather than renunciation. In the context of "tourist art," the clambake is a cultural display that represents, as folklorist Regina Bendix has stated, "a search on the part of _natives_ for what they perceive to be authentic manifestations of their own culture."[8]

The Allen's Neck Clambake is about a lot of things—about how the environment and climate of southeastern Massachusetts has affected the regional food sources and the ensuing eating patterns over time; about the people who were native to the land, and their indigenous foodways; about the settlement of this area by the English, who came with their own eating habits and tastes; and about the later influx of non-English Europeans whose different foodways made comparison and distinctiveness meaningful. It is about the Industrial Revolution, with all its attendant innovations, which conceptually and ideologically transformed the farm, the countryside, and the seashore into a "resort" of the body and imagination; about the success of local farmers in negotiating the potential market for and the capacities of the environment, and their establishment of a secure role within the larger socioeconomic community. And it is also about the ways that human beings seek to commemorate elements of the past in the present, in forms that attempt to assure their future.

The clambake at Allen's Neck is inextricably bound up with the overall cultural pattern, values, history, and aesthetic of the Allen's Neck Friends. In their testimonies, people allude to the clambake as a sacrament of season, a blessing on abundance, and a performance of family. From the ethnographer's perspective, the clambake is also a fleeting but intense celebration of the people of Allen's Neck, expressing and reifying who they see themselves to be—people religious by conviction and birthright, who, having arrived with a witness, have remained Quakers in a world that is largely un-Friendly; Yankees by ethnic inheritance; farmers and fishermen by trade and tradition, dependent on their environment ecologically and historically; and a community at their core.[9]

In 1888, the people of Allen's Neck weren't thinking about the clambake of 1988. Their Sunday school picnic was styled, instead, after a food activity that was both traditional and invented in their region. They were emulating the clambakes of a native American past and of commercial pavilions alike; the historical and symbolic nature of their own clambaking materials, procedures, and aesthetics had not yet developed. After a number of years, repetition, stylization, and a growing awareness of their event's distinctiveness added an interpretive dimension to the clambake, and it began to serve as a repository of cultural norms and nuances.

Today, it is possible to argue that every aspect of the clambake—its organization, the food preparation, building the fire, and serving the meal—carries a wealth of symbols. From the annual decision to hold a clambake to the method for stacking wood to the humble squash pie—participants have involved every procedure with a communal history, every item with communal memory. As a result, the day of Clambake has become like one great symbolic daguerreotype.

Perhaps the strongest message embedded in the clambake concerns the ecological aspect of the community's existence. What is "a proper bake," after all, but the successful manipulation of some rocks, wood, and rockweed, which are, in turn, among the most significant natural elements of the physical world of Allen's Neck. For a person standing atop Bald Hill, at the Allen's Neck Meetinghouse, this world still exists: the stones, worked into walls that stretch in every direction, are testimony to the process of making land arable; the trees have been fashioned into shelter for people and their livestock and the vehicles with which the men set out to sea; and the water has seemingly infinite capacity for life, for plants and animals and sustenance, as well as for destruction. In order to master the bake, people must have first come to terms with their surroundings and have mastered them.

The men who become masters of the bake are the ones who have learned the elements, have achieved success in handling them, and have made their commitment to the place in other aspects of their lives. It is no coincidence that Peter Gonet and Burney Gifford, who have come back to the farms intending to stay in the area, are serious clambakers, or that Raymond Davoll, as master of master bakers, is such a well-respected lobsterman. The community recognizes their talents and depends on them, not only to make a clambake proper, but, on the symbolic level, to hold the physical world together and keep Allen's Neck intact and ongoing. A bakemaster learns the "proper way" to put on a bake by growing up with the clambake, by watching and helping and imitating. He learns about the elemental components of the bake through

Clambake education begins at an early age; toddler Corey Gifford at bake construction. Photograph by Kathy Neustadt, 1985.

his own elemental tools, his senses, so that he will recognize the right color in the rock, the weight of the wood, the feel of the rockweed, the heat of the fire. His internship involves digging in the gravel pits and wading out into the water and cutting and loading wood upon wood, year after year.

When a person has learned how to make a "proper bake," he has learned a lot more than how to pile rocks and wood. In the process of touching it, working with it, listening to and learning its stories, he experiences directly the aesthetics and values of his group. He has been tutored in silence, in Yankee taciturnity; guided into skills without asking or being answered; allowed to maintain the standard of self-reliance. In the process, the clambake becomes a kind of indigenous and organic educational system, a process and method for communicating traditional knowledge, and the bakemaster assumes the position of leader without an attendant hierarchical organization or an increase in power over others.

As with most other efficacious symbolic systems, the clambake, in its reflection of the larger ecological realm, comes to be seen as "natural" and organic; if never quite *wholly* natural, as Lévi-Strauss would argue, it is at least in harmony with the laws of nature. The educational process, the learning of the ways of the bake, is also conceived of in this way. Says Raymond Davoll, "It's more or less something in your head, that's all"; according to Peter Gonet, "It just gets in you over the years."[10] Similarly, the selection of a bakemaster, the emergence of the apprentice's skill and temperament, is also conceived of as an organic process: "See, different people develop as they grow older," Ginny Morrison says; "their temperaments change and you can begin to see how a person is—is this young person reliable? Is this young person responsible? Can you always count on him to do what he says he's going to do?—this type of thing. And after awhile, somebody just begins to stand out as bakemaster."[11]

Using tools that are crafted for other forms of environmental mastery, these master bakers deftly combine and rearrange the elements of earth and air and water and fire into a clambake. The success of the bake depends on their experience and knowledge and skill—the right amounts, the right movements, the right timing, even the right attitude. Within this system, the knowledge of the fire is closely connected to the ordering of the universe, just as the combination of heat and moisture that transmutes the food into a meal by cooking becomes a kind of allegory for the special alchemy of the place.

Related to the messages the clambake contains about the ecological identity of Allen's Neck are expressions of its traditional role as a farming community. As Turner has observed, seasonal changes constitute one rite of passage, and the clambake can be understood as an agrarian mode of "ritually prepar[ing] for a whole series of changes in the nature of the cultural and ecological activities to be undertaken."[12] In Allen's Neck, the clambake marks the end of the summer, the time for harvesting the fruits of the physical and social world—drawing all that is alive and lively together—before the world grows cold, dark, and barren.

Seasons of nature and the seasons of human life overlap. The majority of the guests at Clambake are in the autumn of their years, and many of them are actively entering into winter: for them, re-experiencing summer's waning is not tainted with regret but with exuberance and gratitude. Sarah Orne Jewett wrote about a similar family feast in turn-of-the-century Maine.

> There were enough young persons at the reunion, but it is the old who really value such opportunities; as for the young, it is the habit of every day to meet their comrades—the time of separation has not come. To see the joy with which these elder kinfolks and acquaintances had looked in one another's faces, and the

Clambake reunion, 1985: Gram Gifford visits with Elden Mills, who performed her wedding service nearly seventy years earlier. Photograph by Kathy Neustadt, 1985.

lingering touch of their friendly hands; to see these affectionate meetings and then the reluctant partings, gave one a new idea of the isolation in which it was possible to live in that after all thinly settled region. They did not expect to see one another again very soon; the steady hard work on the farms, the difficulty of getting from place to place, especially in winter . . . gave double value to any occasion which could bring a large number of families together.[13]

The group that is drawn together at summer's end—the local residents, their friends and relations, the perennial summer visitors—only exists once a year, in this time and in this place. In this sense, the clambake is an alchemical model for community, for belonging, for identity. The clambake held in the grove at summer's end establishes for those present their place in nature, in the natural world, in the seasonal process; it provides a place in the social world as well, reuniting, as it does, the producers and the consumers, the food suppliers

and the food eaters. Drawing people together, the clambake establishes and
confirms human bonds, sometimes in the face of the elements and exigencies
of nature that would divide them, that could defeat them.

When they draw together on this biggest of holidays, the hard-working
people of this farming community work. And they work hard. All day long.
The cousins go rockweeding, the Erickson clan sets up tables, people clean
clams, women do double duty in the kitchen, the men rake out. "No one tells
you anything," Florence Smith says; "you just do it."[14] Here is the intensification, not the reversal, of the laboring mode: hours and personnel are extended,
jobs are invented, and new energy-consuming challenges are set and fulfilled.

Play and fun are intertwined with labor in the clambake, just as Turner
found them "inextricably interrelated" in preindustrial societies. "In the universe of work in which the *whole* community goes through the *entire* ritual
round, whether in terms of total or representative participation," Turner
argued, ". . . communal participation, obligation, the passage of the whole
society through crises, collective and individual, directly or by proxy, are the
hallmarks of the 'work of the gods' and sacred human work."[15] Not only does
the *whole* community of Allen's Neck participate in Clambake, but they
complete the *entire* ritual round over the course of a lifetime.

"I heard you ask something like, 'How many times have you been to
Clambake?'" observes Julie. "I think the better question is how many times
have you *missed*."[16] At every stage of development, there are appropriate roles
to be filled and tasks to be performed. Babies come in strollers and playpens
and are often babysat by the older children. As kids, they help throw kindling
on the fire, follow their mothers, and help serve the food. As teenagers, they
gather rockweed, cut fish, and bag tripe. As young adults, they work as
waitresses and waiters. Women go on to become cooks, dishwashers, heads of
tables, and pie makers; men help with the rake-out, oversee the acquiring of
supplies, the distribution, and the clean-up.

Says Elsie of her granddaughter, Sarah: "She helped out last year, when she
was six, and she's pretty much come since she was born." About her own
children, now grown, she recounts, "We used to have the wagon, with a big
water tank on it, and we used to take that up to the bake. . . . So when my kids
were little and wanted to go to the bake but weren't old enough to help, they
always—that was like their playpen: on and near the water tank. . . . So when
they were small, they knew they were safe on this wagon which was their
father's and grandfather's, and they were safe to stay there and we would tell
them to watch out for the water. But it worked out all right; it was fun."[17]

"The stages of man": kids help their mothers serve the clambake. Photograph by Kathy Neustadt, 1985.

Eventually, the ritual round requires abstinence: people decide that it's time to stay home from Clambake altogether, that the time has come to stop; death, too, overtakes them. "I've reached the place now where I don't do anything at clambake," said Mary Davoll at age eighty-seven. "As a matter of fact—do you know the grounds down there?—I hardly dare walk down there without a cane. I have a wonderful family—don't think I'm neglected—but I always think, 'Well, Mary, one misstep, you know, and you won't . . .'"[18] Mary stopped coming to Clambake that year, as Gladys Gifford did the following. The men, like old soldiers, don't so much stop attending; instead, they fade away at rake-out time, to reappear after the sweat work is completed to participate in the banter and recollecting of past, hot fires.

"I can't remember when how excited I used to get: I'm not that excited any more," Hettie Tripp says. "I never thought the time would come when I wasn't ready to go [to Clambake], but I guess nature takes care of it after awhile. You get too tired, and you don't care whether you go or not." It's a hot, muggy day, and the air itself feels depressed. Hettie's anticipation of the end of her clambaking days, although premature, voices her community's understanding that there is, indeed, a time to every purpose under heaven, or at least there still is in the culture of Allen's Neck.

Before she's done talking, however, she has rekindled her own flames: "See, that was a big day, that was a *big* day—well, I guess it still is; well, it 'tis, I guess—I guess I'll go; I guess I'll be there." Speaking with even more enthusiasm of how much she looks forward to watching rake-out, she adds, "It's very fascinating, and something you never get tired of, I don't think." "I'm always

Elder statesmen confer while the bake cooks: Horace Wildes, Willy Morrison, and Ralph Macomber. Photograph by Kathy Neustadt, 1985.

amazed," I say. "That's right, I still am, too,"[19] she replies with a smile, thereby granting herself at least one year's reprieve from the inexorable force of time, which she accepts, from her perspective, as natural and inevitable, but which I, from mine, find poignant and somewhat painful.

For Yankees, hard work is good work, even "the work of the gods"; making some money in the process makes it still better work. One Allen's Neck resident defines Yankee as "self-employed." Burney Gifford's attempt to define it is more associative: "Round here, it's more values than heritage; heritage is part of it, but most of it is values. . . . It's like us, we're a good example: when you want to start a business like this [the herb business], you bust your ass and try to pay for it as you go. . . . The reason there's not a lot of competition is because it's too labor-intensive. . . . It's also a nice feeling at night when you go to bed and the place is paid for."[20] The Yankee stuff that goes into putting on clambakes is the same as it is for starting an herb business: it is inspired by values, labor-intensive, and pragmatic.

According to Protestant apologist Josef Pieper, the essence of a Protestant holiday is the "renunciation of [the] yield of [a] day's labor . . . an offering being made of the yield of labor." At Allen's Neck, the crew voluntarily and self-consciously gives up something of economic value to participate in Clambake—a day's salary, a day's catch, a day's harvest, even a day's vacation—which confirms that their sacrifice is real. That the Meeting is able at the same time to gain monetarily as well as spiritually from this sacrifice is seen as powerful affirmation of the world's goodness and the clambake's festive place in a good world. As Pieper has noted, the "festival joy kindled by a specific circumstance" must be undergirded by "an absolutely universal affirmation extending to the world as a whole, to the reality of things and the existence of man itself."[21]

At a Yankee clambake, the work is hard, but the Yankees like it that way. "I'd be embarrassed to sit down when they were working. I couldn't. I think it's really fun,"[22] says Julie Brown. "Hardly anybody buys tickets from this area," says Florence Smith, "because they prefer to work on it."[23] "When our cousin from Michigan came," recounts Barbara Erickson, "my father gave him two tickets—he'd just been married—as a wedding present, and he didn't enjoy it as much as waiting on. They get to know the different people who are waiting on and have fun with them."[24] Laboring as a group guarantees a way of knowing and respecting one another; it's one of the ways the community became cohesive in the first place. More than a few newcomers to the clambake—a sweetheart brought along for the experience or a person newly married into

nize this ethic; like Kipling's "humphing" camel who refused to work "when
the world was so new and all," it is possible that they may never be able to

make up for the work they didn't do at their first clambake, to erase the stigma    *Thoughts*
of laziness now attached to them.

The Yankee ethos of sweat and toil wears people out. "I wish you could have
been with us and seen what we had to do. . . . You saw ten minutes of it, and
that was nothing compared with carrying sixty-five bags of rockweed up,"
Burney Gifford says. "Where we get the rockweed, it took us an hour and a
half to get the rockweed, which is pretty tedious work. There's about a forty-
foot incline up a stone bank, and you have to carry stuff up it. It's unbelievably
tedious, really strenuous work; it's almost as bad as raking out. It's been non-
stop all day."[25] If tempers rise and feelings are hurt, the difficulty of the work is
often the primary cause, but it is also a source of what is most rewarding.
"Everybody takes pride in what they do—not pride, satisfaction is, I guess, the
word," says Norma Judson. "As meager as it is, you feel needed, you're filling
that slot, you're filling that little gap."[26]

"I don't think there's any favorite part," says Peter Gonet—"have it be over
and everybody happy, I guess."[27] Much of the pleasure that the food brings to
the workers, who are often too exhausted to sit down and eat it, is related to
the amount of toil it represents. Pride in the menu is generally ascribed to its
being "traditional," to its having gone unchanged, but underneath that, and
evident in the stories the women tell, is the recognition and appreciation of
challenges overcome, of the achievement of difficult tasks. Ila Gonet recalls
her mother's story of the men's struggle to secure enough mackerel; in speaking of the squash pie she plans to make for this year's clambake, Mary Davoll
renders poetic the self-sufficiency of her family's farm and the accomplish-
ments of her mother's kitchen. Hard work, well done, with a good outcome.

There are tools and technologies available today that could make the job of
clambaking simpler and easier. When necessity demands it, they are adopted;
otherwise, they are largely avoided. For the men of Allen's Neck, many of
whom are no longer directly engaged in agricultural pursuits, wielding old
hoes and stepping into a fire represents a return to honorable work. For the
women, baking pies from scratch, putting up jams and jellies, and sewing
aprons and pot holders for the sale tables transport them back through
generations of the same activity, putting them in touch with each other and a
world of women's work and culture that hardly exists anymore, but that they
see as still having value. "I like to make jams and jellies," says Priscilla. "I'm a

Women's (handi)work:
Billy Gifford and Pris-
cilla Davoll with pot
holders and aprons.
Photograph by Kathy
Neustadt, 1985.

country girl. My mother always canned; 'course, in those days, years and years
ago, you didn't have freezers, and everything was canned. Blueberries—oh,
everything from the garden was canned. Wild grapes, this year there'll be wild
cherries—that I do like—elderberries, wild blueberries. The wild things have a
better taste than the cultivated thing, I don't know why."[28]

Brown bread steamed for three hours and made from specially ground
johnnycake meal, a bread and cracker dressing that takes several days to make,
and home-baked pies are all "old-fashioned," labor-intensive foods that are
almost impossible to find anywhere else in Allen's Neck at any other time of
the year. Once common and everyday, these foods have become special, even
specialties, with high price tags in the marketplace. Both in spite of and
because of this fact, these foods represent a way of eating that is valued for

being simple and wholesome: it nourishes the body, the soul, and the Yankee
aesthetic. If simplicity and gourmet status seem contradictory, it's the outside
world that has changed, not the essence of the food. At one time, all of the
parts of the meal represented communal toil—the seafood, the vegetables, the
home-baked goods. Today, the toil is still there, even if some of the items are
store-bought.

While the association of Yankees with clambaking has historical roots,
Quaker Yankees certainly have no special claim to the practice. And yet, as
played out in Allen's Neck, there is something particularly resonant between
the "directness" of the clambake as a way of cooking—without pots and pans,
without chefs—and the directness of Quakerism, which, from its inception,
looked to unmediated experience of the divine, without priests, texts, or creed.
Work crews for building the fire, preparing the food, setting up the sale tables,
and serving the meal form without being officially signaled, without being
told: as Norma Judson says, it's "divinely directed, when you don't depend on
human organization."[29]

For Norma, a convinced Quaker of some dozen years' standing, the connection is overt. "To the people that are involved in that clambake, it really is a
very pure expression of Quakerism. . . . Everyone feels responsible, without
saying. I mean, it is an absolute responsibility to be there and to contribute—
very Quakerly. It is unorganized, hardly organized at all, and yet it's carried
out very efficiently: that also is very Quakerly. . . . And this is a day where
calmness and a sense of joy and a sense of happiness is never interrupted. . . . It
is a pulling together, it's a very mystical—Quakerism is a very mystical
experience, anyway—and this is a very mystical day for us."[30] The Quaker
values of being in harmony with nature, of finding harmony within, and of
mastery through love are all subtly implied in Clambake as well.

Lewis Cole, in his last sermon as minister of the Allen's Neck Meeting,
characterized the clambake as a universal religious impulse with a Quakerly
twist.

The expression or the realization of something profoundly spiritual and precious in
some way that you can see is a basic instinct, I think, of all of us. . . . I think that the
principle is universal, and if the denomination has eliminated the familiar eccle-
siastical sacraments, others will pop up.

I'm absolutely convinced that the clambake is one of the most precious sacramental expressions that can be had. I feel that it's a sacrament; I feel that it's
something very visible. The laboring together of good friends and neighbors, the
setting up of the fire, the smoke, the steam, the carrying of the clams, the sitting

down in good fellowship together: all those things are an expression of something we find quite difficult to express—the love that passes between members of the family and members of the community.

How do we express it? By getting together and having such a wonderful time at the clambake. I can't help but think that it's essentially sacramental of something very beautiful, very inward, and very spiritual, that's special to all of us, that we must express, which we must convey to one another.[31]

The tradition of Clambake is also about change. With each new bake, the past is being brought into the present, to be relived and re-experienced in the reenactment. When people talk about the past, they describe it as having been simpler, slower, and less heavily trafficked than the world of today, and to outsiders—particularly those entrenched in their own romantic view of "the folk" or "the olden days"—it may sound like a time when there was a greater integrity of thought, deed, and belief. But this is not necessarily the point the Allen's Neck clambakers are making. Some aspects of life have become less pleasing, surely, but others have gotten better: it's the continuity, the possibility of an unbroken narrative, that makes life and the clambake meaningful.

The tradition of the bake, like the shapes of the houses and barns, has survived the assaults of time. This weathering has given it the patina of venerability. Without the challenges, the changes, and the choices, the value would be missing. If the time comes when there are no more clams, then clambakes will probably cease to exist, but the world will go on, the community of Allen's Neck will survive, and it will doubtless find a new "tradition" to take the place of the bake—even if the folklorists of the world rail against its passing. No one likes to think about this possibility, but radical change is no stranger to this culture: like the end of the mills and the demise of whaling, it is an ongoing fact of their communal experience.

Clambaking at Allen's Neck in 1988 probably differs from as much as resembles what it was in 1888. Lots of things have changed, within the community as well as outside of it. Changes in the world—in large part economic—have had the most obvious impact. Many of the women now work outside the home, for example, and one effect of this change has been the streamlining of some of the food preparation—the introduction of canned onions, the use of paper plates. Another societal shift has affected gender roles, so that women are starting to do some of the "men's jobs"—washing the clams, setting up tables, building the fire, even raking out. What this change in jobs will mean internally, as well as in the world at large, is not yet clear.

As the demise of family farming looms large, the significance of the

Women filling new clambake roles: Julie Brown helps to seal the bake with rock-weed. Photograph by Kathy Neustadt, 1985.

clambake shifts. The relationship of insiders to outsiders changes as they negotiate their relational statuses, their intentions, and even the use of the land itself. In addition, when the "swamp Yankees" mow their nonarable tracts of lawn and the kids from the cities run the mill or grow hydroponic tomatoes on someone else's family farm, the very notion of insider and outsider identities is called into question. In times of intensified social change and shifting power, being native to the land goes up for grabs, as any of the local native Americans can confirm.

As the participation of the Allen's Neck group in the Smithsonian folklife festival clearly demonstrated, the old Yankees are starting to lose their privileged founders' status and are being redefined as a "traditional occupational group" or, even more staggering, as an American "ethnic" group. As power relations shift further due to continuing demographic changes, the clambake may come to demonstrate status inversion more like what anthropological theory has described.

Can a farming culture survive when the farms are gone? Are there going to be any kids who stay around Allen's Neck long enough to take over the men's work at the clambake? Where will the next bakemaster come from, and how will his—or *her*—apprenticeship be carried out? How much change is too much, before the culture and its artifacts—the tradition of the clambake, for instance—are permanently destroyed? Permanence, of course, is a relative thing in culture and symbolic expression, but these questions can feel pressingly real and absolute in the present moment. As housing developments replace the farms and city jobs replace farming, cultural change is undeniably happening; cultural adjustments are being made. In this time of transition, with such large questions abounding, the ritual, the tradition of Clambake—with its implications of permanence, continuity, and identity—is more important, more meaningful, than ever.

Far more than clambaking principles, clambaking techniques, and the manufacturing and maintenance of clambaking artifacts, what the people of Allen's Neck really seem to want to share about the clambake are stories. In a community where silence is valued and emotions are rarely expressed directly, the stories are the most direct form of articulating the meaning of Clambake. In many ways, they constitute the core of its traditional essence. The stories, accrued over time and by theme, communicate deep emotions about a past perceived to be rich and rewarding. For the most part, however, it is not nostalgia—a longing for things passed away—that infuses these narratives. It is more an appreciation and reverence for what has come before, as the foundation for what is now.

Many of the stories are public domain and popular; a number of people tell them with a variety of flourishes. Ila Gonet speaks about the one time the bake didn't cook and only one person asked for money back. In Gordon's version of this story, "some" people wanted a refund. There was the year the Meeting didn't have a minister and "Jimmy Murphy down the road" gave the blessing—"Father Murphy," they still call him occasionally, someone else adds. Another time, according to Karl Erickson, "It was nip and tuck because we didn't know whether it was going to rain. . . . And this man from [the Holy Ghost brotherhood] came up to us and said, 'If it gets so you've got to have the bake under cover, our place is vacant for you.' And I still remember vividly, not only just what he said but his attitude."[32] "Now, wasn't that a nice thing to do?" asks

Florence Smith, rhetorically. "It sure is, and so we really found that we have
friends among all the people in the area, not just the people that go to
Meeting."[33]

Another year, Karl's sister-in-law, Jean Parsons, recounts, "It rained across
the street and didn't rain on the grounds. Were you there that year? We sat
across the street and watched it pouring." "That's an absolute fact," chimes in
Karl, "because I was at the clambake grounds, at the street, and I had just
watched and thought, 'We're going to get drenched'—and here it was really
coming down and we didn't get any. It's a thing that you can hardly say was
true because it was so—almost implausible. And the street isn't more than—
what?—forty or fifty feet wide?, and there it was raining while we have a
clambake."[34] Not exactly a parting of the Red Seas, but pretty close.

"A couple of years ago," Jean continues, "we had two people who were
traveling who bought tickets, and they came and they watched people working and they wanted to work. Now, they had paid for their tickets, and they
waited on and they had the best time. So they were so much a part of it, right
from the beginning to the clean-up." Husband Gordon tells the same story:

> I was there one morning; it was—I don't know—quarter of seven, seven, something
> like that, and, after all, the bake doesn't go on until one. And there was this man
> walking around, snapping pictures, and I assume that it was his wife walking
> around; so you try to make people feel welcome, so I said, "Are you a stranger?"
>
> And he said, "Oh, yeah, we've just come over for the clambake."
>
> And I figured maybe Providence or something. And I said, "Oh, yeah? Where's
> home?"
>
> And he said, "Iowa."
>
> And I said, "What? How did you pull this?"
>
> And he said, "My wife and I usually go to the West Coast for our vacation"—
> and they had a camper—he said, "I was in the barber shop and I read an article
> about your clambake in the American history museum [probably *Natural History*
> magazine]."[35]

In different versions, the couple came from Iowa, Ohio, or Florida.

Many stories are private, individual, and often humorous vignettes that
evoke the textures of the personal past, like Gram Gifford's memory of riding
to Clambake in her father's first car, the Rambler, which had to go up hills in
reverse, or Elsie's image of young Burney sitting on the back of his father's
water truck, eating peanut butter sandwiches because he didn't like the taste of
clambake, or Elden Mills recalling both his fascination and repugnance when,
as a midwestern farmboy, he was first introduced to this bizarre New England
custom. Florence Smith, who as chief ticket seller had learned to say "no" to

the most baroque of pleas and excuses, laughs aloud when she remembers one little man with a cherubic smile who she let in year after year without a ticket because "he just had faith."[36]

Many of these narratives seem to try to capture a message about the goodness of people, particularly as they are inspired by the clambake. "You know," recounts Florence, "two years ago my grandson Jeremy had a problem with his back, and he had to be in a body cast, and so his mother drove the station wagon into the grounds, and he lay in the back there, you know. The kids all took turns playing with him so he wouldn't miss one year of that, and if you'd seen how nice the youngsters were to him and—oh, honestly—people commented on that. They said, 'He was never lonely because either one child or another was playing games with him or doing something.' It really gave you a good feeling."[37]

At the interface between the insider and the outsider—whether between ethnographer and informant, local and transplanted family members, or generations—these narratives construct a vision of the perfect community, laboring together, serving themselves by honoring their neighbors, breaking bread with people who are, in some respects, their enemies. It is a vision not so very far from reality: in ecumenical harmony, the neighbors are all there working, no matter where they go to church on Sunday; the "skewks" eat their meals voraciously but in peace, and forgive their hosts' trespasses, as they, in turn, are forgiven for trespassing against them. Tension among participants, although never totally absent, is remarkably infrequent: generations work together without friction and with respect, and between the work of men and the work of women, a bridge exists that is creative and fertile. "I never heard of anybody getting into a scrap or anything," says Raymond Davoll. "Everybody is always kidding everybody else, giving them a bad time, if they can."[38]

The success of the clambake proceeds from the symbolically powerful and aesthetically rich experience it offers to the community; over time, its symbols have increased in power, its aesthetics in richness. Clambake makes the everyday seem special by holding up its elements for conscious appreciation and dramatic display. But Clambake also transcends and transforms the everyday reality by emphasizing harmony and connectedness among nature, humanity, and divinity. Clambake is both a microcosm of this world and a symbol for its ideal image.

But there is irony in Clambake as a representation of identity, as "truth," and in this irony lies the dynamic nature of perhaps all symbolic expression. For the real and the ideal are not one and the same, and the distance between

them is the ultimate challenge of living. To the extent that Clambake represents participation in nature and control of its elements, the experience of
farming and fishing regularly belies such control. In a world whose natural
ecology is visibly changed and threatened, any balancing of nature is uncer-
tain, and the drawing together of resources—foodstuffs, human energy, the
farm land—is increasingly precarious. Calling people together for a reunion is
proposed in the face of dispersed families and new work habits and schedules;
Thursday, particularly, challenges both fate and practicality.

The clambake seeks to create art through labor, at a time when people feel
they don't have a lot of free time, when the investment of time and self in such
labor-intensive activities as pie-making have been largely given up and self-
sufficiency has been deemed unnecessary, or at least unattainable. It proposes
to affirm identity, culture, history, and faith at a time of increasing cultural
pluralism, social rootlessness, and secularism. In symbolic form, the people of
Allen's Neck hold up their clambake to themselves and others as a symbol of
survival, permanence, tradition, and immortality—"same as last year"—in the
face of change in the world, the mutability of nature, the imperfection of
humankind, and the certainty of their own mortality.

In the tension between the real and the ideal, the clambake represents an act
of faith and faith itself. As people stand around the pile of steaming rocks with
its mound of food, waiting for the first clam to be tasted, there is a corporate
act of breath-holding, of hoping for the best but being prepared for much less.
As each successful bake is uncovered, the world, in a sense, is renewed: faith is
replenished, belief is affirmed, and a slice of the future is guaranteed. "It's
good," Fat Mac decrees: the clam is good, the bake is proper, the tradition has
been maintained, and the world in that place and time is as it should be.

On behalf of those who participate in the event itself—who don't, themselves,
require any confirmation—I have tried to expose the artistry, complexity, and
effectiveness of the clambake as a technical and symbolic experience. To those
who study such events, I have tried to indicate some ways in which the
abstractions and theories our research relies upon might be better grounded.
What Clambake illustrates to me is that life and human situations are less
geometric, tidy, and probably even less knowable than most anthropological
theory proposes: dichotomies and reversals may be meaningful concepts to the
scholar, but if they are not reflected in the experience of the community under
study, then they need to be replaced by concepts that are. The study of human
behavior, as Stoller notes, too often excludes the study of human *being*.[39]

From a theoretical standpoint, the Allen's Neck Clambake represents a kind of subtext within a larger discourse on the relationship between culture and celebration. The meaning of Clambake for the people of Allen's Neck is based on the affirmation of society and an intensification of identity that is, as Bynum would put it, "continuous with *their* sense of social and biological self."[40] Food and food preparation studied within the context of celebration and symbolism is also a kind of subtext that affirms the social and biological self. Particularly in agrarian cultures with explicit religious roots, reaping nature's bounty in a seasonal rite of passage connects the environment, its natural resources, its people, and the spiritual energy that infuses them. The impact of Clambake comes from its ability to reflect, shape, interpret, affirm, unify, influence, and reinforce the group's sense of itself from nourishing and renewing itself, year after year.

As I stand at fire's edge, holding my pitchfork, I am giddy with anticipation, excitement, and fear. The rocks in front of me are white with heat, and my exposed face and eyebrows already interpret the intensity of the temperature as pain. The wool shirts, wool socks, heavy boots, and blue jean pants I wear for protection against the heat make my body heavy and cumbersome. The wooden handle feels cool in my hands, before I sheathe them in leather gloves. I pull the bandana down over my face, just below my eyes, and look behind me to Julie, who adjusts her hat and signals me by lifting her chin that we are about to begin the rake-out. In our last moments of full consciousness, we confer on our strategy: "Okay, you move in to pick up a log, bring it back out, and toss it to the side, over there. When you get too hot, I'll take a turn. After that, we'll do the rocks."

Someone signals the start, and I am aware of movement and communal breathing. The sound of my own heartbeat fills my ears, and sweat breaks out over my entire body as I step toward the fire. The pitchfork is suddenly only inches long: to reach the burning timber is to work against all instincts of self-preservation. It is scorchingly, blindingly hot. Getting the weight of the log balanced on the flat tines seems an impossible task. I shift my body weight: I throw my shoulders forward and my head back to avoid scorching my face. One step backward, and it's cooler. As my vision clears, I look frantically around for a place to discard this living piece of inferno. One or two more rounds in the fire and I turn, nearly exhausted, to hand the pitchfork over to Julie.

My turn comes again, and again, before the cement slab is cleared of wood

"Raking out": the men use long-handled tools for a hot job. Photograph by Kathy Neustadt, 1985.

and rocks, and the men with the rakes begin scraping away the last embers. My body feels stretched, torn, and charred. The rhythm and the strains of the exertion persist within my body. My mind is clouded and hazy, like my eyes; my face is bright red with exertion and drenched in sweat. The blood rushes through my temples, giving a watery quality to the sound that still echoes in my ears, the sound of metal against rock—silence—metal against rock.

As we pitch the rocks back onto the slab, it is cooler but clumsy work. When it is time for the rockweed, I have removed one of the wool shirts and the gloves, and the slick, wet weed is cool against my skin. Its weight is more natural and easier to manage. As the rockweed hits the rocks, I am enveloped in clouds of steam and the pungent smell, and my nose and mouth and eyes are filled to near-suffocation. Suddenly, I am following hand signals, grabbing the handles of a cool wooden box filled with clams, which rattle and shift as I lurch toward the bake. Another hand directs me through the haze. I lower the crate and head unconsciously toward other boxes, shining bright green, then deep orange, and finally to a glistening silver pan of dressing. In a daze, I step out of the way as the sheets of canvas are marched past me, wet and billowing, one after another.

And suddenly it's over. How much time has passed I can hardly guess. My heart rate begins to slow down, and normal breathing slowly returns. I take off the second wool shirt and untie my bandana. Looking around for Julie, I stand with her awhile in silence as we wipe away the sweat and grime, kicking off our shoes and wadding up our socks. While other workers begin to gather in groups around us, our eyes begin to fill with new light. We smile. We did it. I did it. I have actually raked out! At some other time, I might be able to talk about this—about the meaning of the rake-out, the symbolism of the fire, the alchemy of the elements—but now I only know what it felt like. No, not even that; I know that it *felt*. It consumed every part of my body and some primal part of my mind. As far as I am concerned, at this moment, that is what it *means*.

There is no aspect of the bake's process that doesn't have something of this quality of immersion to it. The activities the day before Clambake are decidedly slower and less strenuous, but they are socially and emotionally engaging. Throughout the morning of the bake, all of the preparations have a tempo and mood that envelop the participants and create a shared experience. On the beach with the clams, hands reach into water-filled skiffs to the rhythm of the ocean's pounding; wrapped in the smell of salt water, eyes, fingers, and ears search for cracked shells, snouts that don't respond to touch, and the rattling sound of a single dead clam. At the grove, constructing the bake, the banter along the food table, and cutting the pies all contribute to the anticipation and exhilaration, building toward an unself-conscious transportation. People step outside of this flow from time to time—kids ride around on their bikes, people drive off for supplies, other people talk over family matters—but the current of the events gathers strength.

The rake-out marks the beginning of the most intensified portion of the event, both for those who participate and for those who watch. Similarly, the lull in the baking process marks the beginning of the social rake-out, as people encounter each other, interact, exchange, transmute past relationships into

The fast-paced job of food distribution (foreground, Mary Monteiro; background, Ann Mason). Photograph by Kathy Neustadt, 1985.

present ones, create their own sense of flow. When the time comes for the bake to be opened, the focus shifts again to the food—this time as a meal—and the work of getting the food on the tables is also physically enveloping—fast-paced, intensive, and exhausting. Although seemingly removed from the demands of work, the diners attack their meals with an intensity and speed of their own in an orgy of ingestion, figuratively and literally all-consuming.

This sensory and physical level of experience is essential to what the clambake is about. The memories of Clambake and the stories people tell that attempt to capture its reflection and illustrate its essence are at a remove from this experience. Although they are an integral part of its traditionality, investing it with stratigraphic dimension and complexity and motivating its next performance, they cannot fully capture the sweat and surge and heartbeat of Clambake as lived. The clambake, in its experiential form, is *not* a text, even if

The signified meal: clam juice and melted butter, fish and corn. Photograph by Kathy Neustadt, 1985.

people who aren't covered in sweat and clam juice choose to "read" it that way. The experiencing of Clambake is not metaphoric, metonymic, paradigmatic, syntagmatic; it is far less mediated and conscious than all of this.

I think it is legitimate to say that sometimes a clam is just a clam. It has weight, color, smell, taste, and a distinctive sound when it cooks or dies. Perception of these qualities does indeed require mental functions, but not to the same degree as symbolic or scholarly interpretation does—nor, I am proposing, with the same effect. It has been far too easy in the discourse on representation to forget that the thing being symbolized exists along with the symbol. I offer up slimy honeycombs of tripe, hot, moist clam meat, and butter dripping down one's arms and face as the primary, signified clambake experience.

"Insider" and "outsider," "internal" and "external," "emic" and "etic" are, I

would argue, relative terms. Some people in the Allen's Neck community—
from some perspectives and in some instances—are more "inside" than others;
some "outsiders" can be more "inside" than other "outsiders"; some "outsiders" can be more "inside" than some "insiders." And the same tradition can
be "real" or "invented" depending on where you stand, and for how long.[41]

Just as insider and outsider are not necessarily polarities, sensory perception
is not the opposite of interpretation, nor is the symbolic interpretation of an
Allen's Neck insider the opposite of the cognitive functions of an outside
scholar. Sensation, interpretation, and abstraction are interrelated processes
that overlap and inform each other; as Stoller says, "One cannot separate
thought from feeling and action; they are inextricably linked."[42] Likewise,
although continuity and contiguity may involve greater connection than metaphors and reversals, it still takes energy to maintain them. Keeping the
tradition of Clambake the "same as last year" involves keeping perceptions and
intimations of change at bay.

I have tried to understand as many of the elements of the Allen's Neck
Clambake as I have discerned—historical, symbolic, analytical, experiential—
from as many points of view as possible—the participants', the theorists', and
my own. I know from my experience in the fire that we can share in the
feelings and experiences of others—even if we never can become "one" with
them. Stoller's main informant and friend, Adamu Jenitongo, once told him,
"'Today you are learning about us, but to understand us, you will have to grow
old with us.'"[43] That much, I feel, I have certainly begun to do.

In thinking seriously about the Allen's Neck Clambake as a foodways
tradition, a community celebration, and an event and process loaded with
significance, I would argue that it is possible and desirable to revere both the
Others whom we study and the complexity of the experiences upon which
they, and all of us, build meaning. Beyond that, it seems important to
recognize that what can be known—"truth"—is, like identity and tradition,
negotiated and negotiable: it sometimes resides inside, sometime outside,
sometimes in neither place, sometimes in both.[44] I suspect that the Allen's
Neck Clambake will be telling its stories, telling its truths, far into the future.

# Notes

The citations listed below are abbreviated in form. For full citations, see References.

*Introduction*

1. Sutton-Smith, "Psychology of Childlore: The Triviality Barrier," 1–8.
2. For more on inter- and intragroup folklore, see Jansen, "The Esoteric-Exoteric Factor in Folklore," 43–51.
3. Scott Lillie, a manager of Food and Beverage Project Development for Disney World Corporation, reported to me recently that after several months of operation, the clambake was a big success, although, conceding to popular taste, they had added an "all-American" buffet of fried chicken, spaghetti, and the like to the offerings. A character actor named Harpoon Houlihan serves as the bakemaster and, in addition to tasting the first clam (does he declare, resonantly, "It's good," I wonder?), strolls among the guests telling stories. This interchange with Disney World, which went on for several months, was a real education for me and a cross-cultural experience of a most fascinating variety—something on the order of the commoner, Scholarly Caution, meeting King Cultural Commodifier. I am grateful for the experience, however, if only for the opportunity it afforded me to meet Troy, Scott's secretary, the world's friendliest telephone voice.
4. See Clifford, "On Ethnographic Authority," in *Predicament of Culture,* 21–54, for a history of the development of the authorial voice.
5. As Handler and Linnekin note, "One of the paradoxes of the ideology of tradition is that

attempts at cultural preservation inevitably alter, reconstruct, or invent the traditions that they are intended to fix." See "Traditions Genuine and Spurious," 287.

## Prologue. The Bake

1. The original description of the clambake appears in my article, "Born among the Shells," in Humphrey and Humphrey, "*We Gather Together,*" 89–95.

## Section One. The New England Clambake

1. The term "Indian" is problematic and has been since the mid-seventeenth century, when, according to Berkofer ("White Conceptions of Indians," in Washburn, *History of North American Indians,* 522), "The practice of using a general name for all Native Americans regardless of social organization or cultural complexity was established." However, the proposed term of redress, "native American," has also not found universal acceptance. I have tried to use both terms as self-consciously and judiciously as possible.
2. Evan Jones, *American Food,* 13.
3. Hobsbawm and Ranger, *Invention of Tradition,* 1, 2.

### *1. Early Evidence*

1. See Root and de Rochemont, *Eating in America,* 31, on pit cooking, which "was no doubt invented before cooking pots existed . . . [and] remained in favor long after earthenware vessels . . . were available because of the superior flavor produced by such slow even cooking." Sally Smith Booth, in *Hung, Strung, and Potted,* 21, refers to similar "earth ovens" among coastal Indians. Instead of being dug into the ground, these ovens were built up, and seaweed was added to create steam heat. The "ingenious technique" of cooking "seafood packed in seaweed" over hot stones is the method, Evan Jones asserts unhesitatingly in *American Food* (13), that the Pilgrims learned from the Indians.
2. William Ritchie's excavation of shallow round pits in which shellfish was cooked (*Archaeology of Martha's Vineyard,* 52, 55) cannot be taken by itself to establish clambaking practices, although he does suggest as much. Frank Speck's work among the Passamaquoddy is an example of a professional archaeologist going beyond the data: he asserts clambaking to be a "native procedure" without substantiation (*Penobscot Man,* 65, 97). The work of both men has been cited in subsequent sources as providing "proof" of the existence of prehistoric clambaking: see, for example, Russell, *Indian New England,* 75; Reaske, *Compleat Clammer,* 75; and, more recently, Weatherford, *Indian Givers,* 107.

   Herbert Kraft, director of the archaeological research center and the university museum at Seton Hall University, notes that there is evidence for "stone boiling"—rocks heated in fire and transferred to containers in which liquids were then boiled—in a period before pottery, about 1000 B.C., across this country and British Columbia; however, he adds, baking in underground ovens is not similarly demonstrable. Telephone interview, February 7, 1989.
3. *Handbook of North American Indians,* vol. 15, 65.
4. Ritchie, *Archaeology of Martha's Vineyard,* 52, 233.
5. Snow, *Archaeology of New England,* 285.
6. Russell, *Indian New England,* 123.
7. Simmons, *Spirit of the New England Tribes,* 14. See Little and Andrews, "Prehistoric

Shellfish Harvesting at Nantucket Island," 21–22, for contradiction of the seasonal shellfish gathering hypothesis. Seton Hall's Kraft has specifically argued that the patterns of shell disposal used as evidence of migratory activities would also have been displayed within established settlements and might reflect instead aesthetic and sanitation considerations. Telephone interview, February 7, 1989.

8. See Russell, *Indian New England*, 112, for festive occasions that accompanied the drying of clams and Travers's portrayal of the Wampanoag Autumn Council, based on the early seventeenth-century accounts of Englishman William Wood (Travers, *Wampanoag Indian Federation*, 49–53). A more speculative but popular form of representation can be found in Chris Heisler's do-it-yourself clambaking guide, *Clambake!* (3), in which he ventures this portrait of clambaking's origins:

> It is easy to imagine how it went. After a long tedious walk to the sea and the labor of setting up camp, it is time to prepare the feast to celebrate the end of a diminishing inland food supply. Driftwood is gathered to heat the rocks at a spot where seaweed, clams, lobsters and other seafood are plentiful. The heat of the open fire is a welcome change from the small, smokey fires that keep their longhouses warm. The bright sunshine of the shore contrasts with the darkness of the wooded shade.
> The steamy smell of the cooking seaweed and food fills the air. Children dance around the fire in anticipation of a full stomach. The elders sit with their memories of clambakes past when they seined the fish, dug the clams, snared the lobsters and pulled the waving seaweed from the slippery rocks. . . . The braves lay down their bows and arrows to gather food. The squaws are happy because this is the occasion when the braves take over the cooking duties.

9. People in other areas of New England have claimed the origins of clambaking for other Indian groups: for example, Russell, in *Indian New England* (92), says in general that "the clam bake is considered a modern heritage from the Algonquians"; Haywood, in his *Yankee Dictionary* (30), claims that the clambake was originated by the Abenaki Indians; Speck, in *Penobscot Man* (97), focuses on the Penobscot style of the "native procedure." In the area around Allen's Neck, the clambake is associated exclusively with the Wampanoag.

10. Gladys B. Gifford [not to be confused with Burney Gifford's grandmother, Gladys (Gram) Gifford], *History of Old Dartmouth*, 7. Alexander Cory's store at Westport Point, which outfitted incoming vessels and housed a post office, tailor, milliner, and sail loft, was turned into a restaurant in 1949 and renamed the Paquachuck Inn. See *Westport Heritage Cookbook*, unpaginated.

11. Comiskey, *Secrets of Dartmouth*, 11.

12. Ginny Morrison, audiotape of interview, August 6, 1985.

13. Ralph Macomber, Allen's Neck Clambake, August 15, 1985.

14. See Kopytoff, "Knowledge and Belief in Suku Thought," for observations on anthropological epistemological imperialism.

15. See Clifford, "Identity in Mashpee," in *Predicament of Culture*, 227–46, which concerns the Mashpee Wampanoag land suit in which tribal status had to be first determined; see also 317–25 on the ineffectiveness of the "expert testimony" offered by anthropologists on behalf of the Wampanoag claim.

16. This insight was brought home to me in a vivid and profoundly personal experience where, over dinner with newly made friends, I made passing, probably flippant reference to Trevor-Roper's research on the kilt as an "invented tradition," only to be vigorously and appropriately rebuked by my hostess—an articulate and intelligent woman of Scottish descent—who over the dinner table (and in subsequent correspondence) cited veritable

chapters and verses of historical references and folk traditions to the contrary. The experience catalyzed some considerably deeper reflection on my part on the nature of tradition and its uneasy relationship to history (or, more to the point, to historians), and I offer it as a cautionary note for all who would be too quick to disinherit others from their heartfelt cultural inheritances. Trevor-Roper's work, in Hobsbawm and Ranger, *Invention of Tradition,* does not effectively accommodate the possibility that tradition can be both cultural inheritance and invention.

17. In 1988, Plimoth Plantation dropped the summer clambake from its program, responding in part to the lack of documentation to substantiate it, but also to the increased publicity the history of the clambake was suddenly receiving in the form of inquiries from newspaper journalists writing seasonal feature articles as well as the interest expressed by the Disney people.

18. See particularly Clifford, "On Collecting Art and Culture," in *Predicament of Culture,* 215–51, and Dominguez, "Marketing of Heritage."

19. Handler and Linnekin, "Tradition, Genuine and Spurious," 273; see also Dominguez, "Marketing of Heritage."

20. Nanepashemet, audiotape of interview, June 18, 1988.

21. Clifford, *Predicament of Culture,* 231: "Collecting—at least in the West, where time is thought to be linear and irreversible—implies a rescue of phenomenon from inevitable decay or loss." Folklorists are particularly implicated in this epistemology.

22. Clifford, *Predicament of Culture,* 284.

23. For a brief ethnohistory of the Mashpee Wampanoag community, see Clifford, *Predicament of Culture,* 277–346; see also Weinstein-Farson, *The Wampanoag.*

24. Kupperman, *Settling with the Indians,* vii, presents an example of this self-revealing phenomenon: "When they described the Indians they frequently held them up as an example of a society which had not lost its social moorings as English society had done. England could learn a better way, or could recapture the good old ways by looking at Indian society."

25. Higginson as quoted in Root and de Rochement, *Eating in America,* 52.

26. Mather as quoted in Love, *Fast and Thanksgiving Days,* 104. Love adds in a footnote, "Other historians have attributed this apt quotation of Deut. 33:19 to Elder Brewster." More than a hundred years later, French surveyor-explorer-farmer Michel Guillaume St-John de Crèvecoeur reiterated the account of abundance in a description of nearby Nantucket: "The shores of this island abound with the soft-shelled, the hard-shelled, and the great sea clams, a most nutritious shellfish. Their sands, their shallows, are covered with them; they multiply so fast that they are a never-failing resource." Cited in Trager, *Enriched . . . Foodbook,* 215.

27. Kupperman, *Settling with the Indians,* 172–73, 186–87, discusses how the dependency of the settlers affected their attitudes toward the culture of their hosts.

28. For a culinary history of oysters, see Langone, "From the Kitchen," 34–43. As she notes (35), "Oysters were one of the best loved foods in America from the very earliest European settlement until the nineteenth century when they became an obsession." See also Trager, *Enriched . . . Foodbook,* 237, on East Coast oyster houses; also Towle, *American Society,* vol. 1, 272, on the oyster as the national dish.

29. Root and deRochement, *Eating in America,* 52.

30. See Little and Andrews, "Prehistoric Shellfish Harvesting at Nantucket Island," 22, on the cultural bias against scallops and mussels. At a fund-raising bake at Round Hill (South Dartmouth, Massachusetts), in August 1987, serving mussels elicited lots of negative

response from locals, even as it pleased the more sophisticated palates of the summer folks, from away; the fact that mussels are included in the Wampanoag bake at Mashpee testifies to other aesthetics and traditional uses of local resources.

31. Root and de Rochement, *Eating in America*, 55.

32. Fussell, *I Hear America Cooking*, 291; Fussell also tells of Lydia Child's 1829 clam soup recipe and Mrs. Webster's instructions for cooking clams in a skillet over coals.

33. Fussell, *I Hear America Cooking*, 291.

34. Cited in Baker, "Seventeenth-Century Yeoman Foodways at Plimouth Plantation," in Peter Benes, *Foodways in the Northeast*, 110.

35. *Concise Dictionary of Indian Tribes in North America*, 504. In one account, nine hundred Indians and eight hundred whites died, twenty-five towns were burned, and more than 1.35 million dollars in war debt was generated (*Concise Dictionary of Indian Tribes*, 449); according to another, six hundred whites and three thousand Indians died, twelve hundred houses were burned, and eight thousand cattle were slaughtered; Edmund Randolph, cited in *Handbook of American Indians North of Mexico*, 94.

36. The most extensive account of the impact of King Philip's War can be found in Leach, "Colonial Indian Wars," 134–35, and his *Flintlock and Tomahawk*, throughout.

37. See Berkofer, "White Conceptions of Indians," in Washburn, *History of North American Indians*, 535, on the religious significance attributed to King Philip's War and how this aided in establishing the good Indian/bad Indian motifs in later Yankee culture.

## 2. *The Politics of Feasting*

1. Dulles, *History of Recreation*, 10.

2. In the context of the relatively short-lived Puritan predominance, the focus on the Puritan origins of the new nation at the end of the eighteenth century is particularly interesting. See Matthews, "The Term Pilgrim Fathers," 372–84.

3. Dulles, *History of Recreation*, 42–43.

4. Ibid.; on Boston, 46; on New York, 51; on Newport, 64. The turtle dinners at Newport also involved excursions to Goat Island. See Howell, *The Seaside*, 61.

5. William Woys Weaver, audiotape of telephone interview, May 1, 1988. Even "the father of our country" was involved in this sort of activity, as Tannahill reports in his *Food in History*, 298: "When George Washington ran for the legislature in 1758, his agent doled out almost three Imperial, or 3³/₄ American gallons of beer, wine, cider or rum to every voter. This great man himself was concerned over the extent of this hospitality; he feared that his agent might have been too niggardly."

6. Hobsbawm and Ranger, *Invention of Tradition*, 7.

7. Matthews, "The Term Pilgrim Fathers," 297. I am indebted to Robert St. George for passing along this reference, as well as to James Baker for additional information about the patriotic clubs of New England and their celebrations.

8. Club records cited in Matthews, "The Term Pilgrim Fathers," 299. Compare with the Squantum Club menu in Trillin, "A Real Nice Clambake," 83. Indian pudding seems to have been standard fare at these recreated period meals.

9. Dexter, *Extracts from the Itineraries and Other Miscellanies of Ezra Stiles*, 167; special thanks to Robert St. George for digging out this reference for me.

10. *Boston Gazette*, December 28, 1772, as quoted in Matthews, "The Term Pilgrim Fathers," 304.

11. Hobsbawm and Ranger, *Invention of Tradition*, 2, 6.

12. Matthews, "The Term Pilgrim Fathers," 347. The letter from the *Columbian Centinel* (December 19, 1789) that includes this explanation goes on to talk about the perversion of the original intent by the Federalist Party who, "having gained the seats at the feast of shells . . . polluted the anniversary, with the principles of monarchy."

13. Matthews, "The Term Pilgrim Fathers," 327 n.2. James Macpherson published the epic poems of the alleged third-century Irish bard, Ossian, in the 1760s. After Macpherson's death in 1796, scholars concluded that Macpherson had made up Ossian and written most of the poetry himself.

14. Ibid., 330, 330 n.2; 327–28 n.2.

15. See, for example, Cox, *The Scallop*, for various approaches taken toward the topic of scallops and their shells, especially Gaultier, "The Scallop at the Table," 123, and Christopher Hohler, "The Badge of St. James," 51–61, which traces the development of this symbolism.

16. Matthews, "The Term Pilgrim Fathers," 327–28.

17. Ibid., 340.

18. See Axtell, *Through a Glass Darkly*, on earlier colonial attitudes toward the Indians and how Englishmen perceived native Americans as "a threat and a challenge" to their culture.

19. Old Colony Club records, December 22, 1769, cited in Matthews, "The Term Pilgrim Fathers," 299–300.

20. Ibid., 332.

21. In an interesting historical footnote, during the seige of Boston in 1775 by the British, Mrs. Mary Holyoke noted this event in her diary entry of June 26th: "I went last Thursday in a Calash to a part of the Island called Shimmer where a number of Indians live. We carried our provisions with us. They treated us with roasted Paqwaws (a sort of clam)." Holyoke, *Holyoke Diaries, 1709–1856*, 89. Thanks, again, to Robert St. George for this citation.

22. Rayna Green, "The Tribe Called Wannabee," 31 and throughout.

23. Love, *Fast and Thanksgiving Days*, 423, 76, 44; see also Arnott, "Thanksgiving Dinner," 24.

24. In December 1777, during the American Revolution, Thanksgiving was proclaimed for the first time a national institution; in 1863, during the Civil War, Lincoln declared it a national holiday, and every president after him did likewise. That FDR attempted in 1939 to change Thanksgiving to the third Thursday in November—later returned to the fourth Thursday—in order to extend the commercial activity of the Christmas shopping season is further indication of the political and economic malleability of the event. See Arnott, "Thanksgiving Dinner."

25. *Dictionary of Religion and Ethics*, s.v. "feasting"; an offshoot of this generalized concept is the notion that Americans adopted Thanksgiving from Ingathering, the Jewish Succoth; see Arnott, "Thanksgiving Dinner," 15.

26. Weiser, *Handbook of Christian Feasts*, 291–92. In southern Europe, the feast became known as "Our Lady in Harvest." See James, *Seasonal Feasts and Festivals*, 236.

27. Love, *Fast and Thanksgiving Days*, 93. Arnott suggests that Thursday may have been chosen because a three-day festival could not include the Sabbath; see "Thanksgiving Dinner," 15–16 n.4.

28. Weiser, *Handbook of Christian Feasts*, 28–29.

29. Dulles, *History of Recreation*, 7.

30. Willy Morrison, audiotape of interview, August 6, 1985.

31. This is constructed from the descriptions in *An American Glossary, Dictionary of Americanisms* (1859 ed. and after), and S. G. Goodrich, *System of Universal Geography* (1832) (cited in *An American Glossary*), s.v. "Squantum."

32. See Trillin, "A Real Nice Clambake," on the Squantum Club in Rhode Island, which Bartlett mentions in the 1877 and 1889 editions of his *Dictionary of Americanisms,* s.v. "Squantum."

33. See *An American Glossary, American Dictionary of Americanisms on Historical Principles,* and *A Dictionary of Slang, Jargon and Cant.*

34. Goodrich, cited in *An American Glossary;* see also *American Dictionary of Americanisms on Historical Principles,* s.v. "Squantum."

35. Ibid.

36. Berkofer, "White Conceptions of Indians," 532.

37. Rayna Green, "The Tribe Called Wannabee," 31: "For, I would insist now, the living performance of 'playing Indian' by non-Indian people depends upon the physical and psychological removal, even the death, of real Indians."

38. Berkofer, "White Conceptions of Indians," 532.

39. William Woys Weaver, telephone interview, May 1, 1988. The clambake and the barbecue share similar technologies and styles; of the "Western barbecue" Dulles writes, "Dinner was a gargantuan feast; a barbecued beef or hog, *roasted in a deep hole lined with hot stones;* quantities of buffalo steaks, venison, baked 'posum or wild turkey; and always hominy, corn dodgers, and wheatcakes fried in bear's oil" (italics mine). See *History of Recreation,* 76.

40. Roosevelt, *Superior Fishing,* 289.

41. Historian Carroll Smith-Rosenberg's work on women's history explores the notion of the *body* politic in depth. See also Ann Douglas, *Feminization of American Culture,* in which she argues that the sentimentality of late nineteenth-century American literature was the result of a "feminizing" and Unitarian influence that trivialized art into pop culture and required a remasculinization to set things straight. Most late Victorian American social concerns can be viewed in these gendered "feminizing" and "masculinizing" terms.

42. See Harvey Green, "Political Science and Political Thought Converge," 3–24, and *Fit for America.*

43. From "Picnic Excursions," *Appleton's* (1869), as cited in Hern, "Picnicking in the Northeastern United States, 1840–1900"; see especially 142 on the picnic's "nostalgic respite from industrial life" and 145 on the issue of waging war against neurasthenia.

44. Harvey Green, *Fit for America,* 224–37.

45. Hobsbawm, "Introduction," *Invention of Tradition,* 4.

46. *New Bedford Standard-Times,* June 30, 1975. Miss Martin recalls, "Then the Hornbine Church was over in the woods, farther over—it used to take us all day to drive a horse to get over there." Miss Martin, Clambake day audiotape of interview, August 21, 1986.

47. Howe, *Mount Hope,* 244–45; thanks to Ellen Liberman who, while researching an article on clambakes for the *Boston Globe,* came across this reference and passed it along to me.

48. Lincoln, "A Cape Cod Clambake," 51. See also Lincoln, "The Oldest Inhabitant" in *Our Village:* in 1908, Uncle Seth is 88; in "A Cape Cod Clambake," Lincoln described the bakes that Uncle Seth remembered from when he was a child, making those earlier bakes from at least the 1830s, if not the late 1820s.

49. "Local Twinklings," Fairhaven *Star,* (September 7, 1889) thanks to Bob Demanche for providing me with this citation.

50. *Supplement to the Oxford English Dictionary* (1986), s.v. "clambake": "the Philadelphia *Vade Mecum* reads 'A Clam Bake—Our curiousity [*sic*] has been gratified as to the nature of the festival understood by this term.'"

51. Dulles, *History of Recreation,* 274.

52. Holyoke, *Holyoke Diaries, 1709–1856,* 89.

53. Gifford, *History of Old Dartmouth*, 7.

54. *Americanisms*, 68–69; this is confirmed in *Natick Dictionary*, s.v. "clam."

55. *Dictionary of Americanisms* (1859), s.v. "Clam-Bake"; Roosevelt, *Superior Fishing*, 302.

56. Hart, *Miriam Coffin*, 87–88.

57. Nanepashemet, audiotape of interview, June 18, 1987.

58. *Webster's Third International Dictionary* (unabridged ed. [1986], s.v. "clambake") refers to the bake as "an often noisy and pretentious social entertainment . . . attended to by a great many people . . . esp: a political rally."

59. *Dictionary of Americanisms* (1848 ed.), s.v. "Clam-Bake"; Bowles and Towle, in *Secrets of New England Cooking*, 302, also cite the event but do not cite their source.

60. Subsequently, the 1879 bicentennial celebration of the town of Rochester served a clambake of this size, and other large bakes followed. According to Carl L. Flipp, president of Leighton's Clambakes in South Weymouth, Massachusetts, he has catered a few mass bakes himself, one for eight thousand at U. Mass/Boston, and another for ten thousand booked in 1987. Flipp, audiotape of clambake day interview, July 9, 1987.

61. The Douglas bake is mentioned in the New Bedford *Sunday Standard Times*, January 21, 1934, 3, and in *An American Glossary*, s.v. "Clam-bake." Miss Martin, audiotape of clam-bake day interview, August 21, 1986.

62. Siegafritz's testimony, coincidentally, may well explain the continued idiomatic interpretations of the word "clambake" to mean both high-volume, boisterous gatherings and confusing or garbled transmission of speeches. (See *Supplement to the Oxford English Dictionary*, vol. 1 [1986], s.v. "clambake").

63. Siegafritz as cited in Ingersoll, "The Clam Fisheries," 602.

64. Thomas Anderson, "Old-Home Week," 673, 680; see also *Dictionary of Modern American Usage*, s.v. "Old Home Week."

65. MacCannell, *The Tourist*, 25.

66. Anderson, "Old Home Week," 676.

67. Ibid., 682–83.

68. New Bedford *Evening Standard*, July 29, 1903, 4.

69. See, for example, Robert Rydell, *All the World's a Fair: Visions of Empire at American International Exposition, 1876–1916* (Chicago: University of Chicago Press, 1985).

## 3. Leisure and Industry

1. On the role of the Civil War as the "natural corollary of broader social changes through which it [the nation] was passing," see Dulles, *History of Recreation*, 99; on the rage for theater following wars, see Towle, *American Society*, vol. 2, 13; on war as a stimulant to recreation through the creation of free time, see Kraus, *Recreation and Leisure*, 174; on war as a source for the rise of organized sports, see Dulles, *History of Recreation*, 85.

2. Dulles, *History of Recreation*, 90–91.

3. Trollope, *Domestic Manners of the Americans*, and Gund, *The Americans in Their Moral, Social, and Political Relations*, as quoted in Somers, "Leisure Revolution," 141.

4. Dulles, *History of Recreation*, 30.

5. Weber, *Protestant Ethic and the Spirit of Capitalism.*

6. Kraus, *Recreation and Leisure in Modern Society*, 171.

7. Somers, "Leisure Revolution," 127. Harvey Green likewise points to the transformation "from a homogeneous agrarian and village society to one of great industrial cities with

heterogeneous populations" in *Fit for America*, 322; see also Hale, *Narragansett Bay*, 63; Dumazedier, *Sociology of Leisure*, 9, 13, and throughout; Somers, "Leisure Revolution," 127.

8. Dulles, *History of Recreation*, 85. Somers, in "Leisure Revolution," sets the time later, in the 1880s, and Higham, "Reorientation of American Culture in the 1890s," 25–48, sets it later still.

9. Barrett, *Good Old Summer Days*, 240, 241; Griffin, *Step Right Up, Folks!*", 7, 8.

10. *Centennial Cruise*, 70; Barrett (*Good Old Summer Days*, 251), who subscribes to a trickle-down theory of recreation, has argued that Long Branch lost its charm with the coming of the lower classes.

11. Barrett, *Good Old Summer Days*, 8.

12. Dulles, *History of Recreation*, 149.

13. Hale, *Narragansett Bay*, 63; Barrett, *Good Old Summer Days*, 8, lists some of the older boarding houses by name.

14. Towle, *American Society*, vol. 1, 87–89.

15. Varrell, *Summer-by-the-sea*, 10.

16. Towle, *American Society*, vol. 1, 330. Bourgeois city-dwelling boarders were introduced in the process to rural cultural events.

17. Varrell, *Summer-by-the-sea*, 24, 33; for more details, see Dulles, *History of Recreation*, 221–22.

18. Hartt, *People at Play*, 46. Moreover, Hartt maintains (49–50), urban workers were originally attracted to idyllic pleasures in emulating the recreational lives of the country's well-to-do: "Meanwhile capital, with ever an ear to the ground, has caught murmurs that set it thinking; why not capture the institution, cram it with heathen allurements, put it where the proletariat was already wont to go a-pleasuring, and make the reincarnated and expanded elysium independent, henceforth, of the broomstick train? . . . Expositionism set in. It became epidemic."

19. Willy Morrison, audiotape of interview, August 16, 1986.

20. Hale, *Narragansett Bay*, 58, 59.

21. Lears, *No Place of Grace;* on fatalism, in its impulse toward revivalism, see Harvey Green, "Popular Science and Political Thought Converge," 4, 12.

22. Garfield, as quoted in Kraus, *Recreation and Leisure*, 178.

23. Higham, "Reorientation of American Culture," 27; Kraus, *Recreation and Leisure*, 179–85, attributes the existence of leisure with the Adult Education Movement, the development of parks, the establishment of voluntary organizations, and the Playground Movement, which, in turn, further shaped American leisure.

24. Hale, *Narragansett Bay*, 59; Sagendorph and Hale, *That New England*, 127, say that the rail part was finished in 1845, the water part in 1847; Hale, *Narragansett Bay*, 63.

25. *Appleton's Illustrated Handbook of American Travel*, 85.

26. Grieve, *Picturesque Narragansett*, 120–22.

27. Hale, *Narragansett Bay*, 77. In the 1860s, according to Hale (76), there was little commercial value in shellfishing; in a January 21, 1934, article in the *New Bedford Evening Standard Times*, 1875 is given as the date when shellfishing developed commercially.

28. Mrs. Lincoln's Recipe for a Rhode Island Clambake, from the *Boston Cook Book* (1891), as quoted in Davidson, *North Atlantic Seafood*, 424.

29. In 1881, there is reference to the "daily resort" at Rocky Point, serving a "shore dinner of clam chowder" (Wilkinson, *Holiday Rambles*, 18); in 1886, Glazier, *Peculiarities of American Cities*, 403, recounts that "on moonlight nights in summer, excursion parties . . . glide over the smooth waters to this lovely spot"; in 1900, the "home institution, the Rhode Island

'clam-bake,' which is a mainstay of all the shore resorts, and is considered a connecting link, binding them to the Narragansetts [local Indian tribe], who originated it." See Cook, *America: Picturesque and Descriptive*, vol. 3, 106–7. Rocky Point was flattened in the 1938 hurricane. See *New England Hurricane* for photographs of the devastation.

30. *Centennial Cruise*, 32; according to its chronicler (69), the Centennial Cruise represented "not only . . . private enterprise and munificent hospitality but also . . . the growth of commercial activity in the great metropolis."

31. New Bedford's *Evening Standard Times*, August 19, 1876, as quoted in *Centennial Cruise*, 117; also, from the account of the chronicler (34–35), "the Commodore had telegraphed his arrangements, and the clam bake was ready for the guests soon after their arrival. . . . The dining-room at Rocky Point is large enough to seat a thousand; and this number is often entertained there at one time. The guests of the *Starin* found the 'clam bake' a new feature in the culinary art. . . . The novelty of this entertainment led some of the guests to prodigious feats of gustatory enjoyment, and the quantity of clams that disappeared in this manner was a matter of delightful surprise."

32. From the *Daily Mercury*, August 30, 1876, as recorded in *Centennial Cruise*, 119, 39.

33. Boss and Thomas, *New Bedford*, 179; later, in 1893, the island was given over to more industrial uses.

34. Sisson's establishment was purported to be "the only genuine representative which New Bedford possesses of the reputed Rhode Island clambake institution" in an August 26, 1899 *Evening Standard Times* article (10); "Local Twinklings," *Fairhaven Star*, September 7, 1889, stated the same of Jared Sherman, there designated as the first clambaker in the area.

35. *Evening Standard Times*, August 26, 1899 (10) stated that the pavilion was in business in 1872; the *Sunday Standard*, January 21, 1934 (3) stated that in 1874 or 1875, the business began with "a small building" and by 1877 included a real pavilion with bowling and dancing. For the layout of Sisson's establishment in 1877, see *Evening Standard Times*, August 11, 1877 (3; advertisement); on the dance hall and bowling alley, see *Evening Standard Times*, August 26, 1899 (10).

36. *Evening Standard Times*, August 11, 1877 (3). Also reported in *Rochester's Official Bi-Centennial Record:* here, instead of one hundred barrels, it stated there were one hundred bushels, which, by the current rule of thumb practiced at Allen's Neck, would only serve about twenty-five hundred.

37. *New Bedford Board of Trade*, 313, 314–15, for greater details.

38. Boss and Thomas, *New Bedford*, 83, 105; *New Bedford Board of Trade*, 66; McCabe, ed., *Pictorial History of Fairhaven*, 103, 161, 214–15.

39. Grimshaw's was carried on by family through at least 1949 (*Evening Standard Times*, August 21, 1949, editorial page); Thomas Whitfield's pavilion and W. H. Bennett's at Fort Phoenix were also mentioned in 1949.

40. Arthur H. Brown, "Clambakes: The Development of Rhode Island's Institution Here," *Evening Standard*, August 26, 1899, 10.

41. *Sunday Standard Times*, August 31, 1919, 21.

42. Ann Douglas, *Feminization of American Culture*, 12, describes this as society's attempt "to deal with the phenomenon of cultural bifurcation by the manipulation of nostalgia."

43. *Encyclopedia of World Art*, s.v. "Homer, Winslow."

44. Goodrich, *Graphic Art of Winslow Homer*, 11.

45. *Dictionary of American Biography*, s.v. "Homer, Winslow."

46. Hopkins, *The Clammers*.

47. Lincoln, *Our Village*, 53–54.

48. *New England Hurricane.*
49. *Fairhaven, Massachusetts,* 55.
50. Howland, *Sou'West and By West of Cape Cod,* 124, 131–32.
51. Trillin, "A Real Nice Clambake," 78–90.
52. Ibid. The Squantum Club is also mentioned in Hale, *Narragansett Bay,* 63: "On especially picturesque promontories and rocks private clubs were constructed for the leaders in commerce and industry." Cleveland Amory, in *Last Resorts,* 249, mentions similar clubs in Newport, including the Clambake Club on Easton's Point, limited to one hundred members: "It still features the clambakes and skeet-shooting of yesteryear."
53. During the summer of 1987, my fieldwork included observing several individuals involved in clambakes-for-hire and two catering companies, D. M. Roberts Clambakes and Leighton's Clambakes, which both use rockweed for flavor.
54. Raymond Davoll, audiotape of interview, August 8, 1985.
55. See Jenkins, "As American as a New England Shore Dinner," and Levy, "Taking the Clambake to Texas." But see also Wyss, "Warren, Rhode Island"; Wyler, "The Ultimate Cookout"; Rosso and Lukins, "Summer's Last Fling"; Ferraro, "Great Summer Traditions"; "Gourmet's Menus: Labor Day Clambake"; and, most recently, Liberman, "Clambake Custom Claims More Converts."

## Section Two. The Allen's Neck Bake

1. Yoder, "Folk Cookery," p. 338.

*4. A Portrait of Allen's Neck*

1. Comiskey, *Secrets of Old Dartmouth,* 30–31; Sullivan, *History of Allen's Neck Friends Meeting,* 1–2. Dartmouth was deeded in 1652. For more on the native inhabitants and their "tribal" names and confederacies, see, for example, Travers, *Wampanoag Indian Federation;* Speck, *Territorial Subdivisions and Boundaries of the Wampanoag, Massachusett and Nauset Indians* (New York: Museum of the Indian Heye Foundation, 1928); and Weinstein-Farson, *The Wampanoag.*
2. Russell, *History of Quakerism,* 41–43. Between 1657 and 1660, four Quakers were hanged on Boston Common. On early treatment of Quakers by Puritans, see Matthews, "The Term Pilgrim Fathers," 382–83. Comiskey, in *Secrets of Old Dartmouth,* 35–36, says that the Quakers arrived in Dartmouth in 1657; during an early interview, Florence Smith read to me a section from the book *The Howland Heirs*—compiled after the death of multi-millionare financier Hetty Green as part of the settlement of the Howland family estate—concerning her Quaker relative Zoeth Howland (eleven generations removed), who was thrown out of Marshfield in Plymouth Colony for making a statement that "the devil could teach as good a sermon as the [Puritan] ministers."
3. Anderson, "Racial and Class Boundaries," 37. Anderson also cites Robert Park's use of another term from biological ecology, "natural area," which relates competition and cooperation within a territory, but "ecosystem" seems the better word here, because its stress is on the community and its physical environment.
4. Ernie Waite, audiotape of interview, August 25, 1986.
5. Elden Mills, audiotape of interview, August 7, 1986.
6. See Boss and Thomas, *New Bedford,* 20–21, on older Quaker gatherings. For more on the

development of the regional meetings, see Sullivan, *History of Allen's Neck Friends Meeting*, 3–12.

7. On this split within Quakerism, see Russell, *History of Quakerism*, 280–329; Bronner, *American Quakers Today*, 14–20; and Grubb, *Separations*. See Pease, *Life in New Bedford a Hundred Years Ago* for the disruption within local Quakerism during the early part of the 1800s, which was ushered in by the "New Lights," those in sympathy with the revivalist movement.

   For Elden Mills, raised at the turn of the century in Indiana, stronghold of the Gurneyites, the term Hicksite has a powerful effect: "Well, I hope that the word Hicksite is not used anymore. Of course, I know what you mean. But it had a bitter flavor in my youth. The Hicksites were 'of the devil'—they didn't believe in Christ, they were—Unitarian—or worse." He proceeded to tell me of the cemetery of his Meeting, divided by a driveway, along one side of which the Gurneyites were buried, and along the other, the Hicksites. He continued, "There was a period—and I grew up in it—when Quakers were so unquakerly as to make doctrine central—it never was [meant to be]—George Fox was very outspoken about this. But I remember my mother saying, 'The Hicksites are not of us . . . they were unsound.'" Elden Mills, audiotape of interview, August 7, 1986.

8. There is general agreement about the background influences for the separation—a growing democratic spirit, new rationalistic tendencies, divisions between city and country culture, and effects of the evangelical movement. See Grubb, *Separations*, 5–15, and Russell, *History of Quakerism*, 280–300. On the history of the New England Yearly Meeting, and the split between the Wilburites and the Gurneyites, see Grubb, *Separations*, 84; for further details on the split, see Russell, *History of Quakerism*, 352.

9. Russell, *History of Quakerism*, 427.

10. Burney Gifford, audiotape of interview, July 30, 1985.

11. Elden Mills, letter to author, April 22, 1986.

12. Elden Mills, audiotape of interview, August 7, 1986.

13. Ginny Morrison, audiotape of interview, August 6, 1985.

14. Florence Smith, audiotape of interview, July 25, 1985.

15. Barbara Erickson and Gordon Parsons, audiotape of interview, July 25, 1985.

16. Where the landscape used to be covered with chicken coops of various sizes, today only Allen Gifford still raises chickens for a specialty, ethnic market, and even his business has been greatly curtailed by the outbreak of avian influenza on the farm in 1986, which forced him to destroy all of his birds.

17. Mary Davoll, audiotape of interview, July 26, 1985.

18. Allen Gifford, audiotape of interview, August 12, 1985.

19. Muriel Silvia, audiotape of interview, July 20, 1985.

20. Cathi Rebello, audiotape of interview, August 12, 1985.

21. Mills, *Between Thee and Me*, 122.

22. Muriel Silvia, audiotape of interview, July 20, 1985.

23. Burney Gifford, audiotape of interview, August 5, 1985.

24. Garboden, "Parsimony."

25. For the history of one particular local summer community, see Lyell, *Nonquitt, A Summer Album, 1872–1985*; similar stories could be told about any number of other summer communities in the immediate area, including those of Westport Point and Westport Harbor. In addition, the archives of the New Bedford Whaling Museum contains a variety of materials on the summer colonies.

26. Julie Brown and Burney Gifford, audiotape of interview, August 5, 1985.

27. Mary Davoll, audiotape of interview, July 26, 1985.
28. Allen Gifford, audiotape of interview, August 12, 1985.
29. Willy Morrison, audiotape of interview, August 6, 1985.

### 5. One Hundred Years of Clambaking

1. *Allen's Neck Friends Cookbook,* first page. Note that in the advertisement, the 24th was not the *third* Thursday of the month but rather the fourth.
2. Elsie Gifford, audiotape of interview, August 12, 1985.
3. Mills, "Fiftieth Clambake"; note, again, that the 1889 clambake was held in the fourth, not the third, week in August.
4. Florence Smith, audiotape of interview, July 25, 1985.
5. Clambake day tape, August 15, 1985.
6. Norma Judson, audiotape of interview, August 13, 1985.
7. Imelda Waite, audiotape of interview, August 25, 1986.
8. Willy Morrison, audiotape of interview, August 6, 1985.
9. Ila Gifford, audiotape of interview, July 17, 1985.
10. Elden Mills, audiotape of interview, August 7, 1986.
11. Florence Smith, audiotape of interview, July 25, 1985.
12. Norma Judson, audiotape of interview, August 13, 1985.
13. Mills, "Fiftieth Clambake."
14. Dorothy Gifford, audiotape of clambake day interview, August 21, 1986.
15. Willy Morrison, audiotape of interview, August 6, 1985.
16. Ila Gonet, audiotape of interview, July 17, 1985.
17. Willy Morrison, audiotape of interview, August 6, 1985.
18. Ernie Waite, audiotape of interview, August 25, 1986.
19. J. T. Smith, *Turtle Rock Tales,* 16.
20. Willy Morrison, audiotape of interview, August 6, 1985.
21. Ibid.
22. Ibid.
23. Barbara Erickson, audiotape of interview, July 25, 1985.
24. Peter Gonet, audiotape of interview, August 5, 1985. "Some people do it in a pit," says Peter. "It doesn't matter one way or another." Willy Morrison and Raymond Davoll concur.
25. Morrow, *New England Cook Book,* 1.
26. Jones, *American Food,* 15–16, quoting "a white-haired clambake patriarch."
27. Willy Morrison, audiotape of interview, August 6, 1985.
28. Hettie Tripp, audiotape of interview, August 17, 1987.
29. Leona and John Ashton, audiotape of interview, August 19, 1986.
30. Willy Morrison, audiotape of interview, August 6, 1985.
31. Nanepashemet, audiotape of interview, June 18, 1987.
32. Dave Ramos, interview, July 29, 1987.
33. Willy Morrison, audiotape of interview, August 6, 1985.
34. Ernie Waite, audiotape of interview, August 25, 1986.
35. Cathi Rebello, reporting on the clambakes-in-drum that an older member of the community told her about; audiotape of interview, August 12, 1985.
36. Mary Davoll, audiotape of interview, July 26, 1985.
37. Raymond Davoll, audiotape of interview, August 8, 1985.

1. Burney Gifford, audiotape of interview, July 30, 1985.
2. Ibid.
3. Raymond Davoll, audiotape of interview, August 8, 1985.
4. Ibid.
5. Burney Gifford, audiotape of interview, July 30, 1985.
6. Raymond Davoll, audiotape of interview, August 8, 1985.
7. Ralph Macomber, audiotape of clambake day interview, August 15, 1985.
8. Willy Morrison, audiotape of interview, August 6, 1985.
9. Ralph Macomber, audiotape of interview, August 8, 1987.
10. Peter Gonet, audiotape of interview, August 5, 1985.
11. Gordon Parsons, audiotape of interview, July 25, 1985.
12. Willy Morrison, audiotape of interview, August 6, 1985.
13. Peter Gonet, audiotape of interview, August 5, 1985.
14. Ernie Waite, audiotape of interview, August 25, 1986.
15. Ginny Morrison, audiotape of interview, August 6, 1985.
16. Willy Morrison, audiotape of interview, August 6, 1985.
17. Raymond Davoll, audiotape of interview, August 8, 1985.
18. Burney Gifford, audiotape of interview, July 30, 1985.
19. Ibid.
20. Willy Morrison, audiotape of interview, August 6, 1985.
21. Willy and Ginny Morrison, audiotape of interview, August 6, 1985.
22. Raymond Davoll, audiotape of interview, August 8, 1985.
23. Ernie Waite, audiotape of interview, August 25, 1986.
24. Gordon Parsons, audiotape of interview, July 25, 1985.
25. Burney Gifford, audiotape of interview, July 30, 1985.
26. Clambake day tape, August 15, 1985.
27. Elden Mills, audiotape of interview, August 7, 1986.
28. Ila Gonet, audiotape of interview, July 17, 1985.
29. Willy Morrison, audiotape of interview, August 6, 1985.
30. Ila Gonet, audiotape of interview, July 17, 1985.
31. Ibid.
32. Ibid.
33. Billy Gifford, audiotape of interview, August 19, 1986.
34. Ibid.
35. Ila Gonet, audiotape of interview, July 17, 1985.
36. Raymond Davoll, audiotape of interview, August 8, 1985.
37. Peter Gonet, audiotape of interview, August 15, 1985.
38. Gordon Parsons, audiotape of interview, July 25, 1985.
39. Ila Gonet, audiotape of interview, July 17, 1985.
40. Ibid.
41. Florence Smith, audiotape of interview, July 25, 1985.
42. Gordon Parsons, audiotape of interview, July 25, 1985.
43. Muriel Silvia, audiotape of interview, July 20, 1985.
44. Ibid.
45. Gordon Parsons, audiotape of interview, July 25, 1985.
46. Ila Gonet, audiotape of interview, July 17, 1985.

47. Willy Morrison, audiotape of interview, August 6, 1985.
48. Clambake day tape, August 15, 1985.
49. Mary Davoll, audiotape of interview, July 26, 1985.
50. Ernie Waite, audiotape of interview, August 25, 1986.
51. Marjorie Macomber, audiotape of interview, August 19, 1987.
52. Mary Davoll, audiotape of interview, July 26, 1985.
53. Marjorie Macomber, audiotape of interview, August 19, 1987.
54. Ibid.
55. Billy Gifford, audiotape of interview, August 19, 1986.
56. Muriel Silvia, audiotape of interview, July 20, 1985.
57. Mary Davoll, audiotape of interview, July 26, 1985.
58. Marjorie Macomber, audiotape of interview, August 19, 1987.
59. Elsie Gifford, audiotape of interview, August 12, 1985.
60. Hettie Tripp, audiotape of interview, August 17, 1987.
61. Billy Gifford, audiotape of interview, August 19, 1986.
62. Mary Davoll, audiotape of interview, July 26, 1985.

## Section Three. Clambakes and Meaning

1. See Turner, *Ritual Process,* 106, for a similar listing of binary oppositions.
2. See my article, "The Folkloristics of Licking," in a forthcoming *Journal of American Folklore.* I have been particularly inspired and fortified on this intellectual journey by James Clifford's *Predicament of Culture* and Paul Stoller's *Taste of Ethnographic Things.*

### 7. Food, Ritual, and Festivity

1. Goody, *Cooking, Cuisine and Class,* 10.
2. Richards, *Hunger and Work in a Savage Tribe,* as quoted in Jones, "Perspectives in the Study of Eating Behaviour," 260, and in Goody, *Cooking, Cuisine and Class,* 15. Richards's mentor, Bronislaw Malinowski, had previously posited sex as the main motivating factor behind the structuring of culture.
3. Mary Douglas, "Deciphering a Meal," in *Implicit Meanings,* 249, 260.
4. Ibid., 257.
5. Ibid., 259.
6. Goody, *Cooking, Cuisine and Class,* 32, 37. As Goody points out (32), "For while we accept the need to search for meaningful relations, the problem lies in evaluating what we find. In the end the interlocking nature of these relations must be a matter for empirical validation within a framework of theoretical assumption. The danger of functional and structural analysis lies in unchecked and uncheckable speculation. The burden of proof always rests with the proposer, and the 'fit' must be demonstrated, or at any rate supported, rather than simply assumed. Otherwise, the intellectual enterprise becomes a matter of mere assertion."
7. Mary Douglas, "Deciphering a Meal," in *Implicit Meanings,* 257.
8. Lévi-Strauss, "The Culinary Triangle," 587.
9. Ibid., 595.
10. Mary Douglas, "Deciphering a Meal," in *Implicit Meanings,* 250. Douglas's critique of Lévi-Strauss is particularly interesting in light of Goody's estimation of their common shortcomings.

11. Goody, *Cooking, Cuisine and Class*, 18.
12. Lévi-Strauss, "The Culinary Triangle," 593.
13. Ibid., 589, 590.
14. Ibid., 595.
15. Lévi-Strauss is particularly taken by utensils—that is, cultural objects—which are destroyed in the process of being used. See his discussion of the *buccan*, the wooden frame used by American Indians for smoking meat. Ibid., 592.
16. Elden Mills, audiotape of interview, August 7, 1986.
17. Goody, *Cooking, Cuisine and Class*, 25.
18. It has been noted (Dominguez, "The Marketing of Heritage," 362) that ethnological research entails three major paradoxes, "that intending to depict other cultures it is seeking to complete a depiction of our own, that it rests on a strong historical consciousness but concentrates its work on people perceived to be without history . . . and that it continually depicts 'man' as subject—objectifier, creator, producer—but transforms him into an object and vehicle of knowledge." Each of these points has been leveled as specific criticism of Lévi-Strauss's brand of anthropology, and together they constitute the central themes of my own disaffection.
19. Barber, "Yoruba *Oriki* and Deconstructive Criticism," 514.
20. Turner, *Ritual Process*, vii; this introduction was written eight years after the original publication in 1969, and there had been lots of discussion in between. Turner proposed a definition of social structure and set up abstract systems models on 125–26.
21. Turner, "Liminal to Liminoid," 57.
22. Allen Gifford, audiotape of interview, August 12, 1985. "There's always been a few people from New Bedford that came out to the clambake, you know, acquaintances of the people here . . . storekeepers, guys that ran stables . . . or if he had a summer cottage at Salter's Point or Nonquitt, or something like that."
23. Turner, "Liminal to Liminoid," 58–59; for Turner's debt to Huizinga's and Caillois's theories on play, see Turner, "Carnival, Ritual, and Play in Rio," in Falassi, *Time Out of Time*, 77–80.
24. Turner, "Liminal to Liminoid," 62.
25. Turner, *Ritual Process*, vii.
26. Dumazedier as quoted in Turner, "Liminal to Liminoid," 67, with comments by Turner; Dumazedier's article on "Leisure" is in *International Encyclopedia of the Social Sciences*, 248–54.
27. Nadel from *Nupe Religion* (1954), as cited by Moore and Myerhoff, *Secular Ritual*, 8.
28. Moore and Myerhoff, *Secular Ritual*, 4.
29. Ibid., 7.
30. Ibid., 10–11.
31. Ibid., 24: "Ceremony can make it appear that there is no conflict, only harmony, no disorder, only order, that if danger threatens, safe solutions are at hand." I would suggest that there are different ways of communicating what isn't assured: "made-upness" (24), which is how Moore and Myerhoff refer to the "invention of tradition"—as when Disney performs a bake or a Squantum is held—is one; asserting symbolically that your culture will continue in the face of sociological change is another.
32. Ibid., 19–23.
33. Falassi, "Festival: Definition and Morphology," in Falassi, *Time Out of Time*, 3–6. This characterization of rituals as "things," as units with universal form but individualized contents is "analogous to what Vladimir Propp did for the constituent parts of the folktale,

[and] may aim at an archetype accounting for all festivals, or more accurately, at 'oicotypes' [here invoking the work of folklorist von Sydow] accounting for a class of festivals of the same kind or from the same cultural area."

34. Falassi, *Time Out of Time,* 3, 6, 4.
35. Ibid., 2–3.
36. Babcock, *Reversible World,* 27, 29.
37. Babcock introduces her study of negation as a topic largely unattended to by scholars, "rarely examined" and "ignored" partly because, she asserts, negativity is "potentially dangerous." *Reversible World,* 14.
38. Manning, *Celebration of Society,* viii, x.
39. Ibid., 25: the terms come from Handelman.
40. Ibid., 27.
41. Ibid., 23, 25.
42. If Manning is too negatively disposed toward Protestantism, Josef Pieper's Protestant apologetic, *In Tune with the World,* is almost a caricature of the Protestant Ethic. For example, Pieper describes the "soil in which festivity flourishes" as being "meaningful work" (4–5), in which a holiday represents a sacrifice, a "yield of labor"; he continues, "The only legitimate reason for a day free from work" is the worship of god and assent to the world" (23, 24). Richard Bauman's work, "The Place of Festivity in the Worldview of the Seventeenth-Century Quakers," in Falassi, ed., *Time Out of Time,* would be extremely useful if updated to the twentieth century.
43. Bynum, "Women's Stories, Women's Symbols," 105, 108, 109.
44. Ibid., 109.
45. Ibid., 117, 112.
46. Ibid., 119; see also Bynum, *Holy Feast and Holy Fast,* 289.
47. Abrahams, "An American Vocabulary of Celebrations," in Falassi, *Time Out of Time,* 177.
48. Falassi, "Festival: Definition and Morphology," in Falassi, *Time Out of Time,* 3.
49. Even Babcock's notion of the "negation of a negative" as the basis of the "aesthetic negative" (*Reversible Worlds,* 19) is of a different order, since obversion is actually the double negation of a positive.
50. Turner, "Carnival, Ritual, and Play," in Falassi, *Time Out of Time,* 87.
51. Bynum, "Women's Stories, Women's Symbols," 109.
52. Bynum is a good example of this trend; see also Evelyn Fox Keller on the history of science, the works of Carroll Smith-Rosenberg in history, and Elaine Scarry on literary expression and the body.
53. Stoller, *Taste of Ethnographic Things,* 32.

## 8. Concluding Thoughts

1. Lewis Cole, audiotape of rockweeding interview, August 19, 1987.
2. Norma Judson, audiotape of interview, August 13, 1985.
3. For a more rigorous discussion of "tradition," see Neustadt, "For Want of a Nail," 324–40.
4. Hettie Tripp, audiotape of interview, August 17, 1987.
5. See, for example, Handler, "Authenticity," 2–4; "On Sociocultural Discontinuity," 55–71; and *Nationalism and the Politics of Culture;* and, with Linnekin, "Tradition, Genuine and Spurious," 273–90.
6. Bynum, "Women's Stories, Women's Symbols," 119; on the concepts of "ordinary experience" and "ordinary lives," see 117.

7. Yoder, "Folk Cookery," 338.

8. Bendix, "Tourism and Cultural Displays," 133.

9. Much of the analysis presented here has its origins in my chapter, "'Born Among the Shells,'" in Humphrey and Humphrey, *"We Gather Together"*; passages are presented here without quotation marks.

10. Raymond Davoll, audiotape of interview, August 8, 1985; Peter Gonet, audiotape of interview, August 5, 1985.

11. Ginny Morrison, audiotape of interview, August 6, 1985; this process of selecting a bakemaster was also attested to by the retiring bakemaster at Smith Neck; Smith Neck clambake tape, August 8, 1987.

12. Turner, "Liminal to Liminoid," 57.

13. Jewett, *Country of the Pointed Firs*, 109–10.

14. Florence Smith, audiotape of interview, July 25, 1985.

15. Turner, "Liminal to Liminoid," 64.

16. Julie Brown, audiotape of interview, August 5, 1985.

17. Elsie Gifford, audiotape of interview, August 12, 1985.

18. Mary Davoll, audiotape of interview, July 26, 1985.

19. Hettie Tripp, audiotape of interview, August 17, 1987.

20. Burney Gifford, audiotape of interview, August 5, 1985.

21. Pieper, *In Tune With the World*, 14, 20.

22. Julie Brown, audiotape of interview, August 5, 1985.

23. Florence Smith, audiotape of interview, July 25, 1985.

24. Barbara Erickson, audiotape of interview, July 25, 1985.

25. Burney Gifford, audiotape of interview, August 5, 1985.

26. Norma Judson, audiotape of interview, August 13, 1985.

27. Peter Gonet, audiotape of interview, August 5, 1985.

28. Priscilla Davoll, audiotape of interview, August 14, 1987.

29. Norma Judson, audiotape of interview, August 13, 1985.

30. Ibid.

31. Lewis Cole, audiotape of sermon, August 25, 1986.

32. Karl Erickson, audiotape of interview, July 25, 1985.

33. Florence Smith, audiotape of interview, July 25, 1985.

34. Jean Parsons and Karl Erickson, audiotape of interview, July 25, 1985.

35. Jean and Gordon Parsons, audiotape of interview, July 25, 1985.

36. "Gram" Gifford, audiotape of interview, August 12, 1985; Elsie Gifford, taped interview, August 12, 1985; Elden Mills, *Between Thee and Me*, 113–16; Florence Smith, audiotape of interview, July 25, 1985.

37. Florence Smith, audiotape of interview, July 25, 1985.

38. Raymond Davoll, audiotape of interview, August 8, 1985.

39. Stoller, *Taste of Ethnographic Things*, 40.

40. Bynum, *Holy Feast and Holy Fast*, 289.

41. My favorite insight on this point comes in the form of a grilling of the local anthropologist by a "Native" native informant: "Well, how old does something have to be before it's our own tradition instead of 'borrowed'? We've had the Catholic way for a long time, isn't it our way by now? If it weren't for books, would we really remember all the things that were 'ours' or 'theirs'? What if we borrowed some dance from Hopi—a long time ago, before the whites came? Would it be 'ours' because *you* didn't know and we didn't think about it?" See M. Estellie Smith, "The Process of Sociocultural Continuity," 131.

42. Stoller, *Taste of Ethnographic Things*, 5.
43. Ibid., 6.
44. The discoveries being made by scientists in the new field of chaos studies point excitingly in similar directions. In Edward Lorenz's graphic depiction of weather patterns (Gleick, *Chaos*, 30)—which, like human beings, are aperiodic and unpredictable—the resulting now-famous "Butterfly Effect" is the depiction of "a kind of infinite complexity. It always stayed within certain bounds, never running off the page but never repeating itself, either. . . . The shape signaled pure disorder, since no point or pattern of points ever recurred. Yet it is also signaled a new kind of order." Scholars in the social sciences and humanities are clearly beginning to deal more creatively with the ramifications of human chaos and complexity, and in the fields of anthropology and folklore, where the relevance to the study of human systems of order seems particularly obvious, the enlightenment is already dawning.

While the innocent enthusiasm or the unmitigated hubris of thinking that we would eventually find the universal laws of human existence have, seemingly, been dashed forever in a postmodern world, the thought that the chaos of our experience, throughout history and the planet, might yet have order should provide a certain amount of salve to our anxieties. We need to recognize, as students of humanity and human participants in life, that each of us is involved in our own patterns—personal, cultural, sociological—and that the infinite ways in which people, cultures, and societies come in contact with each other constitute a form of "sensitive dependence on initial conditions" which necessarily changes those patterns forever. If we can give up the need for predictability and certainty—which means, I hope, letting go of our desire to control, intervene, and legislate the lives of others because we "know" best or most—then we can, perhaps, learn better to enjoy, respect, and marvel at the patterns which have been etched and continue to be etched all around us.

If this study of the Allen's Neck Clambake in any way has suggested the need for and the value of moving away from a position of objectifying culture to a more radical subjectivity, from a perspective of symmetrical simplicity to greater complexity, from the purely intellectual stance to one that integrates the body, or from tidy models and self-involved theories toward an ordered sense of chaos, then I have done as much as I could have ever hoped for. But now, as Raymond—the master clambaker of them all—would say, I've "already said [way] too much."

# References

*They sought it with thimbles, they sought it with care;*
*They pursued it with forks and with hope;*
*They threatened its life with a railway-share;*
*They charmed it with smiles and soap.*
—Lewis Carroll, "The Hunting of the Snark" (1876)

On the issue of sources, it should be apparent that I have conceived the "literature" of this work broadly and eclectically. It ranges from archaeological studies to ritual studies, from history books to cookbooks, from "classical" and "experimental" theoretical discussions to oral testimonies, old newspaper ads, travelogues and tour guides, diaries, recent features articles, and "local color" literary renderings. From "the realm of sensual sentiment," as Stoller has termed it in *The Taste of Ethnographic Things* (4), I have also sought and found answers in the auditory, gustatory, visual, tactile, and olfactory experiences of the clambake, and were the technology for it adequately developed, I would gladly include a "scratch and sniff" component to this listing of references.

Although many of these sources are not standard fare in scholarly research, they have increasingly achieved legitimacy within the context of constructing social history, and within folklore studies, at least, objects, performances, and personal "opinions" have been considered valid sources for knowledge for some time. Semiotic studies and communications theories, which look at the ways symbols are constructed and manipulated, have also recognized the importance of looking at the "images" that accumulate and surround a topic or idea, and I have tried to provide at least a sampling of the rich and varied graphic representations of clambaking.

From my perspective, these "documents"—the scholarly works, popular media, oral testimonies, visual representations, material culture, and sensory perceptions—have proved to be of equal value, and as much as possible, I have attempted to set aside the hierarchic divisions usually applied to them and forego privileging, say, an *older* source *written* by a *scholar* over a *recent* explanation given by a *local* resident in an *interview*. The purpose of drawing on both has been to provide the broadest possible representation, and in the context of understanding meaning as well as history—the interpretation as well as "facts" that surround the clambake—I have found relatively few "wrong" answers or "bad" sources. Often the least verifiable historical information has offered the greater potential for uncovering the "facts" of interpretation; in other cases, what is most likely to be "true" is least capable of being proven.

## Books, Journal and Magazine Articles, and Unpublished Papers

Adams, W. E. *Our American Cousins: Being Personal Impressions of the People and Institutions of the United States.* London: Walter Scott, 1883.

*Allen's Neck Friends Cookbook.* Introduction by Marjorie Macomber and Aunt Gladys (Gifford). Acushnet, Mass.: Graphic Stationery/Associated Services, n.d. [about 1983].

*American Dictionary of Americanisms on Historical Principles.* Edited by Mitford M. Matthews. Chicago: University of Chicago Press, 1951.

*An American Glossary.* Edited by Richard H. Thornton. New York: Frederick Ungar Publishing Company, 1962.

*Americanisms; The English of the New World.* Edited by M. Schele de Vere. New York: Charles Scribner and Co., 1872.

Amory, Cleveland. *The Last Resorts.* New York: Harper and Brothers, 1952.

Anderson, Elijah. "Race and Class Boundaries." *Society* 21, 1 (1983):35–40.

Anderson, Jay Allan. "Thanksgiving in the U.S.A.—The Meal as Medium and Message." In *Ethnological Food Research: Report from the Second International Symposium,* 9–13. Helsinki: August 1973.

Anderson, Thomas F. "'Old-Home Week' in New England." *New England Magazine* 34 (March–August 1906):673–85.

*Appleton's Illustrated Handbook of American Travel.* Edited by T. Addison Richards. New York: D. Appleton and Co., 1860.

Arnott, Margaret Louise. "Thanksgiving Dinner: A Study in Cultural Heritage." In *Ethnological Food Research: Report from the Second International Symposium,* 15–26. Helsinki: August 1973.

Axtell, James. "Through a Glass Darkly: Colonial Attitudes toward the Native Americans." *Essays from Sarah Lawrence Faculty* 2, 1 (October 1973).

Babcock, Barbara. *The Reversible World: Symbolic Inversion in Art and Society.* Ithaca: Cornell University Press, 1978.

Barber, Karin. "Yoruba *Oriki* and Deconstructive Criticism." *Research in African Literatures* 15, 4 (1984):497–518.

Barrett, Richmond. *Good Old Summer Days: Newport, Narraganset Pier, Saratoga, Long Branch, Bar Harbor.* New York: D. Appleton-Century Co., 1941.

Bendix, Regina. "Tourism and Cultural Displays: Inventing Traditions for Whom?" *Journal of American Folklore* 102, 404 (1989):131–46.

Benes, Peter, ed. *New England Meeting House and Church: 1630–1850.* Vol. 4, Dublin Seminar for New England Folklife. Boston: Boston University, 1979.

Benes, Peter, ed. *Foodways in the Northeast.* Vol. 7, Dublin Seminar for New England Folklife. Boston: Boston University, 1982.

Booth, Sally Smith. *Hung, Strung, and Potted: A History of Eating in Colonial America.* New York: Clarkson N. Potter, Inc., 1971.

Boss, Judith A., and Joseph D. Thomas. *New Bedford: A Pictorial History.* Norfolk, Va.: The Donning Company Publishers, 1983.

Bowles, Ella Shannon, and Dorothy S. Towle. *Secrets of New England Cooking.* New York: M. Barrows and Company, Inc., 1947.

Bronner, Edwin B., ed. *American Quakers Today.* Philadelphia: Friends World Committee, American Section and Fellowship Council, 1966.

Brown, Linda Keller, and Kay Mussell, eds. *Ethnic and Regional Foodways in the United States: The Performance of Group Identity.* Knoxville: The University of Tennessee Press, 1984.

Bynum, Caroline Walker. *Holy Feast and Holy Fast: The Religious Significance of Food to Medieval Women.* Berkeley: University of California Press, 1987.

Bynum, Caroline Walker. "Women's Stories, Women's Symbols: A Critique of Victor Turner's Theory of Liminality." In *Anthropology and the Study of Religion,* edited by Frank Reynolds and Robert Moore. Chicago: Center for the Scientific Study of Religion, 1984.

Camp, Charles. *American Foodways: What, When, Why and How We Eat in America.* Little Rock, Ark.: August House, 1989.

*The Centennial Cruise.* By One of the Guests. New York: Sheldon and Co., 1876.

Chidester, Lawrence W. *New England's Recreational Appeals.* N.p.: Cooperatively published by The State of Maine Publicity Bureau, The State of Vermont Publicity Department, The New Hampshire State Board of Publicity, and The Recreational Development Committee of New England Council, 1930.

Clifford, James. *The Predicament of Culture: Twentieth Century Ethnography, Literature, and Art.* Cambridge, Mass.: Harvard University Press, 1988.

Comfort, William Wistar. *The Quaker Persuasion: Yesterday, Today, Tomorrow; A handbook for Friends and Friends of Friends.* Philadelphia: Frederick H. Gloeckner, 1956.

Comiskey, Kathleen Ryan. *The Secrets of Old Dartmouth.* New Bedford, Mass.: Reynolds-De Walt Printing, Inc., 1976.

*A Concise Dictionary of Indian Tribes in North America.* Edited by Barbara E. Leitch. Algonac, Mich.: Reference Publications, Inc., 1977.

Cook, Joel. *America: Picturesque and Descriptive.* Philadelphia: Henry T. Coates and Co., 1900.

Cox, Ian, ed. *The Scallop: Studies of a Shell and Its Influence on Humankind, by Eight Authors.* London: "Shell" Transport and Trading Co., 1957.

Cummings, Richard Osborn. *The American and His Food: A History of Food Habits in the United States.* Chicago: University of Chicago Press, 1940.

Cunningham, John. *The Quakers from Their Origins Till the Present Time: An International History.* London: Hamilton, Adams & Co., 1868.

Davidson, Alan. *North Atlantic Seafood.* New York: The Viking Press, 1979.

Dexter, Franklin Bowditch, ed. *Extracts from the Itineraries and Other Miscellanies of Ezra Stiles.* New Haven: Yale University Press, 1916.

*Dictionary of Americanisms: A Glossary of Words and Phrases.* Edited by John Russell Bartlett. New York: Bartlett and Welford, 1848 (and 1859, 1877, and 1889 eds.).

*Dictionary of Folklore, Mythology and Legend.* Edited by Maria Leach. New York: Funk and Wagnalls, 1949.

*Dictionary of Indian Tribes of the Americas.* Newport Beach, Cal.: American Indian Publishers, Inc., 1980.

*A Dictionary of Modern American Usage.* Edited by H. W. Horwill. Oxford: Clarendon Press, 1935.

*Dictionary of Mythology, Folklore and Symbols.* Edited by Gertrude Jobes. New York: Scarecrow Press, 1961.

*A Dictionary of Slang, Jargon and Cant.* Edited by Albert Barrière and Charles G. Leland. New York: Ballantyne Press, 1890.

Doherty, Robert M. *The Hicksite Separation: A Sociological Analysis of Religious Schism in Early 19th Century America.* New Brunswick, N.J.: Rutgers University Press, 1967.

Dominguez, Virginia R. "The Marketing of Heritage." In *American Ethnologist* 13 (August 1986):546–55.

Douglas, Ann. *The Feminization of American Culture.* New York: Avon Books, 1978.

Douglas, Mary. *Implicit Meanings: Essays in Anthropology.* Boston: Routledge and Kegan Paul, 1975.

Douglas, Mary, ed. *Food in the Social Order: Studies of Food and Festivities in Three American Communities.* New York: The Russell Sage Foundation, 1984.

Dulles, Foster Rhea. *A History of Recreation: America Learns to Play.* 2d ed. New York: Appleton-Century-Crofts, 1965.

Dumazedier, Joffré. "Leisure." In *Encyclopedia of the Social Sciences,* edited by David Sills, 248–54. New York: Macmillan and Free Press, 1968.

Dumazedier, Joffré. *Sociology of Leisure.* Translated by Marea A. McKenzie. New York: Elsevier, 1974.

Earle, Alice Morse. *Customs and Fashions in Old New England.* 1893. Reprint. Rutland, Vt.: Charles E. Tuttle Co., 1985.

Eisenstadt, S. N. *Tradition, Change, and Modernity.* New York: Wiley, 1973.

*Fairhaven, Massachusetts.* Written and compiled by members of the Federal Writers Project of Massachusetts, 1939.

Falassi, Alesandro, ed. *Time Out of Time: Essays on the Festival.* Albuquerque: University of New Mexico Press, 1987.

*First Impressions of the New World on Two Travellers from the Old in the Autumn of 1858.* London: Longman, Brown, Green, Longmans, and Roberts, 1859.

Fussell, Betty. *I Hear America Cooking.* New York: Elisabeth Sifton Books, Viking, 1986.

Garboden, Clif. "Parsimony." *Boston Globe Magazine,* November 18, 1990.

Geertz, Clifford. "Blurred Genres." *American Scholar* 49 (1980):165–79.

Gifford, Gladys B. *History of Old Dartmouth from 1602 to 1676.* Unpublished typescript, n.d.

Glazier, Willard. *Peculiarities of American Cities.* Philadelphia: Hubbard Brothers, 1886.

Gleick, James. *Chaos: Making a New Science.* New York: Penguin Books, 1987.

Goodrich, Lloyd. *The Graphic Art of Winslow Homer.* Washington: Smithsonian Institution Press, 1969.

Goody, Jack. *Cooking, Cuisine and Class: A Study in Comparative Sociology.* New York: Cambridge University Press, 1982.

"Gourmet's Menus: Labor Day Clambake." *Gourmet,* September 1989, 134–42.

Green Harvey. *Fit for America: Health, Fitness, Sport, and American Society.* New York: Pantheon Books, 1986.

Green, Harvey. "Popular Science and Political Thought Converge: Colonial Survival Becomes Colonial Revival, 1830–1910." *Journal of American Culture* 6, 4 (1983):3–24.

Green, Rayna. "The Tribe Called Wannabee: Playing Indian in America and Europe." *Folklore* 99, 1 (1988):30–55.

Grieve, Robert. *Picturesque Narragansett, An Illustrated Guide to the Cities, Towns, and Famous Resorts of Rhode Island.* 3d ed. Providence, R.I.: J. A. and R. A. Reid, n.d. [1888].

Griffin, Al. *"Step Right Up, Folks!"* Chicago: Henry Regnery Co., 1974.

Grimes, Ronald. *Beginnings in Ritual Studies.* Washington, D.C.: University Press of America, 1982.

Grimes, Ronald. *Research in Ritual Studies: A Programmatic Essay and Bibliography.* No. 14, ATLA Bibliography Series. Metuchen, N.J.: The American Theological Library Association and the Scarecrow Press, Inc., 1985.

Grubb, Edward. *Separations, Their Causes and Effects: Studies in Nineteenth Century Quakerism.* London: Headley Brothers, 1914.

Hale, Stuart O. *Narragansett Bay: A Friend's Perspective.* Narragansett, R.I.: University of Rhode Island, Marine Advisory Service, n.d. [about 1985].

*Handbook of American Indians North of Mexico.* Edited by Frederick Webb Hodge. Smithsonian Institution Bureau of American Ethnology, Bulletin 30. Washington, D.C.: Government Printing Office, 1910.

*Handbook of North American Indians.* Vol. 15, edited by Bruce G. Trigger. Washington, D.C.: Smithsonian Institution, 1978.

Handler, Richard. "Authenticity." *Anthropology Today* 2, 1 (1986):2–4.

Handler, Richard. *Nationalism and The Politics of Culture in Quebec.* Madison: University of Wisconsin Press, 1988.

Handler, Richard. "On Sociocultural Discontinuity: Nationalism and Cultural Objectification in Quebec." *Current Anthropology* 25, 1 (1984): 55–71.

Handler, Richard. Review of *The Invention of Tradition,* by Eric Hobsbawm and Terence Ranger, eds. *American Anthropologist* 86 (December 1984):1025–26.

Handler, Richard, and Jocelyn Linnekin. "Tradition, Genuine or Spurious." *Journal of American Folklore* 97, 385 (1984):273–90.

Handy, Amy L. *What We Cook on Cape Cod.* Barnstable, Mass.: Barnstable Village Improvement Society, 1916.

Hart, Joseph C. *Miriam Coffin; or, The Whale-Fishermen.* 1834. Reprint. New York: Garrett Press, Inc., 1969.

Hartt, Rollin Lynde. *The People at Play.* Arno Press Collection on The Leisure Class in America, advisory ed. Leon Stein. (Originally, subtitled *Excursions in the Humor and Philosophy of Popular Amusements.* New York: Houghton Mifflin and Co., 1909.) New York: Arno Press, 1975.

Heisler, W. Chris, Neil Williams Ross, and John Long. *Clambake! How to Prepare a New England Clambake—And More.* Wakefield, R.I.: Recreation Publications, n.d. [about 1985].

Hern, Mary Ellen. "Picnicking in the Northeastern United States, 1840–1900." *Winterthur Portfolio* 24, 2–3 (1989):139–52.

Higham, John. "The Reorientation of American Culture in the 1890s." In *The Origins of Modern Consciousness,* edited by John Weiss, 25–48. Detroit, Mich.: Wayne State University Press, 1965.

Hobsbawm, Eric, and Terence Ranger, eds. *The Invention of Tradition.* 1983. Reprint. New York: Cambridge University Press, 1988.

Holyoke, Mrs. Mary. *The Holyoke Diaries, 1709–1856.* Salem, Mass.: Essex Institute, 1911.

Hooker, Richard J. *Food and Drink in America: A History.* New York: The Bobbs-Merrill Company, Inc., 1981.

Hopkins, William John. *The Clammer.* Boston: Houghton, Mifflin Co., 1906.

Howe, George. *Mount Hope.* New York: The Viking Press, 1959.

Howell, Sarah. *The Seaside.* London: Cassell and Collier Macmillan Publishers Limited, 1974.

Howland, Llewellyn. *Sou'West and By West of Cape Cod.* 1947. Reprint. Dublin, N.H.: Yankee Books, 1987.

Humphrey, Linda T. "Small Group Festive Gatherings." *Journal of the Folklore Institute* 16 (1979):190–201.

Humphrey, Theodore C., and Lin T. Humphrey, eds. *"We Gather Together": Food and the Festive Performance of Community.* Ann Arbor, Mich.: UMI Research Press, 1988.

Hymes, Dell. "Folklore's Nature and the Sun's Myth." *Journal of American Folklore* 88 (1975):345–69.

Ingersoll, Ernest. "The Clam Fisheries." In *Fisheries and Fishery Industries of the United States,* edited by George Brown Goode. Vol. 2, *History of Methods of the Fisheries.* Washington, D.C.: Government Printing Office, 1887.

Jacob, Caroline N. *Builders of the Quaker Road, 1652–1952.* Chicago: Henry Regnery Co., 1953.

James, E. O. *Seasonal Feasts and Festivals.* New York: Barnes and Noble, 1963.

Jansen, William Hugh. "The Esoteric-Exoteric Factor in Folklore." In *The Study of Folklore,* edited by Alan Dundes, 43–51. Englewood Cliffs, N.J.: Prentice Hall, Inc., 1965.

Jewett, Sarah Orne. *The Country of the Pointed Firs and Other Stories.* 1896. Reprint. New York: W. W. Norton & Company, 1981.

Jones, Evan. *American Food: The Gastronomic Story, Including a Personal Treasure of More Than 500 Distinctive Regional, Traditional and Contemporary Recipes.* New York: E. P. Dutton & Company, Inc., 1975.

Jones, Michael Owen. "Perspectives in the Study of Eating Behavior." In *Folklore Studies in the Twentieth Century: Proceedings of the Centenary Conference of the Folklore Society,* edited by Venetia J. Newall, 260–65. Totowa, N.J.: Rowman and Littlefield, 1980.

Kirshenblatt-Gimblett, Barbara. "Mistaken Dichotomies." *Journal of American Folklore* 101, 400 (1988):140–55.

Kopytoff, Igor. "Knowledge and Belief in Suku Thought." *Africa* 51, 3 (1981):709–23.

Kraus, Richard. *Recreation and Leisure in Modern Society.* Englewood Cliffs, N.J.: Prentice-Hall, Inc., 1971.

Kupperman, Karen Ordahl. *Setting with the Indians: The Meeting of English and Indian Cultures in America, 1580–1640.* Totowa, N.J.: Rowman and Littlefield, 1980.

Langone, Jan. "From the Kitchen: There Were Always Oysters." *The American Magazine* 4 (1988):34–43.

Leach, Douglas Edward. *Flintlock and Tomahawk: New England in King Philip's War.* New York: Macmillan, 1958.

Lears, T. J. Jackson. *No Place of Grace: Antimodernism and the Transformation of American Culture, 1880–1920.* New York: Pantheon Books, 1982.

Leonard, Jonathan. *American Cookbook: New England.* New York: Time-Life Books, 1970.

Lévi-Strauss, Claude. "The Culinary Triangle." *Partisan Review* 33, 4 (1966):586–95.

Lincoln, Joseph C. *Cape Cod Yesterdays.* Boston: Little, Brown and Company, 1935.

Lincoln, Joseph C. *Our Village.* New York: D. Appleton & Co., 1909.

Little, Elizabeth A., and J. Clinton Andrews. "Prehistoric Shellfish Harvesting at Nantucket Island." *Bulletin of the Massachusetts Archaeological Society* 47 (1986):18–27.

Love, William DeLoss, Jr. *The Fast and Thanksgiving Days of New England.* New York: Houghton, Mifflin and Company, 1895.

Lyell, Anne Morse. *Nonquitt: A Summer Album, 1872–1985.* South Dartmouth, Mass.: Bare-kneed Publishers, 1987.

MacCannell, Dean. *The Tourist: A New Theory of the Leisure Class.* New York: Schocken Books, 1976.

Mangels, William F. *The Outdoor Amusement Industry.* New York: Vantage Press, 1952.

Manning, Frank E. *The Celebration of Society: Perspectives on Contemporary Cultural Performance.* Bowling Green, Oh.: Bowling Green Popular Press, 1983.

Matthews, Albert. "The Term Pilgrim Fathers and Early Celebrations of Forefathers' Day." In *Publications of the Colonial Society of Massachusetts.* Vol. 17, *Transactions 1913–1914,* 293–392. Boston: Published by The Society, 1915.

McCabe, Marsha, ed. *A Picture History of Fairhaven.* New Bedford, Mass.: Spinner Publications, Inc., 1986.

Mills, Elden H. *Between Thee and Me.* N.p., n.d. [about 1985].

Mills, Elden H. "Fiftieth Clambake Set for Thursday by Allen's Neck Sunday School." Unpublished manuscript, Allen's Neck Friends Meeting Library, Dartmouth.

Mitcham, Howard. *Provincetown Seafood Cookbook.* Reading, Mass.: Addison-Wesley Publishing Company, Inc., 1975.

Moore, Sally F., and Barbara G. Myerhoff, eds. *Secular Ritual.* Amsterdam, The Netherlands: Van Gorcum and Company, 1977.

Morrow, Kay, ed. *The New England Cookbook.* New York: 1956.

*Natick Dictionary.* Edited by James Hammond Trumbull. Smithsonian Institution, Bureau of American Ethnology, Bulletin 25. Washington, D.C.: Government Printing Office, 1903.

Neustadt, Kathy. "'For Want of a Nail' (or How A Study of the Allen's Neck Clambake Leads to the Demise of Western Epistemological Imperialism)." Ph.D. diss., University of Pennsylvania, 1989.

*New Bedford, Massachusetts: Its History, Industries, Institutions, and Attractions by the New Bedford Board of Trade.* New Bedford, Mass.: Mercury Publishing Co., 1889.

*New England Hurricane: A Factual, Pictorial Record.* Written and compiled by members of the Writers Project of the WPA in the New England States. Boston: Hale, Cushman, and Flint, 1938.

Nuhn, Ferner. "The Shape of Quakerism in North America." *Friends Journal* (July 1/15, 1983):7–13.

*The Oxford Dictionary of the Christian Church.* Edited by F. L. Cross and E. A. Livingston. New York: Oxford University Press, 1983.

Pease, Zephaniah W., ed. *Life in New Bedford a Hundred Years Ago: A Chronicle of the Social, Religious and Commercial History of the Period as Recorded in a Diary Kept By Joseph R. Anthony.* [New Bedford]: Under the auspices of the Old Dartmouth Historical Society by G. H. Reynolds, [1922].

Pieper, Joseph. *In Tune with the World: A Theory of Festivity.* New York: Harcourt, 1965.

*The Plimoth Colony Cook Book.* Plymouth, Mass.: Plimoth Antiquarian Society, n.d.

Reaske, Christopher R. *The Compleat Clammer.* New York: Nick Lyons Books, 1986.

Ritchie, William Augustus. *The Archaeology of Martha's Vineyard: A Framework for the Prehistory of Southern New England: A Study in Coastal Ecology and Adaptation.* Garden City, N.Y.: The Natural History Press, 1969.

*Rochester's Official Bi-Centennial Record, Tuesday, July 22, 1879. Containing the Historical Address. Also, a Full Account of the Proceedings of the Day.* New Bedford, Mass.: Mercury Publishing Company, 1879.

Roosevelt, Robert B. *Superior Fishing; or, The Striped Bass, Trout, and Black Bass of the Northern States. Embracing Full Directions for Dressing Artificial Flies with the Feathers of American*

*Birds; An Account of a Sporting Visit to Lake Superior, Etc., Etc., Etc.* New York: Carelton, 1865.

Root, Waverly, and Richard de Rochemont. *Eating in America: A History.* New York: William Morrow and Company, Inc., 1976.

Rosso, Julee, and Sheila Lukins. "Summer's Last Fling." *Parade Magazine,* August 30, 1987, 11–13.

Russell, Elbert. *The History of Quakerism.* New York: The Macmillan Company, 1942.

Russell, Howard S. *Indian New England before the Mayflower.* Hanover, N.H.: University Press of New England, 1980.

Sagendorph, Robb, and Judson D. Hale. *That New England.* Dublin, N.H.: Yankee, Inc., 1966.

Sandler, Martin W. *As New Englanders Played.* Chester, Conn.: The Globe Pequot Press, 1979.

Schweid, Richard. "Crazy for Quahogs." *US Air,* August 1985, 10–14.

Shils, Edward. *Tradition.* Chicago: University of Chicago Press, 1981.

Shils, Edward. "Tradition." *Comparative Studies in Society and History* 13, 2 (1971):122–59.

Sickel, H. S. J. *Thanksgiving: Its Source, Philosophy, and History with All National Proclamations and Analytical Study Thereof.* Philadelphia: International Printing Company, 1940.

Simmons, William. *Spirit of the New England Tribes: Indian History and Folklore, 1620–1984.* Hanover, N.H.: University Press of New England, 1986.

*Slang and Its Analogues; Past and Present.* Edited by John S. Farmer and W. E. Henley. London: Printed for subscribers only, 1902.

Smith, Julius T. *Turtle Rock Tales.* New Bedford, Mass.: Viking Press, Inc., 1975.

Smith, M. Estellie. "The Process of Sociocultural Continuity." *Current Anthropology* 25, 2 (1982):127–41.

Snow, Dean R. *The Archaeology of New England.* New York: Academic Press, 1980.

Snow, Edward Rowe. *Marine Mysteries and Dramatic Disasters of New England.* New York: Dodd, Mead and Company, 1976.

Sokolov, Raymond. "An Original Old-Fashioned Yankee Clambake." In *Fading Feast: A Compendium of Disappearing American Regional Foods,* 137–46. New York: Farrar, Straus, Giroux, 1981.

Somers, Dale A. "The Leisure Revolution: Recreation in the American City, 1820–1920." *Journal of Popular Culture* 5, 1 (1971):125–47.

Speck, Frank G. *Penobscot Man: The Life History of a Forest Tribe in Maine.* Philadelphia: University of Pennsylvania Press, 1940.

Stoller, Paul. *The Taste of Ethnographic Things: The Senses in Anthropology.* Philadelphia: University of Pennsylvania Press, 1989.

Sullivan, Mary. *A History of Allen's Neck Friends Meeting.* N.p., 1979.

Sutton-Smith, Brian. "Psychology of Childcare: The Triviality Barrier." *Western Folklore* 29 (1970):1–8.

Tannahill, Reay. *Food in History.* New York: Stein and Day Publishers, 1973.

Tolles, Frederick B. *Quakers and the Atlantic Culture.* New York: The Macmillan Company, 1960.

Tolles, Frederick B. "Quietism versus Enthusiasm: The Philadelphia Quakers and the Great Awakening." *Pennsylvania Magazine of History and Biography,* January 1945, 26–49.

Towle, George Makepeace. *American Society.* 2 vols. London: Chapman and Hall, 1870.

Trager, James. *The Enriched, Fortified, Concentrated, Country-Fresh, Lip-Smacking, Finger-Licking, International. Unexpurgated Foodbook.* New York: Grossman Publishers, 1970.

Travers, Milton A. *The Wampanoag Indian Federation of the Algonquin Nation: Indian Neighbors of the Pilgrims.* Boston, Mass.: The Christopher Publishing House, 1961.

Treat, Rose. *The Seaweed Book: How to Find and Have Fun with Seaweed.* Edgartown, Mass.: The Seaweed Press, 1985.

Trillin, Calvin. "A Real Nice Clambake." In *Third Helpings,* 78–90. New York: Ticknor and Fields, 1983.

Trollope, Anthony. *North America.* Philadelphia: J. B. Lippincott and Co., 1862.

Turner, Victor. "Liminal to Liminoid, in Play, Flow and Ritual." *Rice University Studies* 60 (1974):53–92.

Turner, Victor. *The Ritual Process: Structure and Anti-Structure.* Ithaca, N.Y.: Cornell University Press, 1979.

van Gennep, Arnold. *The Rites of Passage.* Chicago: University of Chicago Press, 1960.

Varrell, William M. *Summer by-the-sea: The Golden Era of Victorian Beach Resorts.* Portsmouth, N.H.: The Strawberry Banke Print Shop, 1972.

Washburn, Wilcomb E., ed. *History of North American Indians.* Vol. 4 of *Handbook of North American Indians.* Washington, D.C.: Smithsonian Institution, 1988.

Weatherford, Jack. *Indian Givers: How the Indians of the Americas Transformed the World.* New York: Crown Publishers, Inc., 1988.

Weber, Max. *The Protestant Ethic and the Spirit of Capitalism.* 1920. Translated by Talcott Parsons. New York: Charles Scribner's Sons, 1958.

Weinstein-Farson, Laurie. *The Wampanoag.* Indians of North America Series, general ed. Frank W. Porter III. New York: Chelsea House Publishers, 1989.

Weiser, Francis X. *Handbook of Christian Feasts and Customs: The Year of the Lord in Liturgy and Folklore.* New York: Harcourt, Brace and Co., 1958.

*The Westport Heritage Cookbook: A Collection of Favorite Recipes from the Kitchens of Westport.* Westport Point, Mass.: United Methodist, 1978.

Whitehall, Walter M., and Norman Kotker. *Massachusetts: A Pictorial History.* New York: Charles Scribner's Sons, 1976.

Wilkinson, Thomas Read. *Holiday Rambles.* Manchester, Vt.: Guttenberg Works, Pendleton, 1881.

Williams, Walter R. *The Rich Heritage of Quakerism.* Grand Rapids, Mich.: Wm. B. Eerdmans Publishing Co., 1862.

Wyler, Susan. "Celebrating Summer with a New England Clambake: The Ultimate Cookout." *Food and Wine,* July 1985.

Wyler, Susan. "The Ultimate Cookout." *Food and Wine,* July 1985, 30–34.

Wyss, Bob. "Warren, Rhode Island." *Yankee Magazine,* August 1984, 54–61.

*Yankee Dictionary: A Compendium of Useful and Entertaining Expressions Indigenous to New England.* Edited by Charles F. Haywood. Lynn, Mass.: Jackson and Phillips, Inc., 1963.

Yoder, Don. "Folk Cookery." In *Folklore and Folklife: An Introduction,* edited by Richard M. Dorson, 325–50. Chicago: University of Chicago Press, 1972.

## Newspaper Articles

Atkinson, John. "It's Traditional It's on [its] Way Out. It's a Clambake." *New Bedford Standard-Times,* September 5, 1976, 37.

Brown, Arthur H. "Clambakes. The Development of Rhode Island's Institution Here. Eighteen Hundred People Fed Weekly at New Bedford Bakes. How a Sunday School Had a Bake Without Clams." *New Bedford Evening Standard,* August 26, 1899, 10.

"Clambake." *Christian Science Monitor,* September 12, 1975, 18.

Converse, Gordon N. "Clam Bake—New England Style." *Christian Science Monitor,* September 4, 1958, first page, second section.

Ferraro, Susan. "Great Summer Traditions." *The New York Times Magazine,* May 21, 1989, 15–18.

Gross, Tanya. "Russells Mills Village: Those Who Love It Battle Change." *New Bedford Standard-Times,* July 12, 1987, 59–60.

Hirsch, Arthur. "Clambake: Allen's Neck Feast is Simmered in a Century of Tasty Tradition." *New Bedford Sunday Standard-Times,* August 26, 1984, 53–54.

Jenkins, Nancy. "As American as a New England Shore Dinner." *New York Times,* July 3, 1985, C1, C6.

Kummer, Corby. "I Hear America Feasting." *The New York Times Magazine.* Part 2, *The Sophisticated Traveler,* March 12, 1989, 10, 12, 16, 18.

Levy, Maxine. "Taking the Clambake to Texas." *Boston Globe,* May 28, 1986, 43, 46.

Liberman, Ellen. "Clambake custom claims more converts," *Boston Sunday Globe,* June 9, 1991, 51, 55.

"Local Twinklings: Clambake at Sconicut." *Fairhaven Star,* September 7, 1887.

"Local Twinklings: Gala Day at Sconicut." *Fairhaven Star,* September 10, 1887.

O'Brien, Dan. "A Good Bake: A Steamy New England Tradition." *New Bedford Sunday Standard-Times,* October 9, 1988, 10–11.

"Sconicut Neck." *Fairhaven Star,* September 17, 1887.

Wood, Bertrand T. "How Famous Clambakes Originated." *New Bedford Sunday Standard-Times,* January 21, 1934, 3.


## Primary Ethnographic Sources


*Audiotaped Interviews*

ALLEN, Cliff: July 30, 1987.
ASHTON, John: August 19, 1986.
ASHTON, Leona: August 19, 1986.
BROWN, Julie: August 5, 1985.
——— July 9, 1987.
COLE, Lewis: August 25, 1986.
DAVOLL, Mary: July 26, 1985.
DAVOLL, Priscilla: August 14, 1987.
DAVOLL, Raymond: August 8, 1985.
ERICKSON, Barbara: July 25, 1985.
ERICKSON, Karl: July 25, 1985.
GIFFORD, Allen: August 12, 1985.
——— August 17, 1987.
GIFFORD, Billy: August 19, 1986.
GIFFORD, Burney: July 30, 1985.
——— August 5, 1985.
——— August 12, 1985.
GIFFORD, Elsie: August 12, 1985.
GIFFORD, Gladys: August 12, 1985.
——— August 14, 1985.

GONET, Ila: July 17, 1985.
GONET, Peter: August 5, 1985.
JUDSON, Norma: August 13, 1985.
KNOWLES, Eliot, Jr.: August 11, 1987.
MACOMBER, Marjorie: August 19, 1987.
MACOMBER, Ralph: August 8, 1987.
MARTIN, Miss: August 21, 1986.
MILLS, Elden: August 7, 1986.
MORRISON, Virginia: August 6, 1985.
—— August 16, 1986.
MORRISON, Wilfred: August 6, 1985.
—— August 16, 1986.
—— July 24, 1987.
—— July 25, 1987.
NANEPASHEMET: June 18, 1987.
PARSONS, Jean: July 25, 1985.
PARSONS, Gordon: July 25, 1985.
RAMOS, Dave: July 29, 1987.
REBELLO, Cathi: August 12, 1985.
SILVIA, Muriel: July 20, 1985.
SMITH, Florence: July 25, 1985.
TRIPP, Hettie: August 17, 1987.
WAITE, Ernie: August 25, 1986.
WAITE, Imelda: August 25, 1986.


*Telephone Interviews*

BAKER, James: March 22, 1988.
KRAFT, Herbert: February 7, 1989.
WEAVER, William Woys: May 1, 1988.


*Audiotaped Events*

Allen's Neck Clambake day: August 15, 1985.
—— August 21, 1986.
—— August 20, 1987.
D. M. Roberts clambake, Cambridge, Mass.: July 23, 1987.
Leighton's clambake, Round Hill, South Dartmouth, Mass.: July 9, 1987.
Rock collecting, Boan's farm: Westport, Mass.: August 8, 1985.
Rockweed gathering, Tuckerman's farm, Westport, Mass.: August 19, 1987.
Russells Mills Fire Station Clambake, Dartmouth, Mass.: July 26, 1987.
Smith Neck clambake, South Dartmouth, Mass.: August 8, 1987.
Table set-up at Allen's Neck: August 7, 1987.

# Index

Italicized page numbers are references for illustrations.